Foreign Policy, Federalism and International Treaties

FOREIGN POLICY, Federalism and International Treaties

Edited by

G. Gopa Kumar
Director General,
Institute of Parliamentary Affairs (INPA),
Government of Kerala.

New Century Publications
New Delhi, India

NEW CENTURY PUBLICATIONS
4800/24, Bharat Ram Road,
Ansari Road, Daryaganj,
New Delhi – 110 002 (India)

Tel.: 011-2324 7798, 4358 7398, 6539 6605
Fax: 011-4101 7798
E-mail: indiatax@vsnl.com • info@newcenturypublications.com
www.newcenturypublications.com

Editorial office:
LG–7, Aakarshan Bhawan,
4754-57/23, Ansari Road, Daryaganj,
New Delhi – 110 002

Tel.: 011-4356 0919

First Published: **July 2011**

ISBN: **978-81-7708-278-4**

Published by New Century Publications and printed at Salasar Imaging Systems, New Delhi.

Designs: Patch Creative Unit, New Delhi.

PRINTED IN INDIA

About the Book

Significant changes are taking place across the world following the advent of globalization and the consequent decline of the nation-state. The conventional parameters of understanding domestic politics and international relations are becoming redundant. New forms of international treaties—relating to regional trade, culture, economy, human security and national security—have become essential. The increasing role played by the civil society has changed the ground rules of foreign policy processes.

The structure, quality and dimensions of Indian federalism are witnessing drastic changes. In this context, the nature and dynamics of federalism in the coming decades will be a pertinent issue for analysis. The concerns of the states in the Indian Union are also changing significantly. Their demand for share in foreign policy dynamics raises new question in the study of federalism.

This book—containing 15 scholarly articles by experts in the field—is an attempt to open up a discourse linking the emerging pattern of international relations to federal management.

About the Editor

Dr. G. Gopa Kumar is presently the Director General of the Institute of Parliamentary Affairs (INPA), Government of Kerala and Professor and Head, Department of Political Science and Dean of Social Sciences, University of Kerala. He has published 10 books and over 130 research articles. His areas of research interest include comparative politics, international relations and Indian politics.

He was Senior Fellow of the Australia-India Council, Melbourne (2009), Shastri Fellow in Canada (McGill, 2006 and Calgary 2000), Salzburg Fellow (1998), Fulbright Scholar in USA (1998), International Visiting Fellow in USA (1996), and UGC-Research Scientist (1998-1999). He was a Visiting Faculty at the Claremont Graduate University in California, USA (1998 and 2003) and University of Calgary, Alberta, Canada (2001). He was recently awarded the three year position of Visiting Research Fellow by the University of New South Wales, Sydney, Australia.

Acknowledgements

This volume is yet another publication of the Institute of Parliamentary Affairs (INPA), Government of Kerala. Established in 2005 in Thiruvananthapuram, INPA has been engaged in research, training and other academic activities for nurturing the values and spirit of parliamentary democracy in Kerala. The stakeholders include students, youth, bureaucrats, media personnel, and other sections of the civil society. INPA is unique in the sense that other state governments have not organized similar bodies so far. Although created by the Government, INPA receives considerable academic freedom to pursue its research goals. INPA started a bi-annual research journal in 2010, titled *Journal of Parliamentary Studies*.

At the outset, the Editor expresses his gratitude to Sri M. Vijayakumar, Honourable Minister for Law, Public Works and Parliamentary Affairs, Government of Kerala for extending all moral support to the activities of INPA. The encouragement received from Sri. A.G. Sasidharan Nair, Private Secretary to the Minister is also acknowledged. The Editor wishes to place on record the co-operation received from the office and research staff of the INPA, especially Sri K. Radhakrishnan, Registrar and Smt. S. Sumangala Devi, Section Officer. The services rendered by Sri Sumesh. N., Smt. Archana V. and Smt. Vidhumol V.S., Research Fellows of the INPA in the proof reading of this work is also acknowledged.

Besides, the support from colleagues in the Department of Political Science, University of Kerala was very consistent and rewarding. Sincere gratitude is expressed to Dr. J. Prabhash, Sri. C. Muraleedharan, Dr. Shaji Varkey, Dr. A. Basheer, Dr. K. M. Sajad Ibrahim and Dr. Josukutty C.A.

The support received from my students, especially Sri P. Anil Kumar, Miss Ashalekshmy B.S. and Smt. Devi Parvathy is also appreciated.

Contents

About the Book v

About the Editor vi

Acknowledgements vii

1. International Treaties and the Distribution of Powers in the Federal State: The Case of Switzerland 1-12
   Markus Schefer

2. Indian Federalism and International Treaties 13-31
   Ashutosh Saxena

3. International Treaties and Centre-State Relations 32-49
   V. Suryanarayanan

4. Indian Federalism as Defined by Devolution and Constitutionalism 50-67
   A. Basheer

5. Indian Federalism in a Transitory Phase: From Asymmetry to Multiculturalism 68-77
   Veena Ramachandran

6. Globalization, Federalism and Democracy in India 78-104
   G. Gopa Kumar

7. Nature of the New Indian State: Federalism in the Current Global Market Scene 105-115
   M.A. Lal

8. Water, Federalism and International Law 116-133
Deepa Karthikeyan

9. Treaty Power and its Implications for Federalism: The Case of Indo-US Civilian Nuclear Deal 134-142
Manu M.R.

10. Parliamentary Control over Foreign Policy: Theory and Praxis 143-154
Sivakumar M.V.

11. New Dimensions in the Indian Foreign Policy in a Multilateral Environment 155-169
T. Krishna Kanth and K. Lalitha Kumari

12. Reorienting Non-alignment: Indian Foreign Policy in the New World Order 170-191
K.S. Pavithran

13. Violence in West Asia: Implications for India's Federalism and Security 192-254
A.K. Pasha

14. India's Quest for New Partnership in West Asia: The Case of Israel as a Strategic Ally 255-270
K.M. Sajad Ibrahim

15. India's Look East Policy: The China Factor 271-284
B. Venugopal

Index 285-292

Contributors and Their Affiliations

A. Basheer	Associate Professor, Department of Political Science, University of Kerala, Thiruvananthapuram.
A.K. Pasha	Professor, Centre for West Asian Studies, JNU, New Delhi.
Ashutosh Saxena	Associate Professor of Political Science, Christ Church College, Kanpur.
B. Venugopal	Formerly Head, Department of Political Science, Sree Narayana College, Kollam.
Deepa Karthikeyan	Research Fellow, Centre for Asia Studies, Chennai.
G. Gopa Kumar	Director General, Institute of Parliamentary Affairs (INPA), Government of Kerala.
K. Lalitha Kumari	Senior Lecturer, Department of Political Science, Kakatiya University, Warangal, Andhra Pradesh.
K.S. Pavithran	Professor and Head, Department of Political Science, University of Calicut, Kerala.
Sivakumar M.V.	Associate Professor, Department of Political Science, Maharajas College, Ernakulam.
M.A. Lal	Research Officer, Kerala State Higher Education Council, Thiruvananthapuram.
Manu M.R.	Research Scholar, Centre for Political Studies, JNU, New Delhi.
Markus Schefer	Professor of Constitutional and Administrative Law, University of Basel, Switzerland.
K.M. Sajad Ibrahim	Assistant Professor, Department of Political Science, University of Kerala.
V. Suryanarayanan	Senior Research Fellow, Centre for Asia Studies, Chennai.
T. Krishna Kanth	Professor, Department of Political Science, Kakatiya University, Warangal, Andhra Pradesh
Veena Ramachandran	Associate Professor, Department of Political Science, Madras Christian College, Chennai.

Introduction

By G. Gopa Kumar

I

This work is an attempt by the Institute of Parliamentary Affairs (INPA), Government of Kerala to open up a new debate on the changing dimensions of Indian federalism and its linkages to foreign policy formulations, particularly in the aftermath of globalisation. While the context of the debate is influenced by the rapid developments in the country following the shift towards neo-liberal agenda, the basic text of the polity, i.e. the Constitution, did not undergo major changes. Given the qualitative and quantitative changes in economy, society and culture during the last two decades and the likelihood of major flow of reforms, it is very likely that the conventional parameters of Indian federalism are not going to hold sufficient for future, Although foreign policy is a subject falling under the Union List and the Constitution is not very vocal about details of foreign policy except making reference under Article 51, the future trends are going to be vastly different. Both inter-governmental jurisdiction and inter-territorial jurisdiction of federal relationships are going to change phenomenally. Hence, it is very likely that states of the Indian Union would demand their role and contribution in drafting international treaties. Moreover, at the international arena, a borderless world is emerging following huge migration, flow of trade, services and technology. Indians working abroad, for instance in Middle East, mainly originate from Kerala state. They face numerous problems in their daily lives like, fake job visas and insecure settlements, issues related to cash remittances, health problems, poor transportation facilities etc. Despite the creation of Non-Resident Keralites Association (NORKA) by the Government of Kerala, it has become pertinent that the demands and concerns of state government must be properly heard before the Ministers of External Affairs finalises the policy for Middle East. Indeed, the remittances from Middle East have been significant for the national and state economy during the last four decades.

Similarly, in regard to the trade relations with ASEAN, the interests of farmers from various states of India are to be properly considered. The free flow of trade and services between countries had placed some of the Indian states in particular advantage while many in a disadvantageous position. Would it be practical for the national bureaucracy to ignore the interests and demands of these performing states? Similarly, the Indian Diaspora contributes significantly to the economy of the country and the states. The specific interest of the diaspora in investing in the states of their origin also raises the need and significance of the state governments in facilitating international economic treaties.

There are already numerous issues in border states like illegal migration, illicit trade, drug-trafficking and problems related to international terrorism originating from foreign soil. Not only that the support of this local machinery is required but also the concerns of state governments are to be properly addressed. The technical and general inputs offered by the concerned state governments would help the Union Government to adopt a viable policy in this regard. The ethnic, cultural aspects are also to be considered since the spill over of these developments has the potentials of generating conflicts. Again, the huge developments in industrial and service sectors following globalisation measures and reforms are not only raising inter-state issues but also state specific related global issues. The expansion of industries like mining, oil and gas, pharmaceuticals, infrastructure, tourism, construction, besides the launch of retail trade by mega corporates, had changed the social, cultural and economic landscape of the region. The flow of job opportunities attracts huge labour migration from different parts of the country to the state's specific industrial belts. Along with the economic changes, there are social, environmental and cultural issues. Although it would be difficult to locate the epicentre of the new problems, the voice of the concerned state government and related pressure groups cannot be ignored. While negotiating with Multinational Corporations, the Union Government will have to provide sufficient policy space for state governments. Sometimes, the big corporates can seek quick licences for a new venture from the local government concerned, by sidelining the responsibilities of the state governments (since the national clearance has been already achieved). All these generate new premises in our federal polity which are to be studied.

Altogether, we get a complex picture in the art and practice of 'new federalism' in India. In fact, dynamic federalism demands 'shared rule and self rule'. The pattern of de-centralised governance since the Panchayati Raj Institution reforms (1993) received a further impetus due to the dismantling of *licence raj system* and opening of the economy. The nature of the state existed in the pre-liberal economy has changed dramatically. But, what is particularly important in the debate on federalism is the emerging trends in foreign policy making. It drives us to the argument that the vital role of states is to be properly considered while policy shifts are made, leading to the signing up of international treaties. The framers of the Constitution could not visualise the vast changing global developments but the architects of the contemporary India cannot ignore these changes. Necessary constitutional changes are needed to place the role of states in foreign policy making. The limited role of the Council of States of the Indian Parliament in federal administration has been made very clear during the last sixty one years. A debate on this aspect is of utmost importance and given the volatile nature of multiparty system and coalition politics, emerging trends in federal practice have to be properly considered. This work is an attempt in the direction so as to grasp the future trends in federalism particularly on the issue of entering into international treaties.

II

Altogether fifteen papers are discussed here covering a wide range of the topic. Aspects related to international treaties and distribution of powers in the case of Switzerland provides the background of this work. Other papers include the role of states in the making of international treaties, the perspective on the issue from Tamil Nadu, re-inventing Indian federalism from asymmetry to multiculturalism, globalisation, federalism and Indian democracy, the nature of the new Indian state, water, federalism and international law, changing power relations and its implications for federalism in the context of Indo-US Nuclear deal, parliamentary control over foreign policy in the multilateral environment, re-orienting non-alignment in the new world order, developments in West Asia and its implications for Indian federalism, issues concerning Indo-Israeli Strategic alliance and the relevance of China factor in the Look East Policy of India are debated.

Markus Schefer's paper **International Treaties and the Distribution of Powers in the Federal State: The Case of Switzerland** provides an exclusive picture of the federal system of the Switzerland by sharpening the active knowledge about the parallel constitutional and federal set up. He made an attempt to answer the problem of federal states in Switzerland and noted that federal states face an additional, more complex problem. It pertains to the relationship between central government and state government in foreign policy issues. As part of the detailed description of the study he made a wide analysis of the articles, provision and sections of Switzerland constitution and sketches the distribution of power between the federal government and the cantons and its entire role in making the international treaties. He underlines the constitutionalisation of the participation of the Cantons in negotiating, ratifying and implementing international treaties to quite a large extent and at the same time estimating its problems and prospects in a meaningful way.

Pluralism and federalism are two existential principles for

organizing heterogeneous societies in to a viable pattern of sharing of power. Ashutosh Saxena in his paper **Indian Federalism and International Treaties** highlights that federalism builds up and sustains the unity of polity and simultaneously preserved and promotes the plurality of society. He concludes his paper by arguing that the federalism in 21st century demands the state members of a federal union should posses a shared capacity to conclude treaties. If such capacity is admitted by the federal constitution and within the limits, they become essential for effective service delivery. The federal spirit of our system is unity with due respect to plural identities. Regional variations in growth develop regional disparities which is harmful for federalism.

In his paper **International Treaties and Centre-State Relations,** V. Suryanarayanan attempts to explain two important issues, which are of vital concern to the government and the people of Tamil Nadu, where the central government ignored the wishes of the state and entered into bilateral agreements with Sri Lanka. The first is Sirimavo-Shasthri Pact of 1964 and the subsequent Sirimavo-Indira Gandhi Pact of 1974. The author argue that these agreements have left a trail of bitterness in the state of Tamil Nadu and the people began to feel that the interests of Tamil Nadu are not safe in the foreign policy for the 'Distant' New Delhi. The author also gives another example to show the insensitive attitude of Government of India towards the interests of Tamil Nadu - the India- Sri Lanka Maritime Boundary Agreements, 1974 and 1976.

A. Basheer in his paper, **Indian Federalism as Defined by Devolution and Constitutionalism** discusses about the federal dysfunctions of Indian federation. He argues that federal functioning faces many challenges with regard to union-state and interstate relations. He also describes the asymmetry and vulnerabilities of federal set up in India. The federal system in India has exposed its weakness, limitations and inabilities in responding to the challenges and problems that exist and emerge in the country. He demands that federal systematic arrangements must be shaped to form a polity that does not seek to deny or disable fundamental local/regional interests and needs.

Veena Ramachandran tells very extensively about the characteristics and changing pattern of the Indian federalism on behalf of a very diversified unity and integrity of the heterogeneous Indian society. In her paper titled **Indian Federalism in a Transitory Phase: From Asymmetry to Multiculturalism** she specifically stressed up on the integrative and disruptive forces which have been simultaneously released by developmental and political dynamics in India. It is the changing balance between these two mutually incompatible forces that defines the characteristics of the ethnic scene in the country. Because of the coercive power of the Indian state and of the inherent strength and resilience of Indian society we will lose "unity in diversity". So she sensibly noted that in the context of the present day multiparty system, the multi cultural federalism appears to offer the greatest scope and possibilities for meeting the requirements of a strong and united India. Indian federalism can only be strengthened by abolishing asymmetry and effective implementation of federalism by all means.

In his paper **Globalization, Federalism and Democracy in India,** G. Gopa Kumar tries to examine the changing and challenging nature of federal democracy in the specific context of India's tryst with globalization. Through out the paper he made a meaningful approach to analyze the brief history of liberalization and globalization, and its deep impact up on the social, economic, political and federalist character of the country during the last two decades. The paper elucidates that as a policy, globalization was not against decentralization process but its strategies included strong neo-liberal approach towards decentralized governance. However, this article defends the growth of local governance but identifies the problem of globalization and the intervention of out side agencies and economies on the local governments. These developments paved the way for the new form of "globalization process" which is changing the conventional parameters of democracy. Indeed, the paper concludes that the federal democracy in India is changing phenomenally taking cues mainly from the framework of globalization.

M.A. Lal in his paper, **Nature of the New Indian State: Federalism in the Current Global Market Scene,** discusses about the influence of globalization and further analyse how this impact upon the Indian federal system. He argues that globalization process has allowed more autonomy of action in favour of the federal units (particularly the states) to reap the benefits of globalization. In his view the role of states in India's reform process is very crucial and politically significant. He concludes his paper by stating that globalization has favoured broadly urban India, organized sectors, richer states and property owners against rural India, unorganized sectors, poorer states and wage earners.

In her paper **Water, Federalism and International Law** Deepa Karthikeyan begins with a brief overview of the evolutionary histories of international and Indian federal law so as to enable one to identify specific divergences that persist between the two. She says that the inconsistency in our understanding of the water laws created a gap between natural water laws and the complex legal systems that govern the use of the same. She explains that Indian Constitution borrows extensively from British common law to regulate and develop the state's water resources. Her major argument is that an overview of the federal constitutional provisions on water governance in India exhibits the presence of several flaws.

M.R. Manu's paper **Treaty Power and its Implications for Federalism: The Case of Indo-US Civilian Nuclear Deal** highlights that the federations' world wide are undergoing a series of changes. This is because of the new developments like the process of globalization, increasing integration of the markets, the emergence of a knowledge based society etc. Thus the monopoly enjoyed by the centre, in terms of foreign relations has also changed. This paper also attempts to analyse the Indo-US Nuclear Deal and implications of the debates surrounding it. He tries to analyse the major aspects of the debates which were set off by the Indo-US Nuclear Deal. He also tries to explain the nature of changing central-state relationship in India. According to him the degree of decentralization in India is not satisfactory and the country has become a product of centre. There is an urgent need to develop political instrumentalities and mechanisms to make foreign policy more responsive to popular concerns and make foreign policy decisions more democratic and representative. The author argues that there is a necessity to ensure state representation in bodies like Finance Commission and Planning Commission and give the power of residual taxation while ensuring larger share of the state in net tax revenue collection.

In his timely contribution on **Parliamentary Control over Foreign Policy: Theory and Praxis,** Sivakumar M. V. tries to highlight the declining role of parliament in the field of foreign policy. He underlines the inevitable problems that have been formulating from the parliamentary order. In the case of foreign policy, theoretically, the unity has been furnishing but in practice the workability of democracy and unity in diversity has come under worthless debates. The paper made an attempt to focus on the parliamentary system in practice. The major part of time and fund has been lost due to disruption and disorder in the each session of the parliament. Because of the competitive and confrontational politics that has overtaken the country today, Parliament cannot appropriately discharge its essential functions. Debates and discussions, the hallmarks of democracy, have been overshadowed by disruptions, confrontations and other non-democratic alternatives, which had reduced the institution as a subject of ridicule. He suggests for the emergence of strong parliamentary conventions which will ensure the dignity of Parliament and rescue our democracy.

T. Krishna Kanth and K. Lalitha Kumari, in their paper, **New Dimensions in the Indian Foreign Policy in a Multilateral Environment,** deals with the dynamic nature of India's foreign policy. In an international situation marked by simultaneous competition and co-operation among the major powers, the government has steadily improved India's relation with all major powers. In their view, India's foreign policy is adaptive to the new challenges of globalization which has now become the principal national objective. As an emerging global power, India cannot be strategically type-casted as an alliance partner of one or the other powers. The paper is concluded by suggesting that federal systematic arrangement be so shaped to help form a policy that does not seek to deny fundamental local/regional interests and needs.

K.S. Pavithran's paper **Reorienting Non-alignment: Indian Foreign Policy in the New World Order,** explains the emergence of India's foreign policy of non alignment. According to him the policy of non alignment implied, a country not joining any of the cold war power alignments while trying to maintain friendly relations with all kinds of nations and helping the preservation of world peace. It is also the idea of neutralism. The author tries to analyse the role of non alignment in the changing manifestations of imperialism. He argues that India's policy of non alignment was against the statuesque situation in international relations that meant opposition to colonialism, imperialism and racial discrimination. It advocates the sovereign equality of all states. But India's foreign policy has undergone major transformation in the post-cold war era. The orientation of non alignment was to that of a pragmatic policy but he believes that the kind of recent transformation is inimical to the people's interests and damaging national strength.

In his paper **Violence in West Asia: Implications for India's Federalism and Security,** A.K. Pasha deeply explains the history of political upheavals in the contemporary West Asia. At the same time he presents a comparative analysis of the character and the dynamics of the Indian federal system. He underlines the fact behind the question, why should India adopt proactive approach on the Gulf States' issue? This paper also tries to search the facts behind India's relationship with Iran which plays a vital role in recent political developments in Asia and West Asia. He also tells us a short background of India's political stand in making and implementing the foreign policy. Besides, Israel-Palestine issue, oil crisis in the gulf region, US political invasion on gulf, India's interest in the West Asia, UN intervention, tactics behind the terrorist attacks etc. are the main points discussed in this paper.

K.M. Sajad Ibrahim's work, **India's Quest for New Partnership in West Asia: The Case of Israel as a Strategic Ally,** tries to explain about the relationship of Israel and India. The author begins with a discussion on India's West Asian policy principles. He also gives a detailed description about the problems of West Asian countries, especially by Israel and Palestine, and the role of India as a moderator to solve this problem. Subsequently he narrates the relationship of India with Palestine and Israel from 1930's to the present. He gives more emphasis for India-Israel relations. According to him the relationship with India and Israel created rifts between India and Iran. But India always takes a soft position towards the Arab countries because it is estimated that more than 5 million Indians work in Arab countries. In his conclusion, he strongly criticize that the new diplomatic initiatives of India target only its vested interest and it is against the traditional principle of solidarity with the third world countries.

In his paper **India's Look East Policy: The China Factor** B. Venugopal points out that since 1962 India is losing opportunities to emerge as an Asian leader, mainly because of our short sighted policies and the in ability to cope with the emerging situations. But after the disintegration of the Soviet Union and the end of the Cold War we could see major change in the policy perspectives of India towards the neighbouring countries. This paper analyses the China factor involved in India's relation with the South East Asian countries. The paper does not go into the economic arrangements between the two, but highlight the China factor. It induces India to forge a close alliance with South Asian countries and vice versa. The paper also examines the areas in which India can overcome Chinese obstacles and create conditions favourable to India's intervention in South East Asia.

1

International Treaties and the Distribution of Powers in the Federal State: The Case of Switzerland

Markus Schefer

Participation of Parliament in Conduct of Foreign Policy

Foreign policy has traditionally been an area of the executive. However, the legislative branch was involved early on, in the first written constitution: The U.S. Constitution in Article II, Section 2, Clause 2 requires the "advice and consent" of the U.S. Senate for the ratification of international treaties by the President. Other Western constitutions like the German Basic Law also involve parliament in some form at least in those instances where international treaties of a certain importance are at stake.

The involvement of the legislature attempts to confer democratic legitimacy on foreign policy decisions and their legal form, international treaties. It tries to ensure that the distribution of powers among the different branches of government remains intact.

One of the main obstacles to this attempt stems from the necessity to conduct treaty negotiations among a relatively small group of participants. Broad participation by the legislature is therefore highly impractical. Article 166, Section 1, of the Switzerland Constitution [1] declares that *The Federal Assembly shall participate in shaping foreign policy and supervise the maintenance of foreign relations.*

On the statutory level, the Federal Parliamentary Act (FPA) specifies this provision. It states that the Federal Parliament "observes the development of international relations and participates in forming the political will about important foreign policy questions and decisions". [2] In order to enable the parliament to fulfil these duties, the federal executive (the "Federal Council") is required to submit periodically a report about Switzerland's foreign policy to the parliament (Article 148, Section 3, of FPA). Of crucial importance for effective participation by parliament are their Foreign Relations Committees. Each chamber established a Foreign Relations Committee. Article 152, Section 1, of FPA requires that they keep close contact and exchange their views regularly. The Federal Council is obliged to inform the Presidents of the two chambers of parliament and their Foreign Relations Committees periodically, precociously, and comprehensively on important developments in foreign policy (Article 152, Section 2, of FPA).

In addition to these duties to inform Parliament, the Federal Council is also obliged to consult with the Foreign Relations Committees on important issues and on the mandates for major international negotiations. The Council informs the Committees on the further development of such issues and on the progress of negotiations (Article 152, Section 3, of FPA). In urgent situations, the Federal Councils consults with the Presidents of the Foreign Relations Committees, who in turn immediately inform their Committees (Article 152, Section 4, of FPA).

Despite these provisions, the possibilities of involving the legislature in the phase of negotiating a treaty remain limited. Binding decisions by Parliament are confined to the need for parliamentary approval of the ratification of international treaties. Such decisions, however, are mainly confined to approving or rejecting the package negotiated by the executive. Parliament has only minimal leeway at best to make changes, without rejecting the treaty as a whole. Even broad powers of the legislature to approve or reject international treaties can, as a consequence, confer only very limited democratic legitimacy.

Foreign Policy in Federalist States: The Problem

Federal states face an additional, albeit more complex problems. It pertains to the relationship between central government and state government in foreign policy issues. This is the problem I want to focus on. The Federal states usually confer the power to conduct foreign policy to the central government. The first federal Constitution, the one of the United States, contains in such a provision. Historically, one of the main reasons for creating federal states in the first place was to centralize foreign policy in order to increase the effectiveness of the foreign representation of small states that share a common goal. Again, this was true for the U.S. in 1789 and, about 60 years later, in 1848, for the Swiss Federation.

Centralizing foreign policy in federal states proved to be essential for an additional reason. To a large extent, internal cohesion and stability of federal states have historically relied on control of foreign relations by the central government. Again, Article I, Section 1, Clause 1 of the U.S. Constitution, allows foreign contacts by states only with the approval of the central government.

Ensuring effectiveness of foreign relations and internal cohesion comes at a price. Focusing foreign policy on the central government raises the issue about the relationship between these powers of the central government on the one hand and the distribution of domestic powers between central and state governments on the other.

Usually, federal states distribute powers between the centre and the states along substantive lines. They typically prescribe which areas of social life should be regulated by the centre, and which areas by the states. Foreign policy, however, does not fit into this scheme, as it may encompass all areas of social life. If, as in Switzerland, the powers to maintain a police force are mainly matters for states and not the centre, international treaties by the centre about police cooperation, such as the Schengen treaty, concur with state powers. Subject matters reserved for the states may be, to the extent that they are internationalized, taken over by the centre. The question arises about how to alleviate the ensuing conflict between states and centre. One recent example in Switzerland is the mentioned Schengen treaty, requiring, among other issues, cooperation between Switzerland police forces with their foreign counterparts. Since the police are mainly a matter for the cantons, the Schengen treaty affects mainly the cantons.

From the perspective of international law, it is quite settled that the federal structure of a country does not affect its obligations from international law [3] International law itself requires that the respective country fulfils its legal obligations. It does not, however, generally mandate which organ in a federal state is competent to implement it. The question of whether state or federal government implement an international obligation is for national law to decide.

International Treaties and Participation of Cantons

So how does Switzerland deal with this situation? Let me first briefly sketch the distribution of powers between the federal government and the cantons. Article 42 of the Switzerland Constitution states the principle that the federal government possesses all those powers the federal Constitution affords to it. Powers the federal Constitution does not (explicitly or implicitly) afford to the federal government remain with the cantons. With this system, the Switzerland Constitution follows the U.S. Constitution.

Irrespective of this distribution of powers, foreign policy is a power of the federal government. The federal government is competent to enter into treaties not only in those areas in which it has domestic powers, but also in those areas in which, on the domestic level, the cantons are competent (Article 54, Section 1, of the Switzerland Constitution).

Since Switzerland follows generally a monist approach to international law, such wide federal powers in the area of foreign policy could be used to override the constitutional distribution of powers. This problem has become significantly more pressing in the last twenty years, as international law has covered an increasingly wide area of social life and state activities. Today, there is hardly any area of domestic law entirely unaffected by international law.

The Switzerland Federal Constitution tries to alleviate this problem on three levels; it includes the Cantons in the processes leading to new international treaties, it allows them to influence the ratification of a signed treaty and it lets them participate in the implementation of a treaty in domestic law. The study has going to describe these three levels of participation by the Cantons in more detail.

Participation of Cantons in the Formation of Treaties

On the first level, the Cantons are involved in the formation of new treaties. In this respect, Article 55, Section 1, of the Switzerland Constitution holds:

- The Cantons shall be consulted on foreign policy decisions that affect their powers or their essential interests.

The following two sections say somewhat more specifically how the cantons have to be consulted:

- The Confederation shall inform the Cantons fully and in good time and shall consult with them.
- The views of the Cantons are of particular importance if their powers are affected. In such cases, the Cantons shall participate in international negotiations in an appropriate manner.

These provisions only very vaguely describe the way the cantons have to be involved in the treaty-making process. Much is left to actual practice.

Probably the simplest guarantee is the mandate to the federal government to keep the cantons informed. The federal government frequently informs the cantons on negotiations of treaties that affect their powers. It often grants them full access to all the internal documents. This allows the Cantons to voice their concerns as the negotiations go on.

More difficult is the problem of how to let the Cantons

participate in international negotiations. There are 26 Cantons in the Federal system of Switzerland. It is not possible to have 26 representatives of the cantons as members of the negotiation team. The problem arose when Switzerland negotiated several bilateral treaties with the European Union about many areas of economic and legal cooperation. The Federal Council decided to include an expert appointed by the Cantons in the Swiss negotiating team. This expert participated as a full member in all negotiations. In order to appoint this expert, the Cantons used one of the pre-existing inter-cantonal bodies, the "Conference of Cantonal Governments". This conference decided on whom to send to the Swiss negotiating team as the representative of the Cantons. As a consequence, the Cantons participated in the formation of new international treaties in a very early stage.

This approach, however, has its dangers. It may threaten the unity of the Swiss negotiating team. If the interests of the federal government and those of the Cantons diverge, it becomes difficult pursue their interests. The other party's negotiating team may well jump on visible differences within the Swiss team and exploit them. It is absolutely crucial the negotiating team resolve their differences internally.

In addition, even the participation of cantonal representatives in the negotiations may come at too late a stage. For these reasons, the federal statute implementing Article 55 of Switzerland Constitution states that representatives of the cantons may participate not only in the actual negotiations, but also in the preparation of the mandate for the negotiations (as in general provisions in Article 5 (4) of the Constitution holds that Federation and Cantons should respect International law). This measure is designed to ensure effective participation by the Cantons and to prevent that differences in opinion between Cantons and federal government are displayed in the negotiations themselves. Opposing views have to be reconciled before the negotiations take place, at the stage of preparing the mandate for them.

Participation of Cantons in the Ratification Process

These mechanisms, however, are not the only ones ensuring some influence of the cantons on possible federal encroachment on their powers through international law? The Swiss political system in general places heavy emphasis on a broad consensus supporting its decisions. This consensus-orientation has helped Switzerland to maintain remarkable stability over the last hundred and fifty years. Even though it was not developed with a view to international law, it nevertheless has very visible effects in this area as well.

One of these consensus-based mechanisms is the necessity for the federal executive to have the sanction of parliament for the ratification of international treaties. Article 166, Section 2, of the Switzerland Constitution states:

The Federal Assembly shall approve international treaties, with the exception of those that are concluded by the Federal Council under a statutory provision or an international treaty.

Only treaties of very limited importance may be ratified without approval by parliament. The relevant statute specifies this exemption as follows. [4]

The Federal Council has the power to ratify international treaties of limited importance without parliamentary approval. Such treaties include, but are not limited to, those, that:

1. Do not create new obligations for Switzerland or do not waive any existing rights;
2. Serve to implement treaties approved by the Legislative Assembly;
3. Certain to issues within the powers of the Federal Council, and whose regulation in an international treaty seems expedient;
4. Address primarily the authorities, govern questions of an administrative-technical nature, or do not entail considerable financial expenditure.

All other treaties that are of some importance need parliamentary approval. How does this measure give influence to the cantons? The Federal Assembly consists of two chambers, very similar to the U.S. Congress: the National Council–parallel to the U.S. House of Representatives – and the Council of States–similar to the U.S. Senate. In the Council of States, each Canton has two representatives. [5] They traditionally represent the specific views of their respective cantons, even though they cast their vote in the Council without instruction (Article 161, Section 1, of the Switzerland Constitution). Since approval for ratification needs to be given by both chambers of parliament, the Cantons' views will be brought to bear primarily in the Council of States.

In addition, the public referendum, under some circumstances, tends to safeguard the views of the cantons in concluding international treaties. Treaties about accession to organisations for collective security or to supranational communities (Article 140 of the Switzerland Constitution is subject to a mandatory public referendum). This provision would, for example, apply to a treaty about the accession of Switzerland to the European Union or to NATO. Switzerland is a member of neither and could only become one with a public vote. In such a vote, particular emphasis is given to the cantons: In order to be successful, the referendum would have to be approved by a majority of the Swiss voters. In addition – and here the Cantons come into play–the referendum also needs approval from a majority of the voters *in a majority of the Cantons*. The referendum only passes, if the voters in 12 of the 23 full Cantons approve of it, in addition to a nation-wide popular majority. A treaty of such enormous importance as becoming a member of the EU or NATO, therefore, can only be ratified if the voters in a majority of the cantons approve of it.

This requirement of a double majority for international treaties is confined to these narrow circumstances, i.e. to treaties about accession to organizations for collective security and to supranational communities. This does not mean, however, that with respect to other, less important treaties the cantons do not have a say. This leads me to another aspect of the public referendum:

Article 141, Section 1 (d), of the Constitution allows for a public referendum against international treaties in the following situations: international treaties that are:

1. Unlimited duration and may not be terminated.
2. Provide for accession to an international organisation.
3. Contain important legislative provisions or whose implementation requires the enactment of federal legislation.

Most treaties of some importance fall under one of these three categories. The referendum is, however, not mandatory, as it is with respect to the accession to supranational organizations and organizations for collective security. Only if 50,000 voters request a referendum within 100 days upon publication, the referendum takes place. An alternative way to put these treaties up for a referendum involves the Cantons: Instead of 50,000 voters, the referendum can be initiated by eight cantons. Eight Cantons can request that any international treaty falling under the quoted provision be put to a public vote. This tool allows the Cantons to challenge international treaties they do not approve of directly and subject them to a public vote. It is up to Cantonal law to decide which Cantonal authority is competent to decide whether to request a referendum. The possibility of a referendum by eight Cantons seems a strong weapon for the Cantons to prevent international treaties they do not agree with. However, the Cantons have never used this tool, not a single time. This may suggest that the other mechanisms involving the Cantons in the treaty-making process suffice.

Participation of Cantons in the Implementation of Treaties

Once an international treaty becomes law, the question arises how to implement it. As a generally monist country, Switzerland does not need statutory transformation of international law. However, those treaties–or at least those treaty provisions–that are not self-executing need legislative implementation to become effective domestically. And here again, the Switzerland Constitution gives some weight to the Cantons.

Even though the federal government has the power to enter into international treaties in all areas of life, it is not competent to implement all of them. If a treaty covers a subject-matter not given to the federal government by the Constitution, but reserved for the Cantons, it is the Cantons that have to implement it. Let me illustrate this mechanism with the Schengen treaty again. The Schengen treaty requires, among other things, the police to co-operate across borders. The power to maintain and operate the police lies mainly with the Cantons. Therefore, it is their duty to implement this aspect of the Schengen treaty. The federal government does not have the power to legislate about this matter; the international treaty does nothing to change that.

This situation strengthens the Cantons, but can have uncomfortable consequences for the federal government. Under international law, responsibility for the fulfilment of Switzerland's legal obligations lies with the federal government. If it does not have the power to implement it with legislation of its own, what happens if a Canton does not pass the necessary laws? The Constitution is silent on this question, but most commentators agree that the federal government must have the powers to legislate itself, if all other measures to get a Canton to implement the treaty fail.

Another problem with this approach is that international treaties typically cover areas that need a unified legal order; unification is often one of the main purposes behind establishing international treaties. Leaving implementation to 26 different Cantons defeats this purpose. The Schengen treaty again is an example on point: It does not make sense to have 18 different legal regimes covering cooperation of Swiss police forces with those of the neighbouring countries (there are 18 cantons with a border to a foreign country). For this reason, the cantons implemented the Schengen treaty not with individual statutes, but they entered into a treaty among themselves, a treaty between the Cantons. This approach guarantees uniformity, even though it is the cantons that retain the power to implement the Schengen treaty.

Conclusion

It has become clear that the Swiss Constitution tries to ensure participation of the Cantons in negotiating, ratifying and implementing international treaties to quite a large extent. One might think that such a system would be too inert because it gives the Cantons the tools necessary to block any meaningful new treaties. However, this danger has not materialized. The powers of the Cantons in the making of treaties and popular participation by public referenda have not blocked Swiss accession to treaties, but have slowed it. For example, Switzerland was one of the last countries to become a member of the United Nations, in 2002. In the public vote, only 12 Cantons were for it, 11 were against it; Switzerland is the only country to join the UN based on a popular referendum decision. In some important areas, however, the extensive mechanisms for participation by the public and by the Cantons left their mark: Switzerland is not a member of the EU and not of NATO. This is mainly due to the necessity of a public referendum for accession and in that referendum, a majority of the voters as well as the cantons would be required.

End Notes

1. An unofficial English translation of Swiss Federal Constitution is available at *http://www.admin.ch/ch/e/rs/c 101.html* (in pdf and html).
2. Translation by the author.
3. Article 27 Vienna Convention on the Law of Treaties of 23 May 1969, UNTS 1155:331.
4. See Government and Administration Organization Act of March 21, 1997, Article 7a Section2 (translation by the author) The authoritative text in German, French and Italian is available at *http://www.admin.ch/ch/d/sr/sr.html.*
5. Six Cantons are – for historical reasons – only – "half-cantons",

are therefore allotted only one representative in the Council of States.

2

Indian Federalism and International Treaties

Ashutosh Saxena

Federal system of governance guarantees the accommodation, protection and development of multi-cultural diversities through federal units. The very notion of division of authorities and powers between federal and unit governments is based on need for recognizing the diversified interests and demands. The system otherwise functions well, as the federal governance is tied through a written constitution which is well guarded by an impartial and supreme institution of arbitration in the form of Supreme Court.

Federalism has been broadly categorized as vertical and horizontal. Vertical Federalism advocate for central dominance over the state, whereas Horizontal Federalism focuses on lateral cooperation among the state units to collectively articulate their interests. [1] The post-modern political culture which believes in recognition of distinctive identities, also prescribe for more downward and horizontal federal structure of polity for stability and development. Today, the federal structure need not be two fold or three fold but power and decision making processes need to be decentralized at the lowest level.

Indian Federalism

Pluralism and federalism are two essential principles for organizing heterogeneous societies into a viable pattern of political sharing of power. Federalism builds and sustains the unity of polity and simultaneously preserves and promotes the plurality of society. It is from this perspective, and ideological premises of federal nation, participatory democracy, secularism and social justice that we should re-examine our federal polity and plural society. [2]

India, the land of unique diversity and heterogeneity, in it's evolution of 5000 years old civilization developed many ethnic, religious, linguistic cultural diversities which have intermingled in evolving a classic plural society under the umbrella of cultural nationalism, which recognizes and respects the concept of "Unity in Diversity". India has never been governed by a single or unitary centre of authority. Throughout the history there has been persistent endeavour to establish sustainable political order in a diverse social framework marked by civilizational unity. Even during the formation of Indian federal state, both 'Centripetal and Centrifugal forces' were in action. Therefore, the framers of the Constitution appeared to have been virtually unanimous on the need for a strong central government with two sets of governments operating at central and state level. Also, nowhere in the Constitution the word "federal" as such is mentioned – indeed, the Constitution says that the nation is a 'Union of states' (Article 1), and it deliberately worked towards building a strong centre.

Indian system has been described, as a "federation without federalism", and variously referred to as 'executive competitive' or 'quasi-federal'. These interpretations are due to the several provisions that permit the centre to infringe on the states' rights. These provisions encompass political, financial and administrative fields. Some of the important provisions are the power of the Parliament to make laws with respect to any matter enumerated in the state list Under Article 249; power of the central government to impose emergency under Article 352; the power of the President, to assume the normal powers of a state, remove a state ministry, dissolve the legislature and empower the union legislature to exercise the respective states' power for a temporary period due to Constitutional failure or political breakdown under Article

356. The Amendment to the Constitution under Article 263, can be initiated only by the introduction of a bill in Parliament which must be passed by 2/3rd majority in both the houses, along with ratification by the legislatures of not less than one half of the states. [3]

However, it is important to mention here that federalism in India is not a static concept. May be it is correct that strong centre was the need at the time of framing the Constitution but as Krishnamachari argued in the constituent assembly debate that federalism is not a definite concept and it has not got any stable meaning. It is a concept the definition of which has been changing from time to time. The demand of 21st Century particularly in view of globalized society and economy is that the nature, content and functioning of federalism need changes constitutionally, otherwise democracy and multi-culturalism will take its own course.

Federalism and Treaty-making Procedure in India

International personality is the source of treaty-making power or we say treaty making power is an attribute of international personality. According to the current status of international law, only states and international organizations possess the capacity to make treaties. Neither private individuals nor transnational corporations possess such capacity. So far as federal states are concerned, there is no doubt that the federal government has the capacity to sign and ratify treaties with foreign countries.

Capacity of the Component Units of the Federation

Whether member states of a federation have treaty-making power or not depends on the federal constitution. After studying constitutions of 24 federal States, a study has concluded that in a majority of federal states the component units have no power at all to conclude treaties with foreign countries and that in some of the federal states a limited power of treaty-making is entrusted to the component units. [4]

Before a critical view of the treaty-making power under Indian Constitution is made, it is proposed to examine similar provisions in other countries.

1. United States of America: Article VI of U.S. Constitution declares that the Constitution and the laws of the United States which shall be made in pursuance thereof; and all treaties made, or which shall be made, under the authority of the United States, shall be the supreme Law of the land; and the judges in every state shall be bound thereby, anything in the Constitution or laws of any state to the contrary notwithstanding. The result of this provision is that a treaty which is made by the Federal Executive with the assent of the Senate must be supreme even though it trenches upon the normal sphere of the States as outlined by the other provisions of the Constitution. Thus, in Missouri vs. Holland, the U.S. Supreme Court held the Migratory Bird Treaty Act passed by the Congress, was valid although the States had a Constitutional title to migratory birds within them. A treaty made by the U.S. may override private rights created by a State law.

In spite of the wide language used in the Article, it merely enlarges the federal power against the states, but it cannot override federal laws or the prohibitions of the Constitution. A valid law of Congress has been placed on the same footing as a treaty. In Unites States the President negotiates treaties on the advice and with the consent of the Senate. The treaty may have no operation in the U.S. although it may involve a breach of the treaty with the foreign state in case the Senate disapproves it.

2. Canada: Section 132 of the British North America Act provides: "the Parliament and Government of Canada shall have all powers necessary for performing the obligations of Canada or of any provision thereof as part of the British Empire, towards foreign countries, arising under treaties between the Empire and such foreign countries." The Dominion Parliament has thus exclusive power to implement a treaty when it comes within Section 132 or where the general residuary power under Section 91 is applicable. But the Dominion Parliament cannot legislate to implement the agreement without the consent of the Provinces, if the international convention was signed by Canada as an independent State, not as a member of the British Commonwealth of Nations, and the matter of the Convention relates to the classes of Provincial subjects. It would thus appear that the Dominion Parliament still lacks the whole of the treaty-making power.

3. Australia: There is nowhere a separate treaty-making power in the Constitution for Australia. Section 51 (xxxix) of the Constitution Act of Australia gives the Commonwealth, the power over "External Affairs". In King vs. Burges case, it was laid down that the external affairs include agreements entered into by Australia and the Commonwealth. Legislation to give effect to such agreement is valid despite its effect on States. It has been suggested in Australia that executive would not ratify a treaty or accept an obligation under the treaty until the appropriate domestic legislation has been passed which would necessarily mean that the ratification treaty has been in principle debated and approved by the Parliament. Furthermore, important that the states will be consulted before entering into treaties and all information will be shared between the various chief ministers of the states.

Role of Parliament and States in Treaty-making: The Indian Position

In the context of treaty making power in practice in India, the states have very little role in the process of treaty making, particularly given that, constitutionally, no role has been set out for them. The power of making international agreements and treaty are vested in executive at centre. Our founding fathers of the Constitution expressly included the treaty-making power within the legislative competence of the Parliament and they incorporated:

1. Article 73: Extent of executive power of the Union (a) to the matters with respect to which Parliament has power to make laws; and (b) to the exercise of such rights, authority and jurisdiction as are exercisable by the Government of India by virtue of any treaty of agreement.

2. Article 253 in Part XI of the Constitution; empowers Parliament to make any law for India for implementing any treaty, even on entry/topic reserved exclusively for state legislature under the Constitution.

3. Article 246 effects a distribution of legislative power between the Union and the States. Article 246(1) says: "... Parliament has exclusive power to make laws with respect to any of the matters enumerated in List I in the Seventh Schedule (in this Constitution referred to as the "Union List". Clause (2) speaks of the concurrent power of Parliament and State Legislatures to legislate with respect to matters in Concurrent List (List III) while clause (3) empowers the State Legislatures to legislate with respect to matters in the State List (List II). Clause (4) empowers the Parliament to make laws with respect to Union territories without any limitation of division of legislative power.

4. The Seventh Schedule to the Constitution contains three Lists: Union, State and Concurrent. Entries 13, 14, 15 and 16 in the Union List are relevant, particularly Entry 14. [5]

5. Articles 73, 246(1) and 253 read in conjunction with the relevant items on the Union List, give the Executive (that is, the Council of Ministers) all the powers necessary to negotiate, enter into and ratify treaties. Even the Parliament is not taken into confidence before such an agreement takes place. And even if the advice is sought through Standing Committee of the Parliament, it may not be finally taken into consideration like in case of TRIPS Agreement.

Absence of Consultation with Parliament in Treaty-making: The Indian Experience

Taking advantage of the fact that Parliament has chosen

not to make any law regulating the treaty-making power, the Union Government has been, taking advantage of Article 73 of the Constitution, freely enter into treaties on its own without reference or taking Parliament into confidence. It would be instructive to notice what happened in the case of TRIPS agreement. India was evidently rattled by the draft Agreement on TRIPS produced by the Conference. The Government probably thought it would be appropriate to bring the matter to the notice of Parliament. Accordingly, the matter was referred to the Standing Committee of Parliament which after due considerations opposed all the major stipulations and terms contained in the draft agreement. But still, the Government of India signed the TRIPS agreement in 1994, practically in the same shape as the draft agreement, without again approaching the Parliamentary Committee or the Parliament.

It needs to be emphasized that TRIPS agreement is not the only agreement signed by the Government of India in this way, there are several such agreements concerning trade, services, agriculture. It is a matter of common knowledge that neither the Parliament nor the people of this country were taken into confidence before signing these agreements having such serious repercussions upon the life and the lives of the citizens of this country. It, therefore, becomes essential to think of subjecting the treaty-making power of the Central Government to appropriate checks and controls, as is sought to be done in several countries all over the world.

Entering into treaties and agreements with foreign powers is, of course one of the chief attributes of Statehood. It is also a fact that international treaties have serious impact upon the economy, social and political life of its society. In spite of the fundamental importance of the treaty-making power to the people of the land, the experience of WTO treaties signed by our Government without consulting or without taking into confidence either the Parliament or the public—the agreements signed on Intellectual Property Rights (TRIPS), trade, agriculture and services, etc., force us to question the legitimacy of treaty-making power under the Constitution. [6]

Executive is not all that Supreme

An international convention or treaty becomes a part of the domestic legal system through incorporation. That happens when the treaty is first signed and then ratified by the executive itself. A legislative backing is not always a prerequisite in the process. Further, if the implementation of these treaties or convention is possible at the administrative level, there is no need for it to have a statutory foundation. [7]

However, in case when the convention or treaty is in deviance with the law of the land they have to be backed with a legislation (that is, if the provisions are not in consonance with the provisions of the domestic law). Any such convention or treaty which seeks to alter the Constitution or any other law in force in India requires an act of the Legislature. Till the time they are not backed with legislation, the treaties and conventions are not enforceable under the Honourable courts of India. [8] With regard to alteration of the laws of the land it has been laid down in the Maganbhai case by Shah, J.: "If in consequence of the exercise of the executive power, rights of the citizens or others are restricted or infringed, or laws are modified, the exercise of power must be supported by legislation." [9] It has also been held by the Honourable court that the treaty obligations cannot have an overriding effect with respect to the municipal law of the land. [10]

The power to enter into treaties and implement them is in terms absolute in India, but having regard to the fact that we have a written Federal Constitution; a court would imply limitation on that power. A treaty, for instance, cannot make provisions which would, in effect, amend the Constitution, for it could not have been intended that a power conferred by the Constitution would, without an amendment of the Constitution, alter or destroy the Constitution. Even while exercising powers conferred by virtue of Article 73 and Article 253, the Executive cannot infringe on the rights of the citizens and create new laws thereof. This has been the established norm even for dealing with the situations that relate to the provisions of the domestic law wherein the executive cannot affect the rights that are guaranteed to the citizens of the nation under the Constitution. Further, no new offences can be created similarly without a confirmatory legislation.

Judicial Interpretation of Treaty-making and Implementation Entitlement in Indian Federal System

After the commencement of the Constitution, quite a few cases have arisen where the Supreme Court had to interpret Entries 14, 15 of List I of the VII Schedule, Articles 73 and 253.

In Maganbhai Iishwarbhai Patel vs. Union of India (1970) 3 SCC 400/AIR 1969/SC 783), regarding the border dispute between India and Pakistan in the area of the Rann of Kutch, where Kanjarkot and a few other villages fell to Pakistan, certain persons approached the Gujarat High Court questioning the power of the Central Government to, what they called, surrender a portion of the territory of India to a foreign power. The matter was ultimately carried to the Supreme Court. M. Hidayatullah, Chief Justice, noted in the case that: "A treaty really concerns the political rather than the judicial wing of the State. When a treaty or an award after arbitration comes into existence, it has to be implemented and this can only be if all the three branches of Government: the Legislature, the Executive and the Judiciary, or any of them, possess the power to implement it. If there is any deficiency in the Constitutional system it has to be removed and the State must equip itself with the necessary power".

The Chief Justice further noted that under our Constitution, treaty-making power is not vested in the Executive or the President–as has been done in some other Constitutions. It is squarely placed within the domain of the Parliament. Theoretically speaking, Parliament can by making a law prohibit the Executive to enter into a particular treaty or a particular kind of treaties; similarly, it can also direct the Executive to enter into a particular treaty or may disapprove or reject a treaty signed and/or ratified by the Executive. It is a different matter that Parliament has not chosen to make a law in that behalf, leaving the Executive totally free to exercise this power in an unfettered and, if I may say so, in an unguided fashion.

Justice Shah J. who delivered a separate but concurring judgment in the above mentioned case dealt specifically with Article 253 and made certain observations which were relevant and which constituted the basis for the judgment of the Bombay High Court in P.B. Samant vs. Union of India (1994 Bombay, 323). It was a petition filed by certain public-spirited individuals seeking the issuance of a writ of mandamus restraining the Union of India from entering into final treaty relating to Dunkel (chairman of the Uruguay Round of GATT negotiations) proposals without obtaining sanction of the Parliament and State Legislatures. In reply, the Union of India relied upon Article 253 of the Constitution and the decision of the Supreme Court in Maganbhai case. It was submitted that not only the Union is entitled to enter into treaties; Parliament alone can make law to give effect to such treaties and international agreements.

Reliance was placed particularly upon the following observations of Justice Shah J. in his separate but concurrent opinion in Maganbhai case. Relying upon the observations of Shah J. quoted above, the High Court held: "The observations made by the learned Judge establish that the executive power conferred under Article 73 is to be read along with the power conferred under Article 253 of the Constitution of India. The observation leave no manner of doubt that in case the Government enters into treaty or agreement, then in respect of implementation thereof, it is open for the Parliament to pass a law which deals with the matters which are in the State list. In case the Parliament is entitled to pass laws in respect of matter in the State list in pursuance of the treaty or the agreement, then it is difficult to appreciate how it can be held that the Central Government is not entitled to enter into treaty or agreement which affects the matters included in the State list." [11]

There is criticism that current practices have led to a 'democratic deficit' or a lack of accountability in the treaty making provision and practices. The concern is that the practice, whereby treaties are entered into by the executive (that is, the Union Government) without significant Parliamentary involvement, is 'undemocratic'.

Federalism in India has always been a dynamic concept and has evolved during the past six decades. The emergence of coalition governments at the national and state levels, growth of regional leaders, impact of globalization and increased people awareness, etc. have contributed in generating need for paradigm shift in federal structure and functioning. There is a strong need for new federal identity and recasting centre-state relations in order to build a more co-operative federal polity where socio-cultural pluralism are accommodated within federal polity and society. [12]

Impact of Globalization: Growing Assertion of States

The federal functioning of the system has undergone a transformation in India widely since the era of globalization began. Until the mid-1990s, the states' involvement in the reforms and development process was less than satisfactory. Guhan [13] says that the Centre was both 'unwilling and unable' to involve the states in the process for a number of reasons:

- External agencies' preference for policy dialogue only with the national government;
- Centre' sole competence in macro-economic stabilization;
- The multicultural-political nature of state governments.

In any case, the states' role is very crucial in the globalization process. Three considerations in this connection arc of vital importance.

First, globalization, as pre-dominantly economic and political processes, is ultimately to be implemented in the states.

Second, constitutionally, the states are responsible for a variety of development works since the Union Government (as all line and no staff!) does not have the bureaucracy to implement its laws; it has to depend on the states for the job.

Third, democratically mandated state governments are more politically vulnerable because being close to the people it is they who suffer/benefit from the after-effects of the policies of globalization.

There have been constant and conscious efforts by the states to be part of the global economic, social and political network directly or indirectly. With the passage of time, the regional identities representing sections of population started demanding share in the decision making processes. These demands should not be treated with wrong intentions. This is the effect or outcome of ongoing process of globalization. States do participate directly with the world community and maintain economic, cultural and social relations with them. The federal government has no other choice but to accept this changing phenomenon and give federal units a fare chance to participate in decision making process. Various state heads, state ministers and bureaucratic officers are visiting abroad and receiving foreign dignitaries in expectation of direct investments and export opportunities.

A group of chief ministers from the North-Eastern States was scheduled to visit Dhaka in March 2009, but was postponed due to internal problems of Bangladesh. However, during her visit to India in January 2010 the Prime Minister of Bangladesh Sheikh Hasina stressed the need for strengthening the relations between Bangladesh and North-Eastern States. The Bangladesh prime minister told them that her country is ready to increase trade and connectivity with the North-Eastern States, especially Assam, Tripura and Meghalaya. The Bangladesh Prime Minister has also invited the North-Eastern

Chief Ministers to visit her country and finalise the modalities to further increase trade and connectivity. Chief Ministers of North-Eastern states also pleaded for more connectivity and trade between the North-Eastern states and Bangladesh, Investors from the ASEAN (Association of South East Asian Nations) countries also visited the region to explore business opportunities.

When seen from the perspective of globalization, the states are today offered more freedom of action in respect of adopting and implementing structural adjustment programmes, the states have become more competitive for inviting investment, industrialization, trade and commerce, entrepreneurial governance for development. With a view to attract foreign investors in their states, many of them are offering incentive packages in the form of various tax concessions, capital interest subsidies, reduced power tariff etc. The Indian government made several reforms in the economic policy of the country in the early 1990s. This helped in the liberalization and deregulation of the Indian economy and also opened the country's markets to foreign direct investment.

As a result of this, huge amounts of foreign direct investment came into India through Non Resident Indians, International companies, and various other foreign investors. The growth of FDI in India boosted the economic growth of the country. FDI in different states in India have increased steadily since the early 1990s when the Indian economy was opened up to foreign investments. The status of FDI in different states of India, during the period beginning from the year January 2000 to October 2006 corroborates the growth of Indian states in sync with the Indian economy. Some of the states in India which have witnessed a massive upsurge in FDI Inflows include Delhi (USD 6,780 million), Maharashtra (USD 5,650.1 million), Karnataka (USD 1,876.1 million), and Tamil Nadu (USD 1,876.1 million). Other states which are in the receipt of FDI Inflows in India include, West Bengal,

Gujarat, Haryana, Andhra Pradesh, Kerala, and Uttar Pradesh. [14]

Various forms of states' growing assertions have also been noticed by acute observers of Indian politics and federalism since the 1990s. C.P. Bhambri says, "The state governments are very important players in the economic development of the country, more pronounced of course since the 1990s. This striking fact has become clear in the 1990s because investors have to contact every state government for launching a project. Since the central state is gradually withdrawing itself from its social responsibilities including welfare-oriented development, most clearly evident, among others, in the shrinkage of the number of centrally-sponsored welfarist development schemes, as Bhambri has shown, centre-state relations have taken often peculiar forms. Persuading and even bribing often could become tactics resorted to by the centre for involving the state governments in the process of economic reforms and restructuring". [15] Rao and Singh (2005) [16] have recognized that the state's role has expanded due to market economy which demands more decentralized levels of governance, but also that all the states are not equally equipped to access the opportunities afforded by the market.

Though the states in India have no direct Constitutional jurisdiction over foreign relations; yet today their growing assertion can be seen to have evolved by extra-constitutional means. The States can also consult with the federal government through the Inter-State Council. Multilateral trading agreements like WTO, with commitments in goods, services, intellectual property and dispute settlement, have reduced the power of the national government. Issues of state sovereignty and federal distribution of power are called into question. The new liberalized economic policies and reforms started in nineties focusing on the realignment of Indian economy to global markets have serious implications for states' economies and electoral fortunes. The regional leaders have got into the mode of demanding partnership in the federal policy-making processes that concern multilateral arrangements with International Organizations like IMF, World Bank and the WTO. Yet another level inter-regional competition of sorts has come to mark the behaviour of state governments in their endeavour to attract more foreign direct investment.

The contemporary phase of the working of federal system in the country which is said to have begun in late 1980s, with the onset of the era of coalition and relatively weaker governments at the centre has been marked by the reversal roles of the sorts for the major players of the game. To put it differently, if during the times of Nehru and Indira Gandhi, the central government by hook or by crook, tried to bully the state governments and over centralized the already centralized constitutional framework of the centre state relation of the country. In the present phase of centre state relations, the overbearing coalition partners with their roots and political visions predominantly if not totally, confined to particular states so much guide and sometimes dictate policies and actions of the central government that India appears to be a classic case of federation where the states are autonomous, with the central government functioning in accordance with their sweet wishes. What is remarkable, however, in this context is the fact even the parties which were staunch supporters of the demand for state autonomy like the National Conference and DMK did not press for any serious effort at recasting the basic parameters in the Constitution, when they were as in the case of former or are as in the case of later, in a position to dictate terms to the centre government.

Recommendations to Amend the Provisions of Treaty-making Power

There is a growing concern all over that executive should not be left free to enter into treaties without taking Parliament or States into confidence. There is need to decentralize the power structure where the lower bodies do have share in decision-making.

- In 1983 Sarkaria Commission was set up to look into the Sub-Regional aspirations and redefine centre-state relations. The Commission observed that federalism was not a static concept but a functional arrangement for cooperative action. The Commission commented that there was not only inadequate territorial and functional decentralization in India when the country became independent, but there has also been a pervasive trend towards greater centralization of powers over the years, due to the pressure of powerful socio-economic forces. The Commission observed that there is special need in a country like India for a conscious and purposive effort to counter it all the time. It recommended decentralization below the state to the local elected bodies. The need for such affirmative action also caught the imagination of jurists, intellectuals and political leaders. Decentralization of real power to local institutions would help defuse the threat of centrifugal forces, increase popular involvement all along the line, broaden the base of our democratic polity, promote administrative efficiency and improve the health and stability of inter-governmental relations.
- On 5th March, 1993, Shri George Fernandes, Member of Parliament, Lok Sabha gave notice of intention to introduce the Constitution (Amendment) Bill, 1993 for amending Article 253 to provide that treaties and conventions be ratified by each House of Parliament by not less than one half of the membership of each House and by a majority of the legislatures of not less than half the states. However, the Bill was not listed for consideration during the life of that Lok Sabha.
- Shri Satyaprakash Malviya, Member, Rajya Sabha tabled a question (No. 6856) enquiring whether the government proposes to introduce any legislation to amend the Constitution to provide for Parliamentary approval of international treaties.

- In India, Justice Krishna Iyer, who presided over Peoples' Commission on GATT, recommended that "it is a matter of constitutional necessity that legislation be enacted so that all treaties go through ratification of the agreement by legislature. It even suggested on the basis of a detailed examination, that the final text resulting in the Uruguay Round is ultravires the Treaty Making Power."
- Justice Venkatchalliah Committee Report of the National Commission to review the working of the Constitution (2002) submitted to Central Government had recognized the delicacy of the situation and recommended for reducing tension or friction between States and the Union and for expeditious decision-making on important issues involving states. The desirability of prior consultation by the Union Government with the Inter-State Council may be considered before signing any treaty vitally affecting the interests of the States regarding matters in the State List.

Conclusion

It can be concluded that the federalism in 21st Century demands that State members of a federal union should possess a shared capacity to conclude treaties if such capacity is admitted by the federal constitution and within the limits there laid down. There have been certain welcome steps in the form of FDI and otherwise growing assertion of states, but States do require proper legal and Constitutional share in decision-making process at national and international level. States represent the multicultural societies. Central executive is sometimes unaware of the demands aspirations and expectations of the diversified cultural societies, this result in regional movements and demands for separate autonomous states as we are witnessing across the state. The better position would be to involve states bodies in decision making process at all important decision making levels irrespective of subject matters of three lists as enlisted in Schedule VII. The states sharing borders with neighbouring countries like North-Eastern States, Punjab, Rajasthan, UP, Bihar, etc. have direct exposure and are more vulnerable. These states must be involved while dealing with or concluding international treaties with their respective bordering countries.

It is not that sharing of decision and treaty-making power with the states is absolutely free from evils. There are lots of apprehended dangers. We have been witnessing a lot of cessionist tendencies in diverse sections of society. People are being segregated on the basis of region, religion, caste, cultural and linguistic identities for political reasons. Happenings in J & K, Punjab, Maharashtra, North-Eastern States and most of others are before us. Thus, though the notion of sharing of sovereign power with the state units is an ideal theoretical formulation, but it has to be implemented with precautions and care.

The federal sprit of our system is Unity with due respect to plural identities. Regional variations in growth develop regional disparities which is harmful for federalism. FDI is welcome, but in the process inter-regional rivalry may creep in, which is dangerous for common national growth. Indian Constitution has provided for setting up of a consensus building and disputes resolution mechanism. It was decided to set up an Inter State Council for mutual consultation and coordination of policies and actions on all matters of common interest between the States and also between the Union and the States. There is a need to further strengthen this body so that the national government and the state governments join hands, in a forum to decide upon the policies, plans and mega projects.

End Notes

1. Allan Erbsen, (2008). *Horizontal Federalism,* the Federal Courts Workshop at American University's Washington College of Law, and faculty workshops at Georgetown University Law Centre and the University of Minnesota Law School.
2. Rasheeduddin Khan, (1997). *Rethinking Indian Federalism,*

Inter-University Centre for Humanities and Social Sciences, Indian Institute of Advanced Study, Shimla.

3. Maj Dalbir Singh, All India Congress Committee. *Democracy, Federalism and Globalisation*, seminar paper presented in Barcelona, 2010.
4. Amna Mirza, *Parliamentarisation versus Federalisation: Treaty Making Power of the Executive in India, Mainstream,* 11 July 2008.
5. Entering into treaties and agreements with foreign countries and implementing of treaties, agreements and conventions with foreign countries.
6. Wali Ullah, *The Treaty-making Power Under the Constitution of India, Hindustan Times,* August 10, 1971.
7. State of West Bengal vs. Jugal Kishore, AIR 1969 SC 1171; State of Gujarat v. Vora Fidali, AIR 1964 SC 1043.
8. Union of India vs. Manmull Jain, AIR 1954 Cal. 615.
9. Jolly George Varghese vs. Bank of Cochin, AIR 1980 SC 470.
10. Khanna H.R., (2001). National Commission to Review the Working of the Constitution, a consultation paper on treaty-making power under our Constitution.
11. Ibid.
12. Sarita, (2009). *Federalism in India: A Quest for New Identity,* Regal Publications.
13. Guhan S, (1995). *Centre and State in the Reform Process,* in Rober Cassen and Vijay Joshi, (eds) New Delhi: Oxford University press.
14. *FDI from Developing and Transition Economies: Implications for Development, World Investment Report,* United Nations, New York and Geneva, 2006.
15. Bhambri C.P., *Political Economy of Federalism in India, Economic and Political Weekly,* 2000: 330.
16. Govinda Rao M. and Nirvikar Singh, (2005). *Political Economy of Federalism in India,* New Delhi: Oxford University Press.

3

International Treaties and Centre-State Relations

V. Suryanarayanan

The Constitution of India, which came into operation on January 26, 1950 introduced a federal form of government, but the extent of federalism, both in theory and practice, was diluted in order to make the Central Government extremely powerful. When the founding fathers were discussing the provisions of the Constitution, a matter of great concern for them was the preservation and promotion of the unity and territorial integrity of the country. The question of incorporation of nearly 600 princely states into India, the problems relating to the accession of Jammu and Kashmir and the volatile situation in the northeast tilted the debate in favour of a strong centre. In fact, the Constitution of India does not use the term "federal" it refers to India as a "Union of States". Dr. B.R. Ambedkar, the Father of the Indian Constitution, has stated that the use of the term "Union" was deliberate. The Drafting Committee was crystal clear that although India was to be a functioning federation, the federation was not the consequence of an agreement among the constituent units. None of the constituent units was sovereign like the thirteen American colonies after the Declaration of Independence or the Swiss Cantons before they decided to enter into a federal compact. Equally important the component units had no freedom to secede from the federation. As a well known scholar has pointed out, in normal times, India would function as a federation, but it can be and has been, in exceptional circumstance, transformed into highly centralized State.

According to the Constitution of India, foreign affairs and

the powers to make treaties vest within the exclusive jurisdiction of the Central Government. What is more, Article 253 of the Constitution empowers parliament to make any law for India for implementing any treaty, even on subjects reserved exclusively for State Legislature. In theory and practice, the state governments do not have any role in this significant area of Indian political system. However, it is essential to keep in mind the reality of Indian geography and how it influences bilateral and multilateral relations. India has land boundaries with Pakistan, China, Nepal, Bhutan, Bangladesh and Myanmar and maritime boundaries with Pakistan, Bangladesh, Myanmar, Thailand, Indonesia, Sri Lanka and Maldives. And, what is more, India's neighbourhood policy has its immediate fallout on contiguous Indian States.

Thus, the vagaries of India-Pakistan relations have their immediate fallout on Punjab, Jammu and Kashmir, Rajasthan and Punjab; the twists and turns in India-Nepal relations affect Bihar, Uttar Pradesh Sikkim and Uttarakhand; the tranquillity in the long Sino-Indian boundary is vital from the point of view of stability of Arunachal Pradesh, Sikkim, Uttarakhand, Himachal Pradesh and Jammu and Kashmir (including Pakistan Occupied Kashmir); India-Bhutan relations will affect Sikkim, Assam, Arunachal Pradesh and West Bengal; India-Myanmar relations impinge on the polity and economy of Mizoram, Manipur, Nagaland and Arunachal Pradesh; India-Bangladesh relations will have their fallout on West Bengal, Meghalaya, Tripua and Mizoram. The fate of thousands of Malayalees working in West Asia is a matter of great concern for the people and Government of Kerala and the State of Tamil Nadu has a vital stake in the political stability of Sri Lanka and also better relations with Myanmar, Malaysia, Singapore and Indonesia.

It is also essential to keep in mind the basic transformation that has taken place in the Indian political system. During the era of one-party dominance, 1947-1977, when the Indian

National Congress was in power in the Centre and in most of the States, the Central Government could afford to ignore the feelings and sensibilities of the regional actors in the name of "good neighbourly relations". After 1977, the reality is that the party, which rules in the Centre, cannot remain in power without the support of regional parties. The regional parties wield considerable influence in the formulation and implementation of domestic and foreign policies. In that process, one may argue, the regional parties have also become "national". Coalition governments have become the order of the day. Unlike the early years of Independence, when the dominant opinion was in favour of a strong centre, today the opinion is veering round to the point of view that strong states and strong centre are not mutually contradictory. A successful co-operative federalism implies greater co-operation and consultation among the various constituent units of the Indian political system.

In this essay, the author have tried to focus on two important issues, which were of vital concern to the Governments and people of Tamil Nadu, where the Central Government ignored the wishes of the State and entered into bilateral agreements with Sri Lanka. The first is the Sirimavo-Shastri Pact of 1964 and the subsequent Sirimavo-Indira Gandhi Pact of 1974, by which New Delhi agreed to confer Indian citizenship on thousands of people of Indian origin in the Island and decided to repatriate them back to India as Indian citizens. The second relates to the India-Sri Lanka Maritime Boundary Agreements of 1974 and 1976, which ceded the Island of Kachchatheevu to Sri Lanka and also sacrificed the traditional fishing rights enjoyed by the Indian fishermen in the Pak Bay region. These agreements have left a trail of bitterness in the State of Tamil Nadu and sections of people in the State have begun to feel that the interests of Tamil Nadu are not safe in the powers that be that determine foreign policy from "distant" New Delhi.

The ideal situation that we should strive to create is for the affected Indian States to make benign inputs into the making of India's neighbourhood policy. This pre-supposes the functioning of vibrant and dynamic research departments in various Universities and research institutions outside the University system with the avowed objective of analyzing various problems in depth and sensitise the general public and the policy planners about various policy options. How can the State Governments be involved in the decision-making process? Should the representatives of the State be included in the decision-making process? Should bilateral treaties be ratified by the concerned State Legislatures? Should Rajya Sabha be reconstituted so that it becomes an institution like the American Senate which has the powers to ratify international treaties? It may be recalled that the establishment of the League of Nations after the First World War was based on President Wilson's fourteen points.

However, the United States itself could not become a member of the League of Nations because the Senate did not ratify the proposal. Similarly, the Comprehensive Test Ban Treaty, in the formulation of which the US State Department played an important, role could not be adhered to because the US Senate did not ratify it. Should India set up an organization like the Committee on Foreign Relations in the United States which plays a dynamic role in US foreign policy? The Committee on Foreign Relations is a Standing Committee of the US Senate. It is the leading body for foreign policy legislation and debate. It is generally responsible for overseeing (not administering) and funding foreign aid programmes as well as funding, arms sales and training for national allies.

The Committee also undertakes hearing on important policy matters in which experts from diverse fields from different parts of the world participate. The Committee has debated, considered and reported on important treaties and legislations. All diplomatic nominations take place after the approval of the Foreign Relations Committee. It is also interesting to note that the federal units in Yugoslavia, before its disintegration, had their own departments of foreign affairs and these departments could formulate foreign policies towards contiguous states, but these should be in conformity with the principles and practices of national foreign policy. However, it should be pointed out that Yugoslavia could continue to exist as a united country because of the towering personality of President Tito. Though federal in theory, it was highly centralized in practice and after Tito's demise, the contradictions, which were lying dormant, came out into the open and the country soon disintegrated. We can learn from the experience of other countries, while establishing our own unique system. The author hopes that, the deliberations in this Seminar will trigger a healthy debate on this issue and related matters.

Sirimavo-Shastri Pact, 1964 and Sirimavo-Indira Gandhi Pact, 1974

According to the bilateral agreement in October 1964 between the Governments of India and Sri Lanka, popularly known as the Sirimavo-Shastri Pact, India agreed to confer citizenship on 5.25 lakh persons, with their natural increase, over a period of fifteen years. The agreement was followed by another in 1974, as a result of which India was to receive another 75,000 persons of Indian origin, within a period of two years, after those under the first Agreement had been repatriated. The entire process was expected to be completed by October 1981. Sri Lanka agreed, in turn, to absorb 3,00,000 persons and their natural increase under the first agreement and another 75,000 persons under the second as its nationals, at the ratio of four Sri Lankan nationals for every seven repatriated to India.

These two agreements sealed the fate of the overwhelming majority of the people of Indian origin in Sri Lanka. They are popularly known as the Indian Tamils. Unlike the Sinhalese and the Sri Lankan Tamils, who are indigenous to the island, the Indian Tamils are the descendants of those Indians who went to Ceylon under the protective umbrella of the British in the 19th and 20th centuries. They were taken to the island to provide the much needed labour for the development of the tea plantations and also construct public works like railways, roads and the harbour. They formed the bulk of labour which turned the malaria infested forests of Sri Lanka into smiling plantations of tea, which sustained the Sri Lankan economy up to modern times. The British government which ruled Ceylon and the Sinhalese leaders, who collaborated with the British, actively encouraged the recruitment of labour from Madras Presidency.

Though in the beginning, the Indian labourers were merely "birds of passage" gradually they began to take roots and became permanent settlers in the island. In 1928, the Donoughmore Commissioners estimated that 40 to 50 percent of the Indian labourers were permanently settled in the island. In 1939, the Jackson Report estimated the permanent settlers to be around 60 percent. The Soulbury Report, 1947 estimated that the degree of permanent settlement was in the region of 80 percent.

As long as the British ruled, the Indian Tamils had the same legal status as the Sinhalese and the Sri Lankan Tamils, for all were British subjects. As Jawaharlal Nehru wrote in 1948, "One of the conditions for emigration to other countries to which the Government of India have always attached utmost importance...has been that an emigrant labourer shall be given facilities to settle in the country...on equal terms with the members of the indigenous population". Colombo did not subscribe to this point of view. According to W.T. Jayasinghe, former Defence and Foreign Secretary to Sri Lanka, the Indian settlers were Indian nationals. In his book, The Indo-Ceylon Talks: The Politics of Immigrant Labour, Jayasinghe has written "The fact of their Indian nationality was never in question". Colombo wanted to absorb only a small fraction of the Indian population as Sri Lankan citizens. From this perspective they argued that it is necessary to prescribe rigid tests for proving the permanent, abiding interest of the Indian community. Herein lies the seeds of the "absorbable minimum" put forward by successive Sri Lankan Governments. Girija Shankar Bajpai summed up the apparent discrimination: "The Indian who has worked in Ceylon is to be thrown back to India as a squeezed lemon".

Despite the restrictions on franchise, in the 1947 elections held under the Soulbury Constitution, the Indian workers elected six representatives of the Ceylon Indian Congress (CIC); where no CIC candidates were fielded, they voted for the Marxist candidates and tilted the balance in Marxist favour in about nine seats. The leftward swing of the plantation voters made the conservative United National Party (UNP) leadership determined to debar the vast majority of Indian Tamils from Ceylonese citizenship after independence. If the government could restrict citizenship and, therefore, the franchise of the Indians, a large number of Marxist candidates could be eliminated and the UNP could win the Kandyan seats very easily.

The Ceylon Citizenship Act of 1948 and the Indian and Pakistani Residents Act, 1949 not only disfranchised the Indian community, but these acts also made them stateless. When applications were invited, nearly 8,25,000 applied for Ceylonese citizenship, which was clear evidence that the overwhelming majority of Indians wanted to permanently stay in Ceylon. But the Government granted citizenship to only 1, 34,618 applicants. All others were characterised as "stateless". It must also be pointed out that the provisions of the Citizenship Act were complicated and cumbersome and naturally the plantation workers were not able to produce certificates to the satisfaction of the Ceylonese authorities. The Indian Tamils were thus ostracized from the political mainstream of the country. Speaking on the Ceylon Citizenship Act, Pieter Kuneman said in Parliament that even Dudley Senanayake would not be able to comply with the clauses because according to his own admission, he could not trace his father's birth certificate.

If the Acts were discriminatory, their implementation was even more tardy and inflexible. By the end of 1953, only 65,714 applications of the total 2,37,034 had been fully investigated and of this number only 7,687 applications, involving 26,360 persons had been allowed. By the end of 1954, a total of 9,672 applications, involving 33,012 persons had been allowed, and by the end of 1955, a total of 37,948 persons covered by 10,875 applications had been registered as Ceylonese citizens.

From the very beginning, it was Colombo's implicit assumption that those who failed to qualify for Ceylonese citizenship were unquestionably Indian nationals and that New Delhi should regard them as such. On the contrary, as far as New Delhi was concerned, its policy was to discourage Indians Overseas from applying for Indian citizenship. In the protracted negotiations that took place between New Delhi and the successive Prime Ministers in Ceylon–D.S. Senanayake, Dudley Senanayake, John Kotelawala and S.W.R.D. Bandaranaike–Jawaharlal Nehru emphatically maintained that except for those who voluntarily opted for Indian citizenship, the Indian immigrants in the island were the responsibility of Sri Lanka. Both C. Rajagopalachari and Kamaraj Nadar, Chief Ministers of Tamil Nadu, supported Nehru's principled stand. The era of statelessness continued and the problem appeared to be interminable.

Following Nehru's demise in 1964, the time tested and principled policy enumerated above was derailed and sidetracked by Prime Minister Lal Bahadur Shastri, Minister for Foreign Affairs Swaran Singh and the Commonwealth Secretary C.S. Jha. During this period, New Delhi was eager to come out of the "diplomatic isolation in South Asia" following the Sino-Indian conflict in October-November 1962. Lal Bahadur Shastri wanted fresh efforts to be made to put Indian-Sri Lanka relations on a sound footing. Officials in the Sri

Lanka Division of the Ministry of External Affairs, who subscribed to the Nehruvian principles on the question of stateless people in Ceylon, were either transferred or sidelined. New Delhi's desire to solve the problem on the basis of "give and take" (which meant more conceding than demanding) becomes evident if one reads C.S. Jha's reminiscences, From Bandung to Tashkent: Glimpses of India's Foreign Policy.

The astute politician that Sirimavo Bandaranaike was, she made the best out of the changed situation. Ably assisted by Shirlie Amarasinghe, the Sri Lankan Government clinched the issue in October 1964. The Sri Lankan team pleaded with Prime Minister Shastri and C.S. Jha that if India could accept 10 million refugees from Pakistan, less than a million from Pakistan would not be a burden. The Indian side had a team, which because of the brief given to them, "was like a set of fishermen who should keep the boat from sinking, but leave it to God to get them to the shore across". The most pathetic member of the Indian team was Ramiah, a Cabinet Minister from Tamil Nadu. According to informed sources, throughout the discussions, Ramiah did not utter a single word on behalf of the Tamil plantation workers, who wanted to remain in Sri Lanka and become Sri Lankan citizens. Finally, these unfortunate people were converted into a merchandise to be divided between the two countries in the name of good neighbourly relations.

As the negotiations progressed, it was apparent that the Sri Lankan team was racing towards the winning post. The number to be accepted by New Delhi as Indian citizens began to increase. As P. Ramaswamy, the well known columnist based in New Delhi, has written, the Ceylon delegation "was chuckling at the rate of progress". 5,25,000 was not far from 9,75,000 and Mrs. Bandaranike was convinced that Colombo could win hands down. Then an unexpected development took place. Ramaswamy informed Kamaraj Nadar, the Congress President that Lal Bahadur Shastri was "going to bring back into the country all those whom Ceylon Government wanted to be repatriated". Kamaraj Nadar knew the complexities of the problem and, what is more, the unwillingness of the plantation workers to come to India and start a new life. Kamaraj Nadar presented his views forcefully to Lal Bahadur Shastri. On the last day of the negotiations, Prime Minister Shastri told a surprised Sri Lankan delegation, "thus far and no further" in a take it or leaves it tone. But since Mrs. Bandaranaike had already won the battle by achieving more than what she had hoped for, the negotiations came to an end with India agreeing to confer citizenship on 5,25,000 people of Indian origin, plus their natural increase, and Ceylon agreeing to confer citizenship on 3,00,000, plus their natural increase on the basis of 7.4. The fate of the balance 1,50,000 was decided in 1974, with India and Sri Lanka agreeing to confer citizenship on 75,000 people with their natural increase.

Few significant features of the Sirimavo-Shastri Pact must be underlined. In his conversation with me, S. Thondaman, the undisputed leader of the Indian Tamils in the island, remarked that the Sri Lankan Government did not permit him to come to India to meet the Indian leaders to explain his point of view. What is more, his plea to the Indian High Commission that it should use its good offices to arrange his visit to New Delhi also fell on deaf ears. It is the tragedy of India-Sri Lanka relations that this agreement, which had a bearing on the lives of thousands of people of Indian origin, was finalized by the two governments without taking into consideration the feelings and wishes of the people concerned. All trade unions in the plantation areas, rivals among themselves, were unanimous in their opposition to the Pact. The Ceylon Workers Congress, the most representative organization of the plantation workers, vehemently opposed the Pact. The continuing trauma suffered by the people made the CWC revise its stand later and co-operate with the Government in its implementation.

The Sirimavo-Shastri Pact was also a bad precedent as far as India's policy towards Indians Overseas is concerned. If you can take a substantial number from Sri Lanka back as Indian citizens, why not from South Africa, Malaysia, Fiji and Mauritius?

What was the fallout of the Sirimavo-Shastri Pact on centre-state relations in India? Bhaktavatsalam was the Chief Minister of Madras Presidency and he deputed Ramiah, his colleague in the Cabinet, to be a member of the Indian team. And, as mentioned earlier, Ramiah was a silent spectator throughout the negotiations. But outside the ruling circles in the State, there was strong opposition to the Pact. C. Rajagopalachari, the leaders of the Communist Party of India, and the Dravida Munnetra Kazhagam expressed their strong resentment and opposition to the Pact. V.K. Krishna Menon, the ideologue of Jawaharlal Nehru, out of power by then, was also critical of the Sirimavo-Shastri Pact. C. Rajagopalachari, the elder statesman, echoed the feelings of the vast majority of the Tamils in India when he stated, "Why should nearly a million children and grand children born in Ceylon to parents who toiled and sweated for Ceylon and who had gone there from South India and settled down in the plantations be disentitled to be citizens of Ceylon? Why should a single child born in Ceylon and desiring to be in Ceylon, and be a working citizen thereof, be turned out to wander as homeless refugees in India?"

India-Sri Lanka Maritime Boundary Agreements, 1974 and 1976

The second illustration, where the Government of India was insensitive to the interests of the State of Tamil Nadu took place in 1974 and 1976, when the India-Sri Lanka maritime boundary agreements were concluded. The Agreements resulted in the ceding of the island of Kachchatheevu, which was a part of the Zamindari of the Raja of Ramnad, to Sri Lanka and also sacrificed the traditional fishing rights of the Indian fishermen in the Palk Bay region. But since fishermen are no respecters of maritime boundaries and since they move wherever there is fish, the Indian fishermen used to move into

Sri Lankan waters and in that process get killed, injured, their boats get destroyed and the fish dumped into the sea. The rich fishing grounds on the Sri Lankan side of the Palk Bay have become a bone of contention among the fishermen of the two countries and the Sri Lankan Navy. If a satisfactory solution is not arrived at amicably and quickly it may bring about tensions between the two countries and between the Central Government and the State Government.

Kachchatheevu is a small barren island in the Pak Bay, with not even a drop of drinking water. Historically, the island was important, because it was leased out for pearl fisheries. It was also used by the Indian fishermen to dry their nets. There is a Church, dedicated to St. Anthony, who is considered to be the guardian angel of the fishermen. The Church was constructed by one Seenikuppan Padayachi, a fisherman from Thakachi Madam. What makes the island extremely important is the fact that the surrounding seas are extremely rich in prawns and the prawns have a good export market. The surrounding waters were also the traditional fishing grounds of the Indian fishermen for several centuries.

The author's argument is that, the island of Kachchatheevu belonged to India is based on the evidence of the Zamindari rights that the Raja of Ramnad exercised over the island. Though the official records have been taken away to New Delhi, there is irrefutable secondary evidence to substantiate these Zamindari rights. New Delhi did not dispute the Zamindari rights, but it was not sure that Zamindari rights conferred ownership. This argument is fallacious and has dangerous implications. It threatens the very unity of India. On the eve of independence, large parts of India were under the Zamindari system. In the nine provinces of British India, the Zamindari system covered 57 percent of the area, the Ryotwari system covered 37 percent and the Mahalwari system 5 percent. In Madras Presidency, 27 percent of the land holdings were under the Zamindari system. It is in this context that the Zamindari rights of the Raja of Ramnad over the Island of

Kachchatheevu have to be viewed.

According to the Gazetteer of Ramnathapuram, published by the Government of Tamil Nadu, the survey number of Kachchatheevu was 1250. What is more, the Raja used to enter into several lease agreements with various parties for the exploitation of marine resources in and around Kachchatheevu. And when the Zamindari was abolished in 1948, Kachchatheevu naturally became a part of the Madras Presidency. As Madhu Limaye, the Socialist leader, mentioned in the Parliament, the island was part of the Ramnad Zamindari system and when Ramnad was merged with the Madras Presidency, it became part of the Ramnathapuram district.

Another significant point needs mention. In the protracted negotiations that took place between India and Sri Lanka on the issue, New Delhi did not maintain that the island belonged to India, it maintained that it was a disputed territory. The reason for this line of argument is that if Indian Territory were to be ceded to Sri Lanka, it required a Constitutional amendment and its ratification by the state legislatures. But if it were a disputed territory it could be transferred to Sri Lanka when the maritime boundaries were delimited. Another point deserves emphasis. In the delimitation of maritime boundaries, the general principle followed is the principle of equi-distance. And if the principle of equi-distance was applied in the Pak Bay, the island would have fallen on the Indian side. Dr. S.P. Jagota, the Director in the Legal and Treaties Division, Government of India has pointed out, "The boundary line between India and Sri Lanka followed the median line, except as adjusted in the Pak-Bay in relations to the settlement on the question of the island of Kachchativu".

It must also be mentioned that the Government of Tamil Nadu was completely kept out of the negotiations which took place between India and Sri Lanka on the delimitation of the maritime boundary. But before the agreement was finally signed, Kewal Singh, Secretary to the Ministry of External

Affairs, came to Madras, met Chief Minister Karunanidhi and a few of his colleagues and explained the background to the signing of the Agreement. According to informed sources, Indira Gandhi requested Chief Minister Karunanidhi to appreciate New Delhi's position and support her stance. Karunanidhi was not happy with New Delhi's position; however, he did not want to confront the Centre on this issue.

According to perceptive observers of the Tamil Nadu political scene, it is very likely that Chief Minister Karunanidhi, in turn, hoped to get Indira Gandhi's critical support in his efforts to consolidate his power in Tamil Nadu, which had come under increasing threat from the AIADMK and its charismatic leader M.G. Ramachandran. If the State Government had resorted to legal remedies in the Supreme Court against the Centre on the ceding of Kachchatheevu to Sri Lanka, or if it had insisted on a reference by the President to the Supreme Court on the ownership claims of the Raja of Ramnad, it is likely that India-Sri Lanka relations might have taken a different turn. It may be recalled that the great Congress statesman, Dr. B.C. Roy, the Chief Minister of West Bengal, approached the Supreme Court when the Central Government wanted to transfer Beru Bari to East Pakistan and got it stalled. In the Kachchatheevu case, legal luminaries like M.C. Setalvad had upheld India's ownership claims. What is more, a few senior officials in the Ministry of External Affairs also subscribed to the same view. But Prime Minister Indira Gandhi unfortunately over ruled them.

The most decisive factor in the ceding of Kachchatheevu to Sri Lanka was the personal friendship between Prime Minister Indira Gandhi and Prime Minister Sirimavo Bandaranaike. The decision was political and it was done to boost the sagging political morale of the Sri Lankan Prime Minister and her political party. Since Sri Lanka, under Mrs. Sirimavo Bandaranaike shared the larger foreign policy concerns of India, it was essential to assist Colombo in stabilizing and consolidating its regime. Kachchatheevu becoming a part of Sri Lanka would enhance the credibility of the government in Sri Lanka and the personal popularity of the Prime Minister. It would also blunt the arguments of the leftist elements in the island, for whom issues such as Kachchatheevu were symbolic of India's hegemonistic designs towards its neighbours.

The personal equation between the two Prime Ministers, which, as pointed out earlier, was the critical factor in the ceding of Kachchatheevu comes out in sharp focus in the following quotation from the book, *Ethnicity versus Nationalism: The Devolution Discourse in Sri Lanka*, written by Professor Partha Ghosh, "Kachchatheevu was the most typical case of a personal equation playing the role of diplomacy. When the negotiations had virtually failed, and the Indian official delegation was pressurizing Indira Gandhi not to give up India's claim on the islet, Sirimavo Bandaranaike made a personal appeal to Indira Gandhi to come to her rescue, as it would otherwise spell political disaster for her. Indira Gandhi appreciated Mrs. Sirimavo Bandaranaike's predicament and manipulated the situation in such a way that it became a fait accompli even before the Indian delegation could react. Sirimavo Bandaranaike remembered this gesture as late as 1990 with immense gratitude".

Having failed to keep Kachchatheevu with India, Chief Minister Karunanidhi's objective was to ensure the continuance of the traditional fishing rights of the Indian fishermen in and around Kachchatheevu. Accompanied by S. Madhavan, then Law Minister in the State Government, Chief Minister Karunanidhi went to New Delhi and had detailed discussions with Swaran Singh. Article 5 of the India-Sri Lanka Maritime Boundary Agreement provides for the continuation of these fishing rights. It must be highlighted that Article 5 does not specifically refer to the fishing rights. It says, "Indian fishermen and pilgrims will enjoy access to visit Kachchatheevu as hitherto". During the debate that took place in the Lok Sabha, Swaran Singh clarified that "although Sri

Lanka's claim to sovereignty over Kachchatheevu has been recognized, the traditional rights of fishermen and pilgrims to visit the island remain unaffected". It must, however, be pointed out that the senior officials of the Ministry of Foreign Affairs of Sri Lanka did not concur with this line of reasoning. They explained to me that Article 5 did not confer any fishing rights, but only the right to dry the fishing nets and the right of pilgrims to visit Kachchatheevu without visa for religious purposes. There is a fallacy in this line of argument. Drying of nets pre-supposes that the nets become wet and this could happen only if the nets had been used for fishing in and around Kachchatheevu.

The desire to maintain friendly relations with Sri Lanka, even at the cost of the livelihood of Tamil Nadu fishermen, becomes further evident if one analyses the provisions of the India-Sri Lanka Maritime Agreement of 1976, which delimited the maritime boundaries in the Gulf of Mannar and in the Bay of Bengal. There was an Exchange of Letters between Kewal Singh, Foreign Secretary to the Government of India and W.T. Jayasinghe, Secretary to the Ministry of Defence and Foreign Affairs, Government of Sri Lanka. The Exchange of Letters, dated March 23, 1976, was held by the Minister of External Affairs Y.B. Chavan to also "constitute an agreement between the two countries". Paragraph I of the Exchange of Letters reads: "The fishing vessels and fishermen of India shall not engage in fishing in the historic waters, the territorial sea and the exclusive economic zone of Sri Lanka nor shall the fishing vessels and fishermen of Sri Lanka engage in fishing in the historic waters, the territorial sea and the exclusive economic zone of India, without the express permission of Sri Lanka or India, as the case may be".

If Paragraph I quoted above, categorical in nature, is applicable to all sectors of India-Sri Lanka maritime boundary, including the Pak Strait, what happened to the fishermen's rights guaranteed under Article 5 of the 1974 Agreement? What happened to the assurance given by Swaran Singh in

Parliament about traditional fishing rights of Indian fishermen? Unfortunately no satisfactory answer has come so far from the Government of India in this matter. The Tamil Nadu fishermen should have resorted to legal remedies, but there was no legal pandit to advise them on these maters. Moreover, India was under emergency rule at that time and it had taken a heavy toll of the rights of democratic dissent and protest. The prevailing atmosphere could be gauged from the fact that Y.B. Chavan's statement in Parliament was not followed by any debate. Even in Tamil Nadu, which had to bear the brunt of the adverse effects of these agreements, there was not much open resentment. What is apparent is the fact that the astute Sri Lankan diplomats played their cards very well and by introducing Paragraph I in the 1976 Agreement they made it crystal clear that the Indian fishermen had no fishing rights in and around Kachchatheevu. As Shri Madhavan, the former Law Minister in the Tamil Nadu Government, explained to the author, the 1976 agreement sounded the death knell of Indian fishermen's rights.

Conclusion

The two illustrations given above substantiate the following points: (1) In the name of good neighbourly relations, the Government of India has sacrificed the interests and views of the federal units. (2) India has not yet evolved a mechanism by which the federal units could make benign inputs into the making of India's neighbourhood policy. In the negotiations which took place preceding the Sirimavo-Shastri Pact, a member of the Tamil Nadu cabinet was included in the Indian team, but he did not carry out his responsibilities as the representative of his government or of the political party of which he was a member. In the case of the maritime boundary agreements, the Chief Minister of the State was formally informed about the provisions, after an informal agreement was reached with Colombo; but the views of the State were not sought on the subject nor were any representative of the State included in the Indian team. (3) The political exigencies of the time and the desire to seek the Congress Party's support in order to remain in power made Chief Minister Karunanidhi not to resort to legal remedies to protect the interests of the State. (4) The University Departments specializing in international relations and non-governmental organizations involved in the study of diplomacy should sensitise the intelligentsia about the pros and cons of international treaties. (5) In the first part of the essay, the author have cited the examples of the United States and former Yugoslavia as to how they strike a balance between the interests of the federal government and the federal units in the pursuit of foreign policy. In depth studies are the need of the hour and we must formulate practical suggestions to solve this conundrum, so that Indian federalism will be an example of how to live together even as we maintain our diversity in a democratic set up.

4

Indian Federalism as Defined by Devolution and Constitutionalism

A. Basheer

It is generally recognised by theorists and ideologists that society, rather than politics, is fundamental in human affairs. As society changes rapidly and evolves and develops, traditional approaches to respond to the changes become obsolete, and new, innovative and more democratic methods will be required. Political arrangements need be adjusted to make them socially just and appropriate to the new societal needs. From 1980 onwards, governments all over the world (nearly 80 governments) started reinventing themselves to reform and make them appropriate to the changing socio-economic conditions and to make them empowered, more open, transparent, participatory, decentralised, accountable and limited.

The reforms initiated under reinventing government sought reforming of government policy, programmes, processes, design and organisation frame. It was a world phenomenon and an international movement having the objective of achieving a comprehensive reform in governance and fostering a performance oriented culture and less centralised government. In India, a Commission to Review the Working of the Constitution started its exercise. The Second Administrative Reforms Commission also undertook an exercise to comprehensively reform the governmental processes, and made path breaking recommendations. It is in this background, the prospects and suitability of India's federal system to address the emerging challenges need fresh examination and suggest how it could be adapted to make suitable to changing requirements.

Notwithstanding the key role that a well-designed and well-functioning federal system plays in promoting the stability and prosperity of a nation, federalism cannot be a steady, static political arrangement. A theoretically determining federal form of government in the conventional, doctrinal sense would matter little for India, given the inner dynamics of Indian society and nation. Constitutional innovations may be needed to meet the emerging people's urges. The elements of a federal system appropriate at a particular stage in the evolution and development of a nation may not be so at a time when the situation is radically changed. When the Indian Constitution came into force in 1950, it, bearing considerable resemblance to the Government of India Act 1935, featured a uniformly prescribed and centrally controlled federalism. [1]

Hence the stated tasks and goals of the federal system of government–protecting security, national unity and integrity, political stability and strength and ensuring overall development, while maintaining local/regional autonomy, freedom, separate and distinct identity—cannot be achieved by simply keeping the federal structure/practices rigid. There cannot be any hard/ideal theory or rigid model of federalism that can have universal values. Each operational federal system is necessarily *sui generic*, reflecting the specificities and uniqueness of the conditions under which it operates. There cannot be any federal orthodoxy or federal fundamentalism. Placing orthodoxy into federation is to hinder political development. Hence, federalism needs be adapted and adjusted to keep it in terms with changing aspirations and needs of society in which it operates. As it is observed, federalism always remains and 'works in progress' or is 'constantly in the making'. [2] The federal structure needs perpetually to be altered, adapted and amended to cope with changing environment and emerging challenges. That is, federal structure must be tailored to be country and culture specific. It does not work in a stable political environment. Hence, it must be dynamic enough to cope with the changes that take place in societal conditions.

Obviously, the shaping and evolution of Indian federal power structure and the nature of federal functioning were influenced by conditions of and concern for unity and integrity of a culturally diverse nation and the experience of partition and the fear of threat to national unity and security from disruptive and disintegrative forces. And with this objective, the founding fathers of the Constitution desired and sought to strengthen the union government against fissiparous pressures, but not to establish centralised power structure. And unity was emphasised rather than uniformity. The regional/local governments form the building blocks, and together make up the whole—the nation. Distinct cultures and identities were sought to be protected while granting regional autonomy in constitutionally assigned spheres. Special provisions were also made in the Constitution to accommodate special cases such as Jammu and Kashmir (Article 370, Schedule IV) and the North Eastern Hill States (Article 371, Schedule, VI) where there is a distinct difference in ethnicity from the rest of India, and several strong divisions based not only on language, but also on culture and other traditions.

The Constitution provides self-government/autonomy to these states under special administrative provisions, demonstrating flexibility of the system to accommodate and adjust emerging socio political pressure/forces. And by conceding the demands for new states such as Jharkhand, Chattisgharh and Uttarakhand carved out from neighbouring states, the social, cultural and economic pattern of living obtaining in well defined regions has been accepted as the rational basis for reconstructing states. This feature in the Indian federalism augurs well for conceding similar genuine and reasonable regional urges. Nevertheless, although the country and its people remain divided into different states for administrative convenience, the country is one integral whole, its people living under a single imperium derived from a single source. [3]

The federal experience in India suggests that the structure of federalism and its inherent resilience can cope with the pressures of conflicts and help resolve some of them provided the imperatives of federal devolution of power and obligations of mutual accommodation and adjustments are observed honestly. [4] Obviously, while federalism has successfully managed linguistic diversity, the conscious approaches followed both at the central and state levels to preserve and promote the cultural specificities of diverse groups have transformed various groups to identify themselves with national mainstream with the effect of strengthening of forces of integration.

Federal Dysfunctions

The functioning of federalism in India has not been problem free. As in any federation, the phenomenon of two sets of government operating on the same community of people creates complex problems. Friction in federal relations occurs when the central government exercises domineering control/power over states or people. As it has been functioning, federalism in India stands distorted in many respects. Centre-state relations have not always been peaceful or tension free and nor so rosy to ensure a co-operative, mutually collaborative relationship among states *inter se*, and between the centre and the states. The issue of unequal and discriminating treatment of different states has been a major irritant in federal relations. Centralization, resulting from the planned development strategy has opened up vast scope for inter-state discrimination in the allocation of resources. While the centre has enormous financial strength to deliver favours to state governments, strong states in politically advantageous position are able to secure substantially higher resources relative to others.

Indian federalism and federal relations are uncontrolled

and unresolved, though not uncontrollable or irresolvable 'turbulence'. Federal functioning faces many challenges with regard to union-state and interstate relations; regional, local grievances against unfair treatment by the centre or by big states against specific regions etc. Many state governments consider that the autonomous status conferred up on them in prescribed area by the Constitution is being circumscribed by the centre, taking the initiative in crucial spheres which tend to erode the state initiative. [5] The political (mis)use of Article 356 of the Constitution to impose presidential rule in a state in the "event of the failure of Constitutional machinery" has been a subject of controversy. Rampant abuse of this provision for political advantage has led to the alienation of Punjab, Kashmir and Assam. The imposition of presidential rule in Nagaland in April, 1992, was interpreted by the then Chief Minister of Nagaland as manifestation of the 'imperial character' of the Delhi Government in its most perverted and brutal forms and an act of perfidy of the central government. The Sarkaria Commission blamed those in charge of the centre for this misuse and centralization of power in the Union.

According to the Commission those in charge of the centre "use diverse strategies and tactics which are not always sound from a long term point of view, to maintain their control over state level forces. Many a time the actions of the centre, its discriminatory approach towards some states, its lack of understanding of local problems, its abject insensitiveness and the blatant misuse of authority vis-à-vis the states have all distanced it from the people. This, in turn, has, it is believed, reversed the process of national integration. [6] The Commission's observations, in fact, took cognizance of the alienation of states resulting from the centre's irrational acts. The sense of alienation due to the overbearing presence of the army and the application of the Armed Forces Special Powers' Act of 1958 and the Disturbed Areas Act in North-East and Jammu and Kashmir are a cause of resentment and alienation of the people of these states from the national mainstream.

Dicey's conviction of a federal state as a political contrivance intended to reconcile national unity and power with maintenance of state rights has not been satisfactorily fulfilled; and protection of state/local interest fairly is a problem. State power in the sense of ability to make decisions and formulate policies in terms of state specific interests and social and political conditions is circumscribed by the union governments' strong centralizing tendencies and dominance and overriding powers which is anti-democratic and unfederal. The central control over their socio-economic spheres has driven the people of North-East as well as Jammu and Kashmir to believe that they have no hope of peace and dignity under the present dispensation. Exercise of sweeping powers by the centre against the sentiments of ethnic/cultural groups has tended to alienate the states based on ethnic/cultural leadership. [7] And when the central government policy makes the state government obliged to carry out central decisions, the philosophy of federalism and federal spirit fails.

The issue of allocation of financial resources by the union government to states has been one of the controversial aspects of federalism in India, despite raising the level of devolution of tax revenue to the states (85 percent) by the Finance Commission. The centralised planning has made all states indebted to the centre. And the way in which central loans and market borrowings are allocated to states is not made rule based and transparent, and there is significant scope for favouring some states over others in the allocation of market borrowings. This system has been resented by some states. In the process of allowing states to negotiate directly with multilateral and bilateral donors, partisanship in the selection of states in this respect has been alleged. As a result, some states seek substantial loans from multilateral donors whereas others have not been able to access the assistance.

Discrimination in the practice of rescheduling and writing off of the loans of some states also creates resentment. Similarly, in the assistance given to states under a variety of central sector and centrally sponsored schemes, which do not have Constitutional sanctity [8], and are given purely on discretionary basis, differential treatment is alleged. Designed by the central Ministries these schemes are mostly uniform across states. There is scope for discrimination between states in the selection of schemes and in their design. New schemes introduced may favour particular states. Transfers under these schemes have been often strongly criticised. The practice of price and quantity controls, and support prices on various commodities has been alleged to be a source of invisible transfer and differential treatment of different states. This practice also results in inter-state discrimination.

The policy of fixing support prices for some agricultural commodities also has a discriminatory impact on different states because the choice of product for fixing prices might be favourable to some states only. Determination of support prices on wheat, rice and other products are controversial with some powerful political parties in a politically advantageous position influencing the centre in determining the prices, resulting in other states losing. The price quantity control system via allocation of subsidised food grains to different states for distribution through fair price shops also results in uneven distribution of resources. The discretion the central government has in this respect can be used to render substantial relief to states ruled by "friendly parties and make token releases to those ruled by unfriendly ones". [9] Similarly, discriminatory tendency in the policy regarding location of central public sector enterprises and industrial units and their head quarters and regional offices also vitiates federal equation.

The situation in Kashmir, North-East and Assam has also been one of economic neglect, discrimination and political exclusion/domination, in the perception of the affected masses. Ethnicity and ethnic conflicts have acquired territorial basis as in Kashmir, and North-Eastern States. It is to be noted that most of the ethnic conflicts are between one given ethnic group and the Union of India, as if there were no ethnic contradictions and incompatibilities between individual groups. The issues involved in such conflicts are invariably mixed with questions of sharing economic resources and decision-making power.

Asymmetry and Vulnerabilities of Federal Setup in India

Despite the defining feature of bargaining between states and the Union government, differences in bargaining strength and opportunities and political advantages of some states have tended to create greater asymmetry in federalism and consequent grievances among some states which have the effect of placing them in confrontational lines with the centre. The federal system as functions in India has exposed its weaknesses, limitations and inabilities in responding to the challenges and problems that exist and emerge in the country. The administrative and political power play resorted to by the ruling coalition for political expediency has caused distortions in the federal system. The difficulty in reorganising a vast and diverse country on perfectly precise linguistic boundaries and the existence of linguistic minorities in the periphery of large linguistic states, and the failure of state governments to address their genuine grievances have precipitated conflicts and linguistic chauvinism in many parts of the country. Interstate water disputes in respect of the use, distribution or control of waters of interstate rivers or river valleys create tension in interstate relations.

Technology led growth, which has been accelerated under globalization-liberalization regime, chooses regions where good infrastructure exists; poor regions do not have the resources to invest in augmenting infrastructure. Foreign investments are not allowed to flow into some border states. Global capital and trade flows into the country have added to regional disparity in its domestic dimension in a massive way. This is glaring in the growth differentials between coastal, rural and inland regions. As a result, growing regional disparity accentuates civil resistance and violence. The rampant discontent among states and regions arising out of their need for overdependence on the centre for financial and administrative support, besides the feeling of neglect and discrimination (as in the case Telengana, Vidharbha, Manipur, North-East, Kashmir, Southern States etc.) gives rise to the demand for more autonomy and even independence.

At times assertion on linguistic, religious, or ethnic identities and self-governance is compounded by discontents arising out of economic backwardness, poverty, and exclusion. Various ethnic and cultural groups seek political expression and assert their identity and demand more autonomy, even independence, as in the case of Naga Nationalists who seek *de jure* independence, Kasmiriat seeking separation and establishment of independent state, and Manipuri nationalists who raise the political programme of attaining sovereign Manipur.

Insurgencies and militancy is the by-product of this discontent, and regional/local assertion. There are contrary pulls and the federal system cannot remain insensitive to such forces and hence needs to address these forces for the very survival of it. Regional/local assertions and new demands call for a new and more pragmatic approach in federal, regional and local governance, the core concern of which must be reduction in disparities among states and regions and narrowing of the distance between the centre and the states. Inept and unintelligent, and often politically motivated approaches towards these issues have tended to alienate the groups of people in these regions from the mainstream.

A Preferred Road Map for Federalism: Towards a Nation of Small States

The Constitution, in fact, envisages a co-operative federalism, with a "high degree of collaborative partnership" which is considered vital for the federal system to endure. Hence, devolution and sharing of decision making authority between the central and state institutions of governance, that form the core aspect of federalism, is essential to manage diversities and conflicting demands and emerging aspirations. Appropriate balance in the relationship between the two levels of government need be maintained with centripetal and centrifugal forces keeping each other in check. [10]

To meet the persistent demand for linguistic, ethnic, religious freedom and cultural identity, which all have now acquired territorial/regional space, as well as local/regional sentiments and specific need, federal structure built on local autonomy/self-government is preferable to centralised unitary structure. The federal type structure that government in India has also needs to be reinvented with innovative democratic and more federalising features in order to accommodate the emerging diverse socio-economic needs and requirements. The gigantic and bewildering diversities of India cannot be successfully managed under one politico-administrative umbrella of a centralised state. And the dynamics of democratic politics in India makes difficult to choose a single, uniform cultural identity, even majoritarian as the basis of nationhood.

To safeguard national unity conflicting interests at the regional/sub-state level need be reconciled in a cooperative, mutually collaborative and dependent federal spirit. Communitarian, regional, sub-state level desires for autonomy cannot be ignored. As long as the people of India live in a wide variety of communities and because of the federal situation is defined by regional differences and disparities, cultural, linguistic diversities, communication problems etc. federalism cannot be dispensed with, but be made more dynamic, viable and capable of responding to these urges and meeting new challenges.

Freedom of constituents for rational bargaining, which is fundamental in a federal set up, must be respected and accepted. Their demand that the Centre concedes their right to self-governance is in accord with the Constitution. The motivation is political, social, economic and cultural empowerment of the group of people. It is to protect and expand economic opportunities and secure freedom from exploitation by larger and more powerful, influential states/regions that special status or separate status or separate statehood is sought by some regions/groups. The objective may be purely political—of enhancing freedom and representation to particular regions/groups or to maximise their political power and influence. It may also be cultural or religious— to preserve group identities or simply be a means of accommodating diverse group interests. Collective rational bargaining could lead to greater decentralization and greater economy for sub-national units.

Some powerful states exerting undue political pressure and influence in the centre to secure special favours to the neglect of politically weaker states, and the centre's tendency to discriminate among states could be checked by such decentralization. Implementation of administrative, political and fiscal systems to meet the sub-national demands or accommodations of their special demands may tend to create asymmetry and upset the balance and stability of the federal system, but also ensure the survival of federalism. A sagacious and pragmatic approach involving rational dialogue between the centre and states can overcome the problem of asymmetry.

In the case of Kashmir, the Government of India has expressed its readiness to offer 'an unspecified assurance of greater autonomy' to accommodate the regional sentiments and demands. This is in accord with the Constitutional provision for self-government under special administrative provisions for Jammu and Kashmir (Schedule IV, Article 370) and to the tribal areas of North-East (Nagas, Mizos, Manipuri, Tripura, under Article 371), which must not be disturbed, but respected to respect people's wishes and their social and cultural pattern of living obtaining in their regions.

Empowerment of local level government institutions will moderate the stirrings for independence at sub-state level as in some parts of North-East and Jammu and Kashmir. And by building capabilities to innovate and work out suitable and appropriate strategies under local/regional conditions, many of the federal problems can be addressed to a large extent. Hence, sub-regional, local, ethnic and socio-economic groups need be empowered to manage their affairs, freeing them from too much restrictive control/ rule by the centre.

Gaining ability to make decisions that affect their lives or to order their own private lives as they choose, people gain dignity by gaining real and concrete power over the institutions which control their lives. It is because of loss/decline of dignity when others decide for them that people become restive and agitated. As these incompatibilities have grown, demands for redefining and restructuring these relations have been most pronounced. Despite the distortions and the consequent turbulence, tension, federalism in India could have the resilience to cope with the pressures of ethnicity and conflicts, help resolve or reduce many of these pressures, if the imperatives of federal devolution of power and obligations of mutual accommodation and adjustments are observed faithfully. Hence, there is a strong case for more devolution of powers and more local/regional autonomy, and strengthening of state/local governments as fully fledged self-government institutions with their own autonomy and self direction. Perhaps devolution of power and state/regional/local autonomy is the essence of federalism.

That localism and local/regional sentiment constitute the federal dynamics must be accepted by the centre. Being a governance system where in functions and powers are shared between the central and state governments under Constitutional guarantees the states must be let to perform "all the tasks that can feasibly be accomplished at the state level" and thus recognise and respect strong regional aspirations. Devolution will not be anti-integral and not a threat to union government. We must recognise the fact that the notions of Grama Swaraj and local self-government that defined ancient

Village republic, in fact, encompassed true federal philosophy.

The fact that Panchayats which had been integral part of rural Indian polity and society have played key roles in organising and maintaining social order in Indian villages provides historical support/defence for more devolution and setting up small states with autonomy and self-direction or conceding demand for creation of new states within the union of India. Further, establishment of new locally/regionally oriented small states and devolution of powers to them will only strengthen the expression of cultural diversity and role of union of India. Small locally sensitive governments remaining closest to the citizens have greatest potential for making a difference in the lives of people. In small communities, common man becomes more articulate than in large 'phantom public' which is inchoate and unorganised. In large states effective citizen participation suffers. Within the many regional/local spaces, people of different 'political persuasions and background' could take part in decisions affecting their area and engage in political process more effectively than in a system comprising a few large units.

Citizens could participate more effectively. Participation can be elevated to a level above that of mere ceremonial. With large number of small states new initiatives can be spurred at the regional levels. Large number of regional governments will enlarge participation, spread political power, check dreadening centralism in administration, and contribute to the creation of a 'democratic community of free, active, self-governing citizens. [11] The people can provide leadership for solving many community problems; contribute to the economic, social and political development of the people facilitated by wider empowerment of local government, and serve as a tool for improving the democratic process. Common, rather than special interest will be served more fairly by the regional than by a central government.

Thus, local/regional grievances against unfairness and discrimination by a central government can be solved. They will introduce new dynamism into the system and entrench pluralism, and make democracy vibrant. Division itself promotes democracy as well as competition. The many small units will easily bring about the more democratic process of mutual adjustments, which is the appropriate method of dealing with diverse interests of the various regions and groups/communities of people. Public interest emerges in a pluralist fashion with policy resulting from an open and continuous contest between opposing groups in a free political market place. Competition, conflict and bargaining between a large numbers of regional units provide scope for open expression of conflicting views and responsiveness to divergent interests that ensure genuine democratic constitutionalism. [12]

Devolution provides new opportunities for civil society to articulate and assert its choice of response at each level. Higher level of devolution of power will operate as an effective restraint up on hyper centralism, abuse of governmental powers by the central authorities and make federalism an integral part of constitutionalism and the mainstay of free constitutional government. [13] Moreover, devolution will enable the centre to lessen some of its responsibilities so that state/local governments will more effectively handle them. Small states are more likely to cooperate and collaborate and enter into more networking in sharing river waters, controlling crimes and violence, developing interstate transportation, trade, check illegal transactions and protect forests and enter into several mutual collaborative efforts on socio-economic welfare programmes. National autonomy, unity and identity will not suffer by this localization/regionalization process but will only be strengthened by improving the particular circumstances of each community's situation. This perhaps is the strongest rationale for local autonomy. Local communities/societies carve for autonomy to protect their identity. The federal system must identify with this urge as it helps strengthening the nation, rather than weakening.

No small state, content with its self-governing status, will entertain any desire to secede from or mobilize forces against the union of India. The creation of new states recently and the hitherto practiced elaborate power devolution has not tended to cause disunity or political instability or disorder, nor tended to disintegrate the nation, but helped to facilitate the management of cultural diversity which in turn helped mitigate pulls toward separatism and disintegration.

The philosophy of democratic pluralism recognises that diverse communities have diverse interests; they all have legitimate democratic rights of decision making and self-governance in matters that affect their lives. It is better India remain a country of small communities and regions enjoying more autonomy and self-governance which will be more democratic than a centralised system. And hence federalism must be sought to be operationalised by creating, operationalising and imbibing the culture of local/regional self-government which are able to pursue self-governance.

Development plans must be devised by local people according to their awareness, aspirations and struggles because people are knowledgeable about their situation and how to manage them within the given necessary resources. We must acknowledge that people have the right to plan their own destinies and determine their life style. The demand for regional autonomy must be seen in this sense. The central government while pursuing any development strategy/public policy must ensure that such a step is in accord with all state/regions which have diverse, conflicting and inconsistent objectives and interests. Hence, regional assertions, even if they are defined by ethnic, cultural or even social identities need be recognised and accommodated.

Uniform and exclusive solution to the problems at the national level alone is no longer feasible. The centre must relinquish some of its traditional functions and powers, which the state can effectively administer (rural development) to state/local governments, and reinvent itself less in terms of too much restrictive control and domination over states, and more in terms of mutuality, partnership and collaboration which must be defining moments in federal relations rather than unilateralism or domination.

By giving every group of people a sense of sharing and access to decision making power such a system will help evolve an ideal paradigm of more participatory and inclusive democracy which would help minimise any sense of exclusion and marginalisation of underprivileged citizens. It will enable the system to acquire the necessary resilience and capability to minimise politically motivated distortions and manipulations of central powers and institutions which will pre-empt conflicts. Moreover, the scope of any political incompatibility and competition between the arty/coalition ruling at the centre and in various states vitiating federal relations can also be reduced. Hence responsibilities of central government must be devolved to state/local governments that are closest and more accessible to the people.

The system, however, must be constitutional, all the central, regional/state/local governments exercising limited powers within their competence. The trend of the centre appropriating and concentrating more and more powers must be reversed. Exercise of centralised power makes for rigidity, insensitivity and authoritarianism in responding to local/regional demands. Similarly, rigidity in devolution of finances, central guidelines on implementation of development programmes and other socio-economic welfare policies, beneficiary selection, addressing local sensibilities and sensitiveness or sentiments are actually hurdles on local/regional development. Central Ministries and departments must provide services to state governments rather than overseeing their operations. Central government must be equally accessible to all state governments.

Inter-governmental relations must be reciprocal, mutually interactional and interdependent; regional governments enjoying power of self-governance. Union as well as state/regional governments share in a partnership basis in the common task of accomplishing the "will of the people". Control and regulation by centre over federal units beyond permissible, rational level is inherently and absolutely devastating to the local spirit and sentiment which must be respected lest it will lead to dangerous situations. To submit or subject a group of people to a central authority which the group treats as outsiders will be counter-productive.

Hence, central government should avoid to the maximum the exercise of direction and control or commanding power over states. The centre must desist from exercising too much control and regulation, and treat itself as one functioning in the midst of several states and is affected by their presence and hence treat the state/local government as partners rather than lower subordinate entities. Building of such inter-governmental relations could facilitate good government and make the country efficient, strong, stable and sustainable democratic society. Supported and nourished by strong and vigorous regional/local governments, union government will govern more democratically. Perhaps, federalism must encompass equality of political conditions, which can be promoted through small states. In such a system democracy cannot be destroyed but will thrive.

Democracy should be made the condition for regional/local autonomy. Governments must be based on moderation, good sense and compromise Federalism must be like social functioning. The blame game by all sets of government must end and they all must not seek to escape/evade responsibility for common problems.

Federal systemic arrangements must be so shaped to help form a polity that does not seek to deny or disable fundamental local/regional interest and needs. A balance between the centre and the local need be kept. Neither side should try to disrupt or devastate this balance. And those who are in charge of the governmental powers must guard themselves against the temptation to resort to politically motivated distortions and manipulation of federal powers and institutions.

End Notes

1. Conrad Dietmar, (1995). Legal *System and Constitution*, in Dietmar Rothermund (ed) *India, Culture, History, Politics, Economy Environment: A Handbook*: 409-426 cited in Patric Hoening Toem and Tabro, *The Case for a Secession Clause in Indian Constitution*, in *Economic and Political Weekly*, Vol. XLV, No. 39, September 25, 2010: 44.
2. *www.unu.edu/u10n press*, accessed on 10th August, 2010.
3. Ideas of Dr. B.R. Ambedkar in the Constituent Assembly debates.
4. Abhishek Singhvi, *Federalism*, *Indian Journal of Public Administration*, Vol. III, No. 4, 2007.
5. C.V.H. Rao, *Evolving Perspectives in Centre-State Relations*, *The Hindu*, Madras, 26, January, 1967.
6. *Sarkaria Commission Reports*, Government of India.
7. M. Govinda Rao and Nirvikar Singh, *Asymmetric Federalism in India*, *www. wikipedia.com*, accessed on 16th September, 2010.
8. According to K.K. Venugopal, Advocate, *giving grants for these discretionary schemes under Article 292 is unconstitutional*. NIPFP 1991.
9. M. Govinda Rao and Nirvikar Singh, op.cit accessed on 10th September, 2010.
10. Bucha nan, (1999). In a debate with Husgrave, *http//wiki.answer.com*, accessed on 22nd August, 2010.
11. Benjami n Barber, (1984). *Strong Democracy*, Los Angels: University of California Press: 217- 312.
12. Basheer A., (2002). *Local Government Federalism in U. S.A: Thrust on Democracy and Constitutionalism*, in Bernard D' Samy, and G. Gopa Kumar, *In Pursuit of American Studies*, South India American Studies Net work:161.
13. Carl J. Friedrich, (1968).*Constitutional Government and Democracy*, Oxford: 190-216.

5

Indian Federalism in a Transitory Phase: From Asymmetry to Multiculturalism

Veena Ramachandran

India's federal democracy functioning in the specific context of its considerable size and diversity, has evolved in response to several challenges.

The need to accommodate socio-cultural diversities within a single political unit has generally been a major motivating factor in the preference for a federal form of government. On the other hand, problems generated by the continued healthy existence of these diversities have frequently occasioned sever stresses in federal systems. All societies can be situated somewhere on a continuum stretching between two hypothetical poles: wholly diversified to wholly integrated. Moreover, there are elements of unity in all diversified societies and vice versa. [1] Before moving on to the core idea of the topic, we will discuss what is federalism and its key features.

Federalism is a system of government in which the power is divided between a central authority and various constituent units of the country. Usually, a federation has two levels of government. One is the government for the entire country, which is usually responsible for a few subjects of common national interest. The others are governments at the level of provinces or states that look after much of the day-to-day administering of their state. Both these levels of governments' enjoy their powers independent of the other.

Key Features of Federalism

1. There are two or more levels (or tiers) of government.
2. Different tiers of government govern the same citizens, but each tier has its own jurisdiction in specific matters of legislation, taxation and administration.
3. The jurisdictions of the respective levels or tiers of government are specified in the constitution. So the existence and authority of each tier of government is constitutionally guaranteed.
4. The fundamental provisions of the constitution cannot be unilaterally changed by one level of government. Such changes require the consent of both the levels of government.
5. Courts have the power to interpret, the constitution and the powers of different levels of government. The highest court acts as an umpire, if disputes arise between different levels of government in the exercise of their respective powers.
6. Sources of revenue for each level of government are clearly specified to ensure its financial autonomy.
7. The federal system thus has dual objectives: to safeguard and promote unity of the country, while at the same time accommodate regional diversity.

Therefore, two aspects are crucial for the institutions and practice of federalism. Governments at different levels should agree to some rules of power sharing. They should also trust that each would abide by its part of the agreement. An ideal federal system has both aspects: mutual trust and agreement to live together. [2]

Balance of Power in Federal Systems

The exact balance of power between the central and the state government varies from one federation to another. This balance depends mainly on the historical context in which the federation was formed. There are two kinds of routes through which federations have been formed. The first route involves independent States coming together on their own to form a bigger unit, so that by pooling sovereignty and retaining identity they can increase their security. This type of 'coming together' federations [3] includes USA, Switzerland and Australia. In the first category of federations, all the constituent States usually have equal power and are strong vis-à-vis the federal government. The second route is where a large country decides to divide its power between the constituent States and the national government. India, Spain and Belgium are examples of this kind of 'holding together' federations. [4] In the second category, the central government tends to be more powerful vis-à-vis the States. Very often different constituent units of the federation have unequal powers. Some units are granted special powers.

India's Ethnic Spectrum and Federalism

India has a highly complex and colourful social mosaic. Yet, although characterized by a vast spread of cultural diversity and heterogeneity, this mosaic is not chaotic. It has a clearly discernible pattern, wherein socio-cultural diversity draws its strength and sustenance from India's composite culture and civilizational thrust. This culture has evolved over centuries, through a process of assimilation and amalgamation of the diverse cultural influxes coming with the hordes of invaders—the Aryans, the Sakas, the Huns, the Pathans, the Moghuls, and the Europeans. Thus, the evolved composite culture of India cannot be compared either with the melting-pot of American society or with the multinational state exemplified by the now defunct Soviet Union. India's socio-cultural mosaic is the true picture of "unity in diversity", like a bouquet of flowers or vegetables in a salad bowl, where every component, while retaining its specific identity, is a part of a larger whole. [5]

Upon this cultural diversity, within civilizational unity, the reality of the multi-ethnic society of India exists. Several cultural markers-language, race, tribe, caste, religion, and region serve as identity axes for ethnic groups and their mobilization. In most of the ethnic groups, more than one of these cultural markers is pertinent for identification. In other words, India's ethno-communities have multi-layered and multi-dimensional identities that impinge on each other in a non-stratified and dynamic manner. The identity composition of ethno-communities has been further complicated by the imposition of class distinctions, not only between one and another ethno-community, but also within each. [6] Multi-layered, non-stratified identity composition has enabled ethnic groups to assert and reshuffle their cultural markers to advance their perceived objectives.

Two other commonly accepted characteristics of the spectrum of ethnic diversity in India deserve attention. One is that there is no subordinate dominant pattern between the ethnic groups. [7] Thus, the patterns of conflicts and contradictions between ethno-communities vary along scales of time and place. Secondly, the ethnic groups do not have territories marked out for them because the cultural markers identifying such groups do not coincide with territorial boundaries. [8] Accordingly, people belonging to specific religions, tribes, castes, races, and languages are found scattered in various territorial regions. We shall see later that not even the reorganization of states in India on linguistic lines has been able to overcome this aspect.

The preference for a federal ordering and articulation of diversities arises from the need for political recognition of territorially-based social pluralism, where it is understood that the denial of articulation opportunities would be tantamount to denying diverse communities the right to exist, the right to continue as distinctive entities. [9] India's federal democracy may thus be viewed as a continuing experiment in discovering the manner and extent to which ethno-linguistic diversity should not only be recognized but also assigned a role in politico-administrative system. [10]

Federalism itself is an institutional device proposed by the colonial power to accommodate diversities. And later the Constituent Assembly also welcomed it. The communal divide had an indelible impact on the subsequent development of federal democracy. [11] Even though the traumatic partition of India extended to viewing the political expressions of ethno linguistic regional identities with suspicion and unease, and federalism is a natural necessity in India. It has developed a unique model of federalism and the first phase, of federal reorganization (in the 1950s) on the basis of language breathed life into this model; the second phase, of reorganization in the north-east, protected the model by giving the new states a stake in India's territorial integrity; and the third and most recent phase of reorganization also, fits this model well. [12]

Each state will try to bargain terms and conditions advantageous to join the Indian Union, while the federation will try to attract entry situation, by maintaining symmetry in intergovernmental relationships which may not be possible always. "Asymmetric federalism" is understood to mean federalism based on unequal powers and relationships in political, administrative and fiscal arrangement spheres between the units constituting a federation. [13] Asymmetry in the arrangements in a federation can be viewed in both vertical (between Centre and States) and horizontal (among the states) senses. If federations are seen as 'indestructible union of indestructible states', and Centre and states are seen to exist on the basis of equality; neither has the power to make inroads into the defined authority and functions of the other unilaterally.

However, the nature and basis of relationship between Centre and states is not the objective of this paper. Unequal arrangements and special treatment for some units within a federation are the points where I focus on. Such an arrangement is quite feasible in a system, evolved from bargaining and accommodation. It may also be desirable to have special powers and asymmetric arrangements to accommodate diverse group interests and identity and therefore, has an important role in 'coming together' federalism as well as 'holding together' federalism. But such accommodation can only be at the margin and cannot violate the basic fabric of equality and fair treatment of jurisdictions.

This would also require transparency in the arrangements. It is important to make a distinction between unequal arrangements or symmetries that are (i) transparent and rule based; evolved to facilitate the smooth functioning of the federation and (ii) those that are opaque and discretionary; caused by the balance administrative and political power and expediency. [14] The first may be built into the constitutional arrangement itself or may be evolved through conventions for the smooth functioning of the federation. This type of asymmetry is transparent and rules based and play an important role in building the nation. In contrast, the second type of asymmetry cans simply the result of administrative and political power play in a federation. In India for example, the dynamics created by the end of single party rule at the centre and states, emergence of coalition government at the centre and regional domination of regional parties in the coalition and wielding power in the states can create asymmetries in the functioning of the federation on political considerations. This can have serious repercussions for the future of the federalism.

Political Elements in Asymmetric Practices

A major source of asymmetric treatment of different states has to be found in the nature of Indian polity and the way in which political institutions have functioned over years. In the initial years of Independence, the issue did not come to the fore because, the Indian National Congress, which was in the forefront of independence movement had little opposition and had a virtual monopoly in forming the government at the centre as well as states. Since at both central and state levels a single party ruled, and as the party itself was centralized, there was little scope for disharmony between the centre and individual states and for discrimination between the states. However, four important developments in Indian federalism have impacted to create asymmetric treatment of States in Indian federation. These are discussed as follows. [15]

The first important development is the increasing economic centralization of Indian federalism. The Constitution adopted in 1950 had a strong centripetal bias to be considered 'quasi-federal'. The centralization bias became stronger with the adoption of planned development strategy that required the concentration of economic powers and centralized allocation of resources. The concentration of economic power reached the pinnacle with the nationalization of Insurance and the important commercial banks in 1969.The concentration of fiscal and financial resources with the Centre opened up vast scope for frontier-state discrimination in the allocation of resources. The second important development is the end of single party rule at the centre and states. The continuation of the single party rule for relatively long period left two notable implications for intergovernmental relations.

First, strong authority of the party, more particularly the Prime Minister had to be accepted and when there was a feeling of discrimination, it was ignored in the larger euphoria of planning for economic progress. Second, the concentration of power in the party and resolution of Centre-State and inter-state issues through informal means through the party forum with the Prime Minister wielding paramount authority meant that sufficient scope for development of formal and rule based intergovernmental systems did not exist. The third important development was the emergence of parties with regional identity as ruling parties in some important states. In many states from time to time, electorate perceived that the regional interests and their distinct identity will be preserved better if they voted the regional parties to power.

The emergence of two Dravidian parties alternating as ruling parties in Tamil Nadu, Telugu Desam reigning power in Andhra Pradesh, and other parties such as Haryana Vikas Party in Haryana, Biju Janata Dal with a distinct regional identity in Orissa are cases in point. This has shifted the perspective of parties on power at the State level towards strongly safeguarding regional interests even if that may beat the cost of the rest of the country. Fourth, is the formation of coalition governments at the Centre. [16] As none of the National parties emerging victorious during the last general elections, they had to forge alliances with other parties including regional parties to form governments. The regional parties could force their agenda and try to extract the maximum for their beneficial arrangements. This is particularly true when the parties had a pivotal standing in the coalition. Thus, on the one hand, the central government continues to have enormous financial strength to dispense favours to state governments and on the other, has lost enormous power to prevent the strong states from bargaining and securing the allocation of resources in their favour. The states ruled by regional parties with significant strength in the Parliament have become pivotal and have been able to secure substantially higher resources relative to other states. This has been achieved by the fact that significant proportion of explicit and implicit transfers in Indian federation is discretionary.

Due to all these factors the present Indian model of federalism is in transitionary phase from asymmetry to multiculturalism. Instead of linguistic reorganization now the emphasis is on cultural and ethnic identities of the population and each ethnic groups are demanding separate statehood. From the north eastern states to Telengana, Vidharbha and Gorkhaland, umpteen number of demands started rising. In a land of multiple diversities and socio-cultural pluralism, it is very difficult to suppress such waves. Since federalism is very much a political reality in India such new waves should also be accommodated. Further, federalism itself is not a static or unidirectional concept but a dynamic one. [17]

Conclusion

It is clear from the foregoing discussion that both integrative and disruptive forces have been simultaneously released by developmental and political dynamics in India. It is the changing balance between these two mutually incompatible forces that defines the characteristics of the ethnic scene in the country. Looking at the prevailing situation, one cannot avoid the impression that over the past few years ethnic conflicts and disorders in India have gained in ascendancy and ugliness. However, the battle of preserving and promoting "unity in diversity" in India is far from being lost. It can be won not because of the coercive power of the Indian state, but because of the inherent strength and resilience of Indian society. Notwithstanding the raging ethnic conflicts in the Punjab, Kashmir, Assam, and the North-East region, the ethnic situation in India is still not unmanageable.

Keeping in view India's vastness and diversity and the challenge of externally inspired subversion, it must be recognized that the Indian masses, not the power elites, are strongly rooted in their composite culture and secular commitments, evolved over centuries of cultural synthesis. This composite culture's vitality and resilience have not been lost even in the face of distortions brought about by India's power elites, its developmental dynamics, federal polity, or democratic politics. In the context of the present day multiparty system the multi cultural federalism appears to offer the greatest scope and possibilities for meeting the requirements of a strong and united India and Indian federalism can only be strengthened by abolishing asymmetry and effective implementation of federalism by all means.

End Notes

1. Mukherji, Nirmal and Balveer Arora,(1992). *Federalism in India Origins and Development,* Delhi: Vikas Publications: 2.
2. Rod Hague, Martin Harrop and Shaun Breslin, (2004). *Comparative Government and Politics: An Introduction,*

London: Macmillan: 268-270.

3. Ibid.
4. Ibid.
5. S.D. Muni, (1994) *Ethnic Conflict, Federalism and Democracy in India* in S.D. Muni (ed.) *Understanding South Asia: Essays in the Memory of Late Professor (Mrs.) Urmila Phadnis,* New Delhi: South Asian Publishers: 145.
6. Ibid.
7. Ibid.
8. Ibid.
9. Mukherji Nirmal and Balveer Arora, op.cit:2.
10. Ibid.
11. Ibid.
12. Gurpreet Mahajan, *The Multicultural Path : Issues of Diversity and Discrimination in Democracy,* Delhi :Sage publications:82.
13. M. Govinda Rao and Nirvikar Singh, *Asymmetric Federalism in India, Scholarship.org*, UCSC, UC Santa Cruz, 2004:.2.
14. Ibid.
15. Ibid.
16. At ul Kohli, (1992). Democracy and Discontent: India's Growing Crisis of Governability, Cambridge: Cambridge University Press: 340-342.
17. Ibid.

6

Globalization, Federalism and Democracy in India

G. Gopa Kumar

The transition of India towards democracy itself was a historical and complex process and this was further complicated by the arrival of globalization and the neo-liberal policies that the country followed. Indeed, the nation accepted the new economic reforms in 1991 much ahead of its maturing of federal democracy. Many of the trends and discourses in the political system were altered once globalization policies began influencing the various dimensions of the country—economic, social, environmental, cultural, educational, political and historical factors. The conventional competition in a federal system, viz. the centripetal and centrifugal forces that also dominated the discourse in Indian federalism has succumbed to the pressures of market forces. It also reduced the significance of the role attributed to state and national governments in regard to welfare and economic functions. New market forces attracted the entry of Multinational Corporations and national corporates in significant sectors of the economy and this had affected the incremental pace of economic growth.

The paramount role of agriculture in the Indian economy changed giving way to other sectors like manufacturing, construction, information technology, tourism, bio-technology, pharmaceuticals etc. Consequently, a new thrust was given to service sector and industrial sector and this shift was by and large accepted by the urban middle class in the country. The rural-urban divide, gender divide, digital divide, problem of effecting decentralized governance and other challenges of development including low productivity in agriculture, overpopulation, widespread poverty, ignorance and illiteracy in BIMARU states (Bihar, Madhya Pradesh, Rajasthan and Uttar Pradesh) and North-Eastern region etc had sharpened the polarization between emerging middle class and the poorer sections in the country.

The priorities of the corporates sidelined the welfare functions of the state and the approach of national and state governments underwent drastic changes. Major political parties at the national and the regional levels had limited options in the emerging context other than joining the official bandwagon of neo-liberal paradigm. Of course, negative reactions to these developments produced conflicting pressures from various sources. These include liberal as well as extreme reactions emerging from different sectors. The non-governmental organizations, human rights bodies and environmental activists constituted the evolutionary reaction whereas the rise of Maoist forces and religious fundamentalist forces highlighted the growth of political extremism. The predicament of the state in the emerging context is very clear. This paper attempts to examine the changing and challenging nature of federal democracy in the specific context of India's tryst with globalization.

Of course, the early trajectory of globalization, as a process, has been well documented in human history. But globalisation as an organised socio-economic activity and political process is rather a 20th Century phenomenon. The western countries had accepted it during early 1980ss and prompted the Latin American countries to follow it up. Mostly, Third World countries beginning with India accepted the neo-liberal process since 1991 at a time when bipolarism in global politics gave way to unipolarism led by USA. The formal disintegration of USSR on December 31, 1991 was a major watershed. The decline of Cold War actually started much earlier and intensified further in 1989 with the collapse of the Berlin wall.

The dismembering of Soviet Union did not bring a peaceful transition towards liberal democracy as witnessed in the events in Eastern Europe and Central Asia. Although Francis Fukyama came up with the theory of the "End of History", taking few threads from Immanuel Wallenstein's critique of "World System Analysis", the global events marked conflicting developments. While ethnicity and religious fundamentalism intensified in many parts of the Third World, economic developments leading to a process of global integration could also be evinced in this context. The consensus evolved since the Mastrich Treaty strengthened the European Union whose membership went beyond Western Europe and accepted the fragile economies of Eastern Europe and Turkey.

Almost the same time when USSR was disappearing from the world map, India was facing acute Balance of Payment crisis and many western leaders predicted the bankruptcy of Indian economy. The country of course had limited option in the emerging situation and joined the neo-liberal world, accepting the dictates of World Bank and International Monetary Fund. This was a paradigm shift from India's conventional position in creating a welfare state with a socialist nature. The series of economic reforms that followed since 1991 opened up avenues for the private sector to enter in to the economy in a big way affecting the social values, attitudes, culture, profession, mobility and development. The mainstream India changed drastically since then.

Hardly there were very few areas India did not open up for private and foreign sectors. The neo-liberal reforms brought changes in the sectors like telecommunications, information technology, higher education pharmaceuticals, bio-technology, food and agriculture, tourism, education, health care, aviation industry, infrastructure, arts and culture, environment etc. Even in the area of decentralization process, which the country had otherwise ushered through Constitutional reforms in 1993 (73rd and 74th Amendments), the globalisation policies contributed its own share of ideas and strategies. For instance, as a policy, globalisation was not against decentralisation process but its strategies included strong neo-liberal approach towards decentralized governance.

The corporatist forces find it convenient to approach local governments for expanding their markets and exploiting local resources. The "globalisation" theme has much to do with the neo-liberalist expansion of markets in the villages and urban pockets. Not only that, it facilitated the appropriation of indigenous knowledge to the global market, affecting the lives of the tribals and villagers. The union-state local governments could not develop a common strategy to counter the threat from corporatist forces. It is very clear in this context that not only the conventional nation-state had declined, affecting the national values and sentiments, the federal equation and balance (even if it was favouring an upper hand for the union government) also underwent a drastic shift, benefiting the new actors of globalisation process.

Perhaps one area that requires a serious discussion is the changing priorities in our foreign policy and perspectives towards international relations. As a tradition, two things are important here–the formulation of foreign policy was elitist through out, involving a small group of diplomats, strategic experts and foreign policy specialists. [1] Again, our conventional position towards newly independent countries, approach towards bi-polar conflict, relations with major powers, and the effective leadership we took for strengthening Non-Aligned Movement etc. had underwent transition. Indeed, both aspects are witnessing changes in the new context though not everything is moving in a negative direction. For instance, the controversy that followed the issue of Indo-US nuclear co-operation beginning with the CPI(M)'s strong objection brought the debate in to the national discourse. [2]

It could be possible that in future foreign policy issues would be debated more outside including in the fora of civil society, rather than restricting itself into an elitist discourse.

Again, globalization process had intensified international and cross cultural migration and mobility in an unprecedented manner involving the concern of Indian states rather than leaving everything to the Union Government. Although foreign policy and foreign relations are items belonging to the Union List, in the contemporary situation states are equally interested and concerned. The Malayalee migration to West Asia is a strong case in point here. The bulk of gulf expatriates from India originates from Kerala state and it is natural that state government would influence the central government on many urgent issues. This trend received greater attention with the result a new minister for looking after Overseas Indian Affairs was appointed in 2006.

The LDF government in Kerala really complained that the centre is not giving security clearance to its project on Vizhinjam port in Trivandrum because the Build-Operate-Transfer (BOT) auction was won by a Chinese company, 'Tunes'. At the same time the LDF pointed out that the bilateral agreements are being signed by Government of India and Chinese Government. It highlighted that the central government has no hesitation in signing treaties with China but at the same time prevents Kerala state in allowing a Chinese company to start the working of the project for security reasons.

The border states in India are vulnerable to illegal migration and international terrorism which would demand better interaction between union and state governments for curbing the troubles and challenges across the border. Again, with the increasing level of foreign trade and investment, every state would be interested in formulating its share in foreign policy which would facilitate their economic and human security interests. It is well known that the concept of "Vibrant Gujarat" is linked to the substantial contribution and linkages of Gujarati expatriates settled in foreign countries. All these call for a fresh looks at Indian federalism.

Once we had practically abandoned Non-Alignment policy

in the post communist era, it also signalled a shift towards US and other western powers. The Pro-US shift began since 2000 and strengthened further with the civil nuclear agreement and defence treaties signed between India and the US. The shift also brought strong objection from states like Kerala and West Bengal for ideological reasons. Very soon the foreign policy leadership at the instance of coalition government at the centre, agreed to develop a policy in favour of multilateralism. This was also a product of our globalised policies in favour of trade, business and migration. The new trading class preferred to support the government in its "Look-East Policy", besides encouraging economic relations with Russia, France, U.K, Japan, Brazil and countries in West Asia.

The economic growth witnessed in the country during the last two decades, the rise of India as 'soft power', contribution of Information Technology, professionals since Y2K issue, the predicted emergence of China as a potential super power by 2020 etc. had altogether shifted the external and internal dynamics. The potential market for the developed countries looking at the fast growing middle class (estimated at 360 million), was another factor in India's favour. Therefore, a multilateral policy even while keeping a pro-active tilt towards United States became the hall mark of the nation's foreign policy in the era of globalisation. Obviously, critics had noted the rise of market fundamentalism destroying the social security and welfare functions of the state in post-independent India. The new political discourse demanded for an' "inclusive development" rather than falling an easy prey to the interests of corporatist forces and crony capitalism.

Globalisation and Nation State

It has been generally accepted that the impact and working of globalisation has considerably weakened the Westphalian concept of nation-state and state sovereignty. Viewed from this angle, globalisation process directly challenges national unity and the spirit of nationalism. The process of globalisation hinges upon inter-state treaties and international bodies and therefore we are caught between the dynamics of global integration and imperatives of identity. [3] The present wave of globalisation is contingent to the expansion of economic space beyond the nation state through global market mechanisms. [4] The continuous decline in the capacity of the state and the legitimacy of the government as a consequence to the increasing role of transnational institutions and global integration is promoting the politics of identity instead of citizenship based politics of nation building. [5]

The experience of India is not different we could notice not only the changing role of the State consequent to the economic reforms but also the rise of identity politics at the regional and local levels. On the other hand, powerful multinational enterprises are able to transfer investment across political boundaries, control the terms of technology transfer and enhance global business strategies through radical changes in information technology and telecommunication. These flows of investment, technology, communication and profit access across national boundaries are clear evidences of the global challenge for nation state. [6] As a contradictory phenomenon, globalization is driven by the complex logic of geopolitics and capital and the apparent decentralization of nation-states. [7]

Indeed there are many evidences to suggest regarding the set back and decline of nation states since the end of Cold War and the current march of globalization. The nation state was put under pressure from two ends–the pressure for transcendence and amalgamation of nation states for economic goals (the European Economic Community and North American Free Trade Agreement are the best examples) and the pressure towards decomposition in to constituent linguistic, national, religious or ethnic components as witnessed in the decomposition of Soviet Union, Yugoslavia, Czechoslovakia, Ethiopia and Somalia. The consequent effect of the diminishing nation state would lead to the polarization at two levels-democracies with out empowerment and power inaccessible for democratization. [8]

These are dangerous trends because the emerging world order will be controlled by the powerful sections with out any humane national commitments. Given the social and cultural diversity of the Third World nation-states, the challenges have far reaching consequence. However, in the Indian case, an apparent consensus seems to have emerged although the social heterogeneity has made the reaching of concrete policy decisions difficult. Baldev Raj Nayar argues that political parties in India were forced to enter into alliance-building, which has moderated the extreme ideological positions of individual parties. [9] The centrist tendency generated in Indian political system is also a practical attempt to keep the balance between the appeals of globalization and the demands and struggles exerted by the nationalist and regional groups. It acts as a safety valve to prevent the onslaught of globalization on national values.

The contradictory forces of globalization coupled with the pressures of post-communist world system had significantly affected the fortunes of democracy in the Third World. While scholars like Larry Diamond, and earlier Samuel Huntington, speaks about the rise of the fourth wave of democracy since 1991, the empirical scenario in Afro-Asian political systems were quite different. More than at any time in the history, issues like identity crisis, ethnic and military uprising and decline of national feelings were noted. This has led to the disintegration and failure of many Third World political systems.

Globalization and Democracy

Did globalization facilitate or hinder democracy? It is hard to find a scientific response to this question. Jagdish Bhagavathy, on the other hand, notes that successful and robust development in developing countries requires two strong pillars: democracy and market. [10] He feels that the effect of globalization process on national sovereignty have an obvious relationship to the ability of the citizens to participate effectively in the democratic choice of policies with in the nation-state. Through trade, investment, foreign education, free mobility of people and expansion of the medium of television and flow of information, the quality of democracy has certainly improved. [11]

However, this analysis can be easily contested in a country like India where, despite the presence of a growing middle class, the status of Human Development Index has fallen (128th rank out of 178) and a huge majority of people live below poverty line. Further, the polling figures in national elections show a two point decline during the last fifteen years. However, some scholars attribute the rationale for the fractured verdicts, series of hung parliaments and the inevitability of coalition politics as the trend of increasing political awareness of the Indian electorate. Indeed, these developments had compelled the political elites to speed up economic reforms and maintain the tempo of inclusive development.

In the recent World Economic Forum (2011) Summit, the remarks made by the Deputy Chairman of Planning Commission of India, Montek Singh Ahluwalia and noted critique of globalization, George Soros are worth stating here. While the former reminded the participants that political stability is crucial for the success of economic reforms and policy continuity, the latter commented that democracy is crucial for the globally integrated society. George Soros particularly compared China and India in this context. While China achieved higher economic growth with out political reforms and democracy. India has been maintaining reasonably good growth rate while sustained democracy in her political system.

The political dimension of globalization advocated for a "universal political culture" with a high priority to democracy and democratic institutions. The enthusiasts of globalization championed the cause of democracy and viewed globalization and democratization to between the two sides of the same coin. [12] However, we cannot ignore the role and interests of market forces in this context. Actually, the whole idea of democratization here is related to market democracy with emphasis on money, materialism, global capital, information flow, environmental issues etc. Traditional democratic concerns for human dignity and equal opportunity have been replaced by obsessions for managerial efficiency and product quality". [13] The citizenship values are replaced by the interests of share holders of a private company.

The negative results of this shift had resulted in the formation of anomic groups who believed and struggled for immediate reversal of the whole situation. These groups come from a complex background-environmentalist, human rights groups, other NGOs, religious fundamentalists and terrorists, causing uneven developments in domestic and international political systems. Indeed, the attempt to formulate globalised political culture under the agies of market forces produced dysfunctional results. This trend can also be seen in Indian political system. Therefore, a complex mix of responses, with some people adopting or adapting alternative ideas and joining global networks, while others reject competing universalisms in hostiles localized reactions can be vividly seen. [14]

Castells (1997) views the relationship between state politics and transnational politics as paradoxical: "the more states emphasise communalism, the less effective they become as co-agents of a global system of shared power. The more they triumph in the planetary scene, in close partnership with agents of globalization, the less they represent their national constituencies". [15] This apparent contradiction diminishes the potentialities of an emerging democratic system. The welfare state model with emphasis on centralized planning received a huge set back in India in the given context of economic reforms. The competing and conflicting demands of the states, the struggles of the communal organizations, the decline of nation-state sentiments, rise of localized struggles etc are clear reactions to the phenomena that emerged since 1991.

The changing role of civil society is worth discussing here. Unless civil society institutions emerge as effective mechanisms of citizen empowerment as well as regulators of state and market players, democracy with concern for the weak will not develop. Mere reduction of civil society to NGO's, with little regard for movements for people's rights is not at all a positive development. [16] The privileging of 'consumer' over the 'citizen' in matter of rights has far reaching implications for principles of democracy. Survival, sustainability, equity, democracy and social justice stand to lose out to consumer rights in case of a conflict in this kind of discourse. [17] In developing countries, the transition from the status of a citizen to consumer is not an easy process. Even before the basic imperatives of citizen empowerment has been completed, the new market forces are insisting for a shift in favour of consumers and further making the citizens as if they are share holders of a private sector. Thus, globalization process widens the priorities and preferences between developing countries and developed countries and forces a typical polarization which is not facilitating to the growth of democracy.

The Federal India and Democracy

Federal idea and federal systems are old but as democratic forms of government emerged, federal systems worked in harmony with modern political systems. Conventionally, the confederal idea was to organize diverse political systems under a common umbrella social as to face a common threat, or strive for particular political goals. Even today, confederal systems like the European Economic Union and Common wealth of Independent States operate with a weak centre on the one side and strong states on the other. However, in major modern political systems, one of the two conventional features are prominent–the centripetal federal system and the centrifugal federal system. In the former, the federal trend is towards reaching a powerful centre where as in the latter, the system itself is trying move away from the centre. The United States which originally emerged as a confederation, before the 1789 Constitution was implemented, was a classical example of a centrifugal federal system. Most of the federal systems, particularly with parliamentary framework are clear cut centripetal systems. Canada, India, South Africa, Australia, Nigeria are the best examples. Switzerland, although a small country, remained as a confederal system with partial forms of direct democracy.

Ideally, huge and diverse political systems are suitable for federal forms of government. Most of the countries in the world lack homogeneity due to historical and contemporary factors. Hence, many of those countries qualify to be brought under federal systems. Conventionally, as argued, federal system is a political contrivance in which multiple layers of government are organized. Like an arch dam, the system is accepting pressures, eventually moving towards a centripetal or centrifugal pattern. Again, a federal system can easily accommodate diversity and differences. Especially in a democracy, diversity and accommodation are the hall marks of a federation. Regional, sub regional and national interests are intertwined here. Cultural, social and economic integration are quite possible in this context by providing special rights and privileges in the Constitution.

For instance, according to the Constitution of 1982, Canada has given special veto power to five regions including Quebec Province in the law-making process. Quebec's distinct identity is protected through other provisions as well as including the provision for one-third members of the Supreme Court originating from Quebec province. As an economic imperative, in every federal system, sufficient checks are provided for the distribution of resources in a meaningful manner. Again, in a modern federal system, every citizen qualifies to be serviced by a variety of governments–local, sub regional, regional, state and national. Now with the globalisation process, further diversity and accommodation has become contingent since market relations cut across horizontal and vertical dimensions. Both the citizens and variety of governments in the federal system are provided with numerous challenges and opportunities. This trend could after the vertical governmental relationships in a significant manner.

Some of the federal scholars had argued that the sub continent was strong and united under a strong centre. This was true even during the Ashoka period and once we compare with the Mughal period, it witnessed disunity and disruption. The colonial India was also centralized although, in theory, princely states enjoyed some elements of political and administrative freedom. The provisions of Government of India Act, 1935 also clearly leans towards a centripetal federal system. But once the goal of freedom was reaching closer, the confederal idea came up and sought for classifying Indian states into A, B and C categories. Probably India without the partition would have become a confederal state.

The impact of partition and the painful process of the integration of Indian states seem to have changed the attitude and approach of the makers of the Indian Constitution. Of course, integration of the former princely states was one of the major experiments in the history of nation building. [18] Despite many challenges, this process was completed more or less successfully. It was a remarkable achievement in the modern history of national unification.

Probably the second dilemma was the re-organisation of Indian states in the Union. The provisions of the Constitution particularly the dominance of the Parliament to enact various items in the Union List and Concurrent List, besides the possibility of shifting an item from the State List to Concurrent List had practically moved the system towards a centripetal federal system. The 'parliamentary-federal character' of the Indian constitution had made the federal system more centralized.

Even the existence of state boundaries, formation of new states, financial powers of the Union government, the prominence of All India Services, Emergency powers of the President of the Union, single citizenship, integrated judiciary with Supreme Court as the apex court had all practically made the system vulnerable to unitary features. K.C. Wheare had long back reviewed Indian constitution as 'quasi federal'. Even in the language policy, we can find several issues despite the fact the country is deeply multi-lingual and multi-cultural. Of course, the state reorganization process had more or less addressed these issues and India's record in shaping a linguistic federalism is satisfactory. There could be few more states and official languages coming through in the context of few years but the democratic process had successfully accommodated the diversities to a great extent.

The pre-globalisation period's economic policies and party system require further discussion, in this context. The nature of the Indian state was centralized and planning was officially organised from top to bottom. With a mixed economy, India had given high priority to public sector to emerge as the commanding highlights of the economy'. The creation of Planning Commission as statutory body with powerful provisions; planning, supervising and advising the Union cabinet, the significance of Finance Commission, a constitutional body, competent to decide on apportioning national revenues had drifted the federal status more towards the Union Government. The Indian welfare state model gave high prominence to the Centre and most of the centrally sponsored schemes plus the Community Development Plan energised the union government. The history of uneven development of the Indian states, economic the neglect and discrimination to certain regions had raised many issues-political, economic, ethnic and cultural. Over a period, this had affected the administrative and party system.

The centralised nature of the Indian state had two quick

problems even from the beginnings: (1) the emergence of the 'licence raj' where the Indian bureaucracy sluggishly performed quota distribution and licence permits for all imports and exports, and (2) the slow pace of decentralisation process, although under Article 40 in the part relating to Directive Principles of State Policy of the constitution, provision for strengthening local governments were provided. Both these problems had significant impact in arresting development and social progress in the country. Critiques had attributed this to the existence of one party dominance system in the country besides the legacy of bureaucracy inherited from British power.

It is true that a post-independent polity like India could not quickly transform towards multi party democracy. The Congress dominance was through out, except Kerala, and few states for the first three decades. Yet the party was federal to a great extent until it was nationally split in 1969. Rajini Kothari (1965) conceptualized the 'Congress System' as democratic though not competitive. He analyzed that dissent had become strong inside the Congress and therefore the scope of opposition is weak outside the Congress. [19] The non-competitive, non authoritarian party system collapsed in the wake of Internal Emergency clamped on June 25, 1975. The sudden unity among major opposition parties and the over centralized misrule finally brought down the one party dominance system in 1977. Although Congress regained its popularity in 1980 and 1984, it was never the same again. Moreover, the second national split on January1, 1978 further weakened the organizational base of the Congress party. Its typical shift towards 'High Command' politics in the subsequent years revealed the inner dynamics of a centralised political leadership as the best bet for rallying party unity and popularity.

The rise of regional and state centric national parties was also evident right from 1967 elections. States like Tamil Nadu, Kerala, Punjab, and Rajasthan, Jammu and Kashmir were examples to this phenomenon. Once the Congress suffered electoral setback and organizational schisms, the political space became much more competitive. In the federal discourse, this trend added another dimension when the non-congress parties ruling few states alleged 'step motherly attitude' of the Centre towards the states. The demand for revising the Centre-State relations became prominent as series of non-congress party conclaves demanded for strengthening the Inter State Council, reducing the power and changes in the mode of appointment of governor, strict measures for preventing the misuse of Article 356, more allocation for the states by the Finance Commission etc. This trend was on the rise. With the arrival of globalization process, a new form of caste and ethnic politics began to emerge. The fragmentation of multiparty system deepened in 1990's providing more avenues for the rise of identity politics. The neo-liberal age raised fresh challenges to parliamentary and federal system.

Shift towards Neo-Liberal State

The competing forces of nationalism, regionalism and globalism are working with divergent trends including antagonistic, overlapping and some times co operative features towards each other. [20] This presents a very complicated profile of contemporary Indian polity. India's global integration is more in terms of information technology and open book printing, market and brain-drain than in economic and fiscal forms. The neo-colonial cultural and educational and information domination of the West is more threatening Indian cultural setting and ways of life than neo-colonial economic domination. [21] Therefore, the cultural impact of globalization is attacking the basic values and traditional premises of the Indian society. It should be noted that one of the prominent factors of the unity of India is the existence of civilizational values including secularism and multi culturalism. Despite the uneven nature of societal development, a broad civilisational unity was found in the country. Unfortunately, the cultural invasion of globalization is attacking at the very root of the basic values of Indian society. The reaction emerges in diverse forms including the rise of political extremism and religious fundamentalism. In other words, the post-modern trends of globalization produced dysfunctional results among some sections of the society.

In this context, it will be interesting to look at the impact of liberalization in the federal structure of the country. The flow of foreign direct investment (FDI), dismantling of 'license raj' system, competitive attitude of some of the states in India for attracting FDI and joining the bandwagon of global trade, the influence of Persons of Indian Origin (PIOs) in pressurizing their foster land to help business and trade (especially the case of states like Gujarat, Punjab, Maharashtra, West Bengal and Andhra Pradesh) in their motherland had deep impact in the hitherto federal balance and relations. Another aspect is the influence of World Bank, International Monetary Fund and the Washington Consensus groups support to strengthen decentralization process and governance in the country. While the tradition of decentralization and good governance was problematic, the neo-liberal setting provided an ideological and policy oriented setting for the promotion of these two goals. It may be coincidental that 73rd and 74th Amendments to the Constitution came in 1993 but the slow and steady pace of decentralization process in some of the Indian states worked in harmony with the goals of neo-liberalism.

Lawrence Saez (2002), argues that liberalization policy promoted a change in federal relations from intergovernmental co-operation towards inter-jurisdictional competition among the states. Although there witnessed a concentration of FDI in few states, the transformation from co-operative federalism to inter- jurisdictional competition had prompted states to compete each other for further flow of FDI. This development has increased the polarization between states. [22] Nevertheless, a broad multi-partisan political consensus in favour of measured economic liberalization has emerged. However, the gradual move to a market economy did not significantly alter the central governments financial relationship with the states.

The reforms had prompted some states to adopt major strategic and structural change towards internal development. State like Maharastra, Gujarat, Tamil Nadu and Andhra Pradesh offered specific incentive packages for foreign investors. Saez concluded that political party realignment combined with the impact of foreign investment inflows has shifted the debates about federalism from inter-governmental cooperation to inter-jurisdictional competition. The transformation has several implications for federal relations. However, the role of inter-governmental institutions may become weak and it will weaken state capability because the state will be unable to either regulate or mediate inter-jurisdictional competition. In order to cope up with the emerging developmental challenges, he suggests the creation of strong inter-jurisdictional institutions to address the problem of horizontal integration of the states in India. [23]

The irony of Indian federalism in the age of globalization was that it was accepting forces with divergent characteristics. For instance the strengthening of Inter State Council (initiated in 1990 lapsed during 1992-96 period) since 1996 points out the willingness of the Indian state for promoting intergovernmental jurisdiction and cooperative federalism. On the other hand, the selective growth of some states making use of the virtues available in globalization brought two results– the growth of inter-jurisdictional competition between states and the polarization between performing and non-performing states.

Thus, while a shift from vertical federalism to horizontal federalism becomes inevitable, the role of government becomes very much limited. The market friendly federalism has phenomenally reduced the role of inter-governmental institutions. Again, the contemporary trends indicate the decline of centralization process, due to the impact of market forces and the rise of political awareness in favour of decentralization. However, in both these aspects, there is no homogeneity among the performance of states. Some states, especially BIMARU region, are still lagging behind making the work of "new federalism" really difficult and challenging.

In a sense, rigidity and formalism attached to operation of Indian federalism seem to have declined in the neo-liberal age. The country witnessed rapid political developments and realignment among political parties since 1989 and it is very evident that the new economic reforms had influenced the political parties. Although many of them were critics of globalization (interestingly there was internal opposition inside the Congress party also), a broad consensus had developed compelling them to moderate in the new context. The contradictions proliferated when regional responses of national parties differed (look at the position of West Bengal unit of CPI (M) with that of Kerala until 2006) and the manner in which casteist and regionalist parties responded to globalization. The DMK, a party in Tamil Nadu, committed for achieving social justice became the arch supporter of neo-liberalism. The Bahujan Samaj Party led by Mayawati, while promoting identity politics in Uttar Pradesh, was demanding for more foreign direct investment to flow in her state. The approach of Samajwadi Party led by Mulayam Singh was no different. Again, the major opposition party, BJP also changed its stance compared to its approach in 1991.

The Indian National Congress emerged as the chief architect of globalisation reforms in the country. By abandoning Nehruvian policies of planned economy, socialist ideas and self reliance, Congress was instrumental for shifting the conventional role of the state in India. However, it has realised the significance of 'inclusive development' after the NDA lost power with its pet theme of 'shining India' in the 2004 elections. Therefore, it is trying to perform a balancing act between large scale economic reforms in major sectors of the economy while trying to uplift the vast majority of the poor through a series of popular policies like MGNREGS (Mahatma Gandhi National Rural Employment Guarantee Scheme) and National Rural Health Mission.

The CPI (M) has been a major critic of globalization policies and all its frontal organisations took very clear ideological position regarding this. But it was supporting industrial and business development in West Bengal attracting strong criticism from its arch rival Trinamool Congress. The latter objected the development of car industry in Singur in favour of the settlement issue of the rural people. Eventually, the business lost to West Bengal was a gain for Gujarat. Similarly in Kerala, the conventional anti-industrial policy of CPI(M) frustrated economic growth but in the new context, particularly since 2006, the LDF government modified and welcomed business and industry, though with caution. Indeed, it was a hectic struggle for CPI(M) to fine tune with economic growth and social justice. On the whole, the attitude of left parties underwent major changes during the neo-liberal era.

Parties with strong regional base like Samajwadi Party (Uttar Pradesh), Rashtriya Janata Dal (Bihar), Janata Dal-(United) (again, in Bihar), Biju Janata Dal (Orissa), Nationalist Congress Party (Maharashtra), Janata Dal-Secular (Karnataka) maintained twin imperatives in the context of their orientation towards reforms. First, they have the pressure for appear as pro-people and not pro-MNCs. Second, they have to produce conducive environment for the entrepreneurs for investment and employment generation. [24] It is a win-win formula of selective use of reforms and foreign investments and promotion of self-reliance but eventually there exists considerable confusion on issues like agricultural subsidies, privatisation of sectors like health and education, encouragement of FDI and increasing the cost of urban services. [25]

Baldev Raj Nayar (2004) finds out two major factors which brings BJP little to differentiate with Congress Party or

United Front: (1) the centrist tendency of Indian politics in the context of country's immense social diversity and the institutionalised nature of its political framework of democracy and (2) the asymmetric yet interdependent world economy which assures substantial initiatives to participate. [26] There are many areas where BJP shifted from its conventional ideology of 'Swadeshi' or economic nationalism-Free Trade Areas (in fact preferential trading areas), sale of equity of a PSE to benefit a strategic partner in the private sector to assume management control of the enterprise, patents policy and the Insurance Regulatory and Development Authority (IRDA) policy. [27] The centrist tendency generated by India's political system is the major explanation for the change in the BJP to a moderate economic policy and Nayar holds the view that "in an era dominated by economic globalisation, the acceptance of economic liberalisation is a manifestation of the centrist tendency in Indian politics' [28]

These are strong evidences to suggest how the major, medium and regional parties cutting across the traditional ideological positions of right left and centre had modified its policies to suit the context of globalisation. Obviously, the decline of the centralised role of the Indian state is very much evident leading us to suggest that the conventional and unilateral tendencies of federalism are undergoing serious changes. In a parliamentary federal system, parties and their positions are extremely important. Given the above background, the increasing role of the international market is driving federalism in hitherto unexplored areas. Paradoxically, though it may appear, decentralization measures are also becoming stronger which again formulates new federal trends. The emerging role of Self-help Groups, other NGOs, new social movements, civil society etc. is to be noted with significance.

The emerging interaction of national, state and local governments with foreign governments and corporations is not only redrawing state-market boundaries but also reconfigure federal institutions. [29] In the case of the first, financial sector reforms, assignment of regulatory, infrastructure reform and development are included while in the case of the latter, tax reforms, Centre-State fiscal transfer mechanisms and local government reforms are included bringing new dimensions of political economy and issues of regional inequalities. [30] Differential growth across states and the continued inequalities across the states and regions are found during the last two decades of reform.

While some states were able to achieve independent growth, co-ordination between federal institutions in designing and implementing reform policies becomes most essential. On the whole, Indian federalism is facing new challenges due to greater openness to world economy and growing regional disparities. [31]

Conclusion

The two decades experiences of economic reforms have brought significant changes in the country. A new middle class has emerged in the country that holds professional skills, higher and technical education, mobility and dynamism. The foreign policy initiatives underwent drastic changes. But, on the other hand, the decline of the welfare state has brought many negative results. It had widened inequality among people and regions, increased the poverty ratio, and weakened the social security net work, created new power lobbies like mining giants and land mafia groups. The rural-urban and digital divide has become more polarized.

At the federal level new trends had emerged. The conventional, political-legal dimensions of the centre- state relations are getting increasingly outdated. Earlier, the arrival of 'cooperative federalism' strengthened the position of the centre even though the roles of states were becoming equally significant. It was not possible to implement pro-poor and popular policies with out the joint effort of union and states. The emergence of a strong multi party system and coalition politics in the backdrop of the decline of 'one- party system' facilitated the process. However, the effects of the new economic reforms since 1991 had changed the trends altogether and opened up fresh debates on the theory and practice of federalism.

Market friendly federalism is fast replacing parliamentary federal status in the country. Emphasis is more on trade and business relations, inter-state migration, approach of private sector and Non-Governmental sectors in directing neo-liberal agenda. The role of the Union and State governments is that of a facilitator to these reforms and efforts. The primacy of the new economic actors had overshadowed the conventional role of political leadership. Of course, the inter-state competition continues to drive the economy. Nevertheless, the political leadership could not prevent the growing inequality between states. Few states have emerged as the economic role models while many others on the other side are struggling to cope up with the challenges of ensuring basic elements of development like education, health, infrastructure, food security etc. This apparent inequality between performing and non-performing states or between developed and underdeveloped regions will produce friction and tension areas in Indian federalism. A recent estimate has also shown that 75 percent of foreign direct investments is flowing to the five leading states of the country.

Critics had noticed the evolution of apolitical attitudes among people in the context of globalisation. While the environmental and economic effects of land mining are huge, in many states there did not witness any rapid protest movements. While the mainstream political forces had silently assimilated to the new process of development, there witnessed localised struggles led by marginalised groups and human rights movements. Thus, apolitical attitude of the middle class is creating a vacuum in the functioning of democracy. The response of the civil society especially in urban areas was notable. One should also notice the rise of Maoist groups in more than seven states challenging parliamentary democracy and the neo liberal state, compelling the Prime Minister Manmohan Singh to state that political extremism of Maoist groups constitutes a major challenge to the country.

The rise of inter-jurisdictional competition sidelining the centre-state and inter-state conflict marks another emerging trend in Indian federalism. The economic activities following the march of globalisation have shifted the dynamics of vertical federalism to horizontal federalism. This process was facilitated by the intense competition by the market forces cutting across the territorial aspects and sidelining the role hitherto played by state governments. Business and trade relations, demand for infrastructural developments, technological break through are beyond the geography of states. Internalised territorial dimension is becoming weak in this context. Infrastructural facilities needed in specific regions can bring a sea change in future. Once trade related developments take place, jurisdiction becomes wider and wider and this would impact upon federalism in newer forms.

The impact of globalisation in foreign policy of the country has been discussed. With the emergence of multilateral, polycentric world, India will actively engage with the host of countries including economies of South-East Asian region besides European Union and US. China is a strong competitor globally acknowledged, but India can initiate for fresh economic relations, there by cast an indirect influence over Pakistan. The relevance to this discussion is that the priorities of international relations are changing fast and many of these are determined by global developments. In the move towards an integrated economy, new issues are emerging. Problems of illegal migration, interest of non-resident Indians (NRIs) in investing in the Indian economy, issues of NRIs in Middle East etc. have federal dimensions too.

Therefore, the Government of India, at the instance of some state governments, had initiated reforms and set up institutions to look after these affairs. International issues and developments are therefore going to create both national and state specific reactions. An alignment of domestic policies with international policies has become the order of the day. International terrorism, issues of human security and human rights, poverty, malnutrition etc require global and regional attention. All these are bound to impact on federalism in India.

While local democracy in India is growing in an uneven form, the influence of the neo-liberal agenda could also be noticed here. Some of the pet themes of World Bank and Asian Development Bank in regard to infrastructural development were borrowed by the state and local governments and used for infrastructural development. The increasing role of voluntary organizations and civil society movements in local governance is evidence in this direction. The support extended by outside agencies and their sponsored agencies is impacting local leadership through material and policy oriented guidance. The new form of "globalization process" is changing the conventional parameters of democracy. Altogether, federal democracy in India is changing phenomenally taking cues mainly from the framework of globalization.

End Notes

1. Prakash Karat, Indo-US Civilian Nuclear Agreement and the Strategic Relations: Whither Independent Foreign Policy and Strategic Autonomy?, *Journal of Parliamentary Studies,* Vol. 1, Issue 1, June 2010:30.
2. Ibid.
3. Roberts, J.T and Amy Hite (2000). *From Modernization to Globalization* London: Blackwell cited in Anand Kumar *Modernity, Nation Building and Globalisation: An Indian Anxiety*, in Kameshwar Choudhary (2007). *Globalisation, Governance Reforms and Development in India* New Delhi: Sage Publications: 525.
4. Anand Kumar, Ibid: 526.
5. Ibid: 533-534.
6. Vidhu Verma, *Globalisation and the State in India* in Kameshwar Choudhary (2007). op. cit.:470.
7. Kavita Philip, *Reflections on the Intersections of Environment,*

Development and Human Rights in the Context of Globalisation, in Mahmood Monshipouri et al., (eds.) (2004). *Constructing Human Rights in the Age of* Globalisation, New Delhi: Prentice Hall of India: 55.

8. Claude Ake, *Dangerous liasions: the Interface of Globalization and Democracy* in Axel Hadenius (ed.) (1997). *Democracy's Victory and Crisis,* Cambridge: Cambridge University Press: 286-287.
9. Bal Dev Raj Nayar, *BJP's Economic Nationalism in Theory and Practice* in Ashuthosh Varshney (ed.) (2004). *India and the Politics of Developing Countries,* New Delhi: Sage Publications: 253.
10. Jagdish Bhagwati, "*Globalisation, Sovereignty and Democracy*" in Axel Hadenius (1997). op. cit:273.
11. Ibid: 27 8.
12. Peu Ghosh, (2009). *International Relations,* New Delhi: PHI Learning Private Limited: 314-315.
13. Ibid: 31 5.
14. Mah mmood Monshipouri et al (Eds) (2004).op.cit.: xiii.
15. Mann uel Castells (1997). *The Power of Identity: The Information Age- Economy, Society, and Culture* Vol.2 Malden, M.A. Blackwell, cited in Mahamood Monshipouri et al. (eds.) op.cit: xvi.
16. Doll y Arora, Globalisation and Reorganisation of Institutional Space: Meaning for Democracy and People's Rights in Kameshwar Choudhary (ed.) 2007 op.cit.: 91.
17. Ibid p: 93.
18. V.P. Menon, (1955). *Integration of Indian States,* Hyderabad: Orient Longman Publishers: 3.
19. See for details in Rajani Kothari (1964), *The Congress System in India, Asian Survey,* December.
20. Arie M.M. Kacowicz, *Regionalisation, Globalisation and Nationalism: Divergent or Overlapping? Alternatives,* Vol. 24, No. 4, October-December 1999: 5-7 cited in M.P Singh and Rekha Saxena (2010). *Indian Politics: Contemporary Issues and Concerns,* New Delhi: PHI Learning Private Limited: 71.
21. M P Sing h and Rekha Saxena, op.cit: 73.
22. La wrence Saez (2002). Federalism with out a Centre: The Impact of Political and Economic Reform on India's Federal System, New Delhi: Sagc Publications:135.

23. Ibid: 13 9-158.
24. A nand Kumar (2007). op.cit: 531.
25. Ibid.
26. Bal Dev Raj Na yar (2004). op.cit: 228.
27. Ibid: 24 1-250.
28. Ibid: 25 4.
29. Nirrikar Singh and TN Srinivasan, *Indian Federalism, Economic Reform and Globalisation* (2002).*http://en.wikipedia.org/wiki/United States public debt*, accessed on 9.2.2011, 2 pm.
30. Ibid.
31. Ibid.

7

Nature of the New Indian State: Federalism in the Current Global Market Scene

M.A. Lal

The impact of globalization to the nation-states all over the world reveals that state sovereignty is diminished and state crisis has become more complex. A notion of a post-traditional or post-classical nation-state is being theorized by scholars of state formation. Theoretically, it is being argued that globalization may be a threat for the centralized nation-state known for its over-emphasis on uniformity and homogeneity in political, social, economic and even cultural sectors. At the same time, it has contained some disguised blessings for the respect for diversity by allowing more decentralized levels of governance which help transfer of power to the people, and more autonomy of action for the constituent units of federations. The changes due to globalisation are more economics rather than politics or even more commerce rather than economics. However, the benefits of market-driven federalism are being positively assessed by established scholars of federalism.

Globalization has produced paradoxical results in India. It has allowed more autonomy of action in favour of the federal units (states) to reap the benefits of globalization. This has at the same time prepared the long-term basis of crisis in Indian federalism itself. Major crises include the following:

- The political autonomy of the states has been compromised in favour of the market.
- The states have been engaged in fierce competition among

themselves for foreign direct investment and special economic zone models of development giving rise to a new division among the states such as forward and backward states, inter-jurisdictional competition in place of inter-state cooperation, and weakening loyalty to the Union.

- With the weakening of the welfare state, the newly created conflicts out of disparity in regional development, and widening inequalities remain unmitigated.
- Local governance is more and more exposed to direct penetration by global and corporate power structures.
- There is mass protest against globalization led by various forms of grass-roots political activism. This cuts into the very democratic basis of legitimacy of the parties in power in the states.

The term 'globalization' has attracted the attention of scholars, rulers, opinion-makers and commoners, for a variety of reasons. While the first three groups often find common ground of looking at it and assessing some 'positive benefits' out of globalization, the commoners have become most often compelled to look at globalization more critically since it hit them the hardest. If jobs are made insecure, if lands are taken away, if habitat is disturbed, and the inhabitants are displaced in the wake of 'development', and if social security nets are withdrawn, they will not have a particularly pleasant attitude to the process responsible for them.

If social and economic inequalities are increased; if regional disparities are increased in a multi-regional and multi-cultural country, as a result of the so-called competition among the regions and the states for foreign capital, and for development, this does not augur well for national identity and unity, and cohesion. If the Central State, in the 'rolling the state back' mould (much propagated by globalization), withdraws itself from its social welfare activities, from its job of an arbiter in the inter-regional/state disputes, or does not plan any longer for removing intra-regional and inter-regional gaps in development, the field that is left open is dangerous. If in the society, class, group including ethnic tensions are accentuated and 'the forward' and the 'backward' states (in terms of development) are created as a result, they pose a threat for 'national identity'.

The typical international political atmosphere followed by the end of Cold War, and the gaining in widespread popularity of various regional, and transnational political associations, most notably the European Union, have meant that the classical nation-state based on homogeneity and uniformity is much condemned in favour of a genuine federal state respectful of diversity and heterogeneity. Globalization, in other words, has created the congenial conditions for federalism. This has been reflected in the growing literature on federalism. The established scholarship on federalism strongly suggests that thanks to market-driven globalization in recent times there has been a kind of renaissance in federalism. It is widely believed that federalism has been proving itself to be the form of government for the contemporary world whatever the kind may be. About 40 percent of the world's population is said to be living under federalism, and some more, under some kinds of federal arrangements including that of the European Union.

According to Ronald Watts, the desire for progress, a rising standard of living, social justice, and the growing awareness of the interdependence of the world in conditions of revolutions in communication, transportation, technology and industrial organization has encouraged, on the one hand, smaller, self-governing political units, and governments more responsive to citizens' preferences as well as to some primordial group attachments based on language, culture, regions and so on, and on the other hand, larger political units (transnational, global and so on) where states pool their sovereignties for various common interests. The renewed emphasis on contractual relationships, non-centralized character of the market-based economies, entrepreneurial self-governance, consumer rights, diversity and the recognition of the difference etc is closely connected with globalization and supportive of the federal idea. In this context, there is no wonder in the fact that revealing in the growing literature on federalism which witnesses a paradigm shift from statism to increasingly decentralized forms of governance in the context of what Thomas Fleiner has termed 'diminished state sovereignty.' Also, Americanisation in the style of governance became the central character of a globalized federal setup. This is because of copying the legitimate and convenient definition of federal government spoken in the constitution of United States, by the modern nation states. [1]

Changes in Indian Federal Structure

The real globalisation process had its beginnings in India in the mid-1960s. In the initial approach paper on the Fourth Five Year Plan it was stated: "within the broad framework of control in strategic areas, there is an advantage in allowing the market much fuller play". [2] India's liberalisation until the end of the 1960s took a variety of forms: 16 items were decontrolled in 1963; cement was decontrolled in 1966, and cotton in 1967; controls on investment were liberalized, and several industries were also decontrolled. However, the process of India's liberalisation has since been slow and halting, and passed through phases, and even during the Emergency regime (1975-77) of authoritarianism and excessive state control, the process of liberalization, paradoxically enough, was broadened and accelerated. Hardgrave and Kochanek have noted as follows: during the emergency, the government tried to further liberalize the industrial licensing policies, relax price controls, and provide tax incentives for industrial investment in an effort to accelerate the rate of economic growth. [3]

What remained basically a guarded process of liberalization until the early 1990s became ever since a combined process of liberalization, privatization and globalization (LPG). The so-called 'structural reforms', as is heard a lot these days, encompass the combination: 'decontrol and deregulation of industry, changes in monetary and fiscal policy, liberalization of trade policy, changes in foreign exchange regulations, encouragement of foreign direct investment, financial sector reforms, promotion of private foreign investment in infrastructure, partial privatization of public sector units, and the promise to enact labour reforms, and an exit policy that allows bankrupt private sector firms to go out of business.'

The states in Indian federation are the most crucial strategic players in implementing the agenda of globalization. The Indian Constitution entrusts the states with the major tasks of development including infrastructural development. Globalization, really, has increased the importance of the states. Observers of Indian politics have noted how the Central State induced, or coerced many states which were unwilling to join in the process of structural reforms. C.P. Bhambri has noted how the Central government made use of such tactics as cajoling, persuading and even bribing the unwilling states in the reforms process more particularly in the case of structural reform of the State Electricity Boards. [4]

Most of the states in India have joined in the process of structural reforms followed by globalisation, in order to benefit from it. This situation paved way for a fierce competition among the states for FDI, and other benefits. This takes place in the environment in which the socially interventionist state (Central State) gradually withdraws itself from public welfare activities leaving the field to a series for 'regulatory authorities'. Here, the characteristic of federalism implied in Wheare's definition that the powers of the Central government are exercised directly over individual citizens and private groups rather than, as in a confederacy, through the states or provinces alone, becomes irrelevant. [5]

Indian States in the New Pattern

The nature and working of the states in Indian federation

in the process of globalization is an interesting area to be understood. Globalization is at the same time is beneficial and harmful to the Indian states. It is not entirely true to say that globalization signal the decline, or regeneration of Indian federalism. To be sure, a federation provide for a different space for policy interaction and implementation from that of a unitary state, and hence, the constituent units of the federation become strategically important in this respect. In the Indian constitutional system, the most important key sectors which are central to India's globalization are competences of states in the fields of industrial infrastructure, power development, agriculture, and its allied sectors and irrigation, roads, health education, medical services, nutrition, water supply and urban development and so on. And yet, until the mid-1990s, the involvement of states in the reforms process was less than satisfactory. The Centre was both unwilling and unable to involve the states in the process for a number of reasons. Various external agencies preferred for policy dialogue only with the national government. Only the Centre has sole competence in macro-economic stabilisation, and the variegated nature of state governments. This situation became changed dramatically with the advent of new millennium.

Indian federalism has been drastically changed so that it needs to be redefined. Rudolph and Rudolph argued that as a result of the impact, the interventionist state in India had given way to a 'regulatory state' [6], which again was more suited to a growing multi-party system. Critics of this view do not subscribe to this because they believe that India's redefined federal system requires the central government to play a critical role. They are also not sure that a regulatory state will be able to mitigate the growing competition among the Indian states in the era of globalization. However, Indian federalism has undergone some major transformation from the intergovernmental co-operation to inter jurisdictional competition among the states.

State governments are very important players in the

economic development of the country, more pronounced of course since the 1990s. This striking fact has become clear in the 1990s because investors have to contact every state government for launching a project. Since the central state is gradually withdrawing itself from its social responsibilities including welfare-oriented development, most clearly evident, among others, in the shrinkage of the number of centrally-sponsored welfarist development schemes, as C.P. Bhambri has shown, centre-state relations have taken often peculiar forms. Cajoling, persuading and even bribing often could become tactics resorted to by the centre for involving the state governments in the process of economic reforms and restructuring. [7] Rao and Singh (2005) have recognized that the role of states has expanded due to market economy which demands more decentralized levels of governance, but also that all the states are not equally equipped to access the opportunities afforded by the market.

The Indian federal system offers both opportunities and constraints for structural reforms. The constraints refer to the variegated political complexion of governments at the centre and at the states. This may facilitate the reforms process or, stand in the way of implementation of any uniform reforms package if the rival rules in the states. The coalition governments thus often become worse victim of such eventuality. When seen from the side of globalization, given that the states are today offered more freedom of action in respect of adopting and implementing structural adjustment programmes, the states have become more competitive for inviting investment, industrialisation, trade and commerce, entrepreneurial governance for development. Globalization thus is encouraging for more rights for the states although it is hard to conclude that all the states will benefit equally from out of globalization, and also that people in each state will be able reap the benefits of globalization equitably. Much depends on the policy preferences of the state governments concerned, and space for the exercise of such preference.

In short, the role of states in India's reforms process is very crucial and politically significant. Globalization which is predominantly economic and political processes is ultimately to be implemented in the states. As per the Constitution, the states are responsible for a variety of development works since the Union Government does not have the bureaucracy to implement its laws. Also, democratically mandated state governments are more politically vulnerable because being close to the people it is they who suffer from the after-effects of the policies of globalization. The states being distinct socio-cultural units, the political vulnerability of state governments, especially in the face of rival mobilisation of popular discontent is particularly of concern to the party in power. The globalization may create risks and uncertainties for the legitimacy of governing parties of states since an uncritical approach to and implementation of the reforms process inevitably adversely affects the socially and economically vulnerable sections of society, and paves the way for undemocratic practices.

According to Livingston, the structural and institutional features of federalism have been given far more attention than the actual working of the political systems which they sustain. He contends that the institutions and the constitutional arrangements roughly reflect the nature of society, in the context of globalisation. However, the institutional arrangements and the constitutional structure are by themselves no guarantee that a given system is federal. How the institutions work in the context of a given society and how they operate is more important than the form. Federalism is indicative of the social and political thinking of a society. [8]

Globalization-propelled current assertion of the states for autonomy of policy and action occurs in the age of 'retreat of the state', i.e., the increasing withdrawal of the states from social welfares. Thus, the rights of the states may not be as much people's rights assuring. It must not be forgotten that this re-federalization of the Indian polity, or true federalization ever taken place, is market oriented and pro global. There is growing inter-state and inter-regional disparities in terms of investment. This will create genuine ground for fear that the situation will accentuate inter-regional tensions and encourage ethnic conflicts, which will affect adversely the sense of national identity. The researchers are already making the distinction between the forward states and backward states in development terms, which have immense ideological and political implications for India's unity and integrity.

Conclusion

Growth due to globalisation has favoured, broadly urban India, organized sectors, richer states, and property owners against rural India, unorganized sectors, poorer states and wage-earners. The result is a huge polarisation of the economy and society resulting from a policy of growth with inequality. The strategically most significant effect of globalization, from the viewpoint of national unity and integrity, is the growth in inter-state and intra-regional disparity in development. Historically, India's regions have lacked balanced development. The centuries of colonial exploitation and plunder of India left the country at the point of independence not only underdeveloped, but with huge unevenness in regional development. Regionalism and separatism have had their roots in the sense of regional deprivation in development. This has called for the most judicious management of ethno-regional conflicts in post-Independence period on the part of the socially interventionist state for ensuring political unity and cohesion. Globalization process seems to be upsetting all that by re-creating bases of ethno-regional conflicts.

As a result two groups of states, namely, 'have' and 'have-not' states have been created. The so-called 'have' states such as Maharashtra, Gujarat and Tamil Nadu account for 40 percent of the all-India value added in manufacturing; also two-thirds of foreign investment during 1991-98 were in these states also. [9] Of these three states, Gujarat and Maharashtra were the largest beneficiaries (36.7 percent) of the above investment during the same period. [10] By an estimate made by the Economic and Political Weekly, in 2000, the categories of forward states and backward states in India became a reality in terms of urbanity, female literacy, female infant mortality, per capita income, percentage of the poor, infrastructural development, and consumption of power per capita.

Thus, the forward states were Andhra Pradesh, Gujarat, Haryana, Karnataka, Kerala, Maharashtra, Punjab and Tamil Nadu, and the backward states were Assam, Bihar, Madhya Pradesh, Rajasthan, U. P and West Bengal. [11] Some of the so-called backward states must have caught up since, especially West Bengal which in the above categorisation was found to be very close to Tamil Nadu in terms of most indicators. But then, the competition among states is fiercer today for attracting foreign investment and other private investment for development. The disparity among the states in terms of FDI inflows has also been growing. During the same period, West Bengal received only 1.4 percent of the total inflow of FDI compared to Karnataka (7.53 percent), Maharashtra (20.28 percent), North-Eastern states together (0.05 percent), Bihar and Jharkhand (0.00 percent).

It is difficult to build a cohesive national identity in the midst of manifold, complex diversity coupled with mass poverty, illiteracy, extremes of social and economic inequalities and so on in India. But the country's achievement in this regard, when compared to many post-colonial and even the industrially advanced former socialist systems, has been remarkable indeed. But in the wake of globalization, followed by withdrawal of the public welfare state, when a certain paradigm of development produces disparities of many sorts, and polarises the society sharply, ultimately it is the sense of national identity, unity or cohesion that is the victim. For over five decades, in the context of a social welfare state, people's wishes and aspirations have informed programmes of decentralization and autonomy. That was how democracy could be blended with diversity. But today when the very domain of the public is fast shrinking due to globalisation, harnessing democracy for national unity would be very difficult. Classical federalism gave way for the creation of market friendly federalism; there the federal units are just markets of corporates, shaping New India; New Federalism; Globalised Federalism.

End Notes

1. K.C. Wheare, (1963). *Federal Government,* London: Oxford University Press: 1.
2. Hardgrave R. L., and Kochanek S. A., (2000). *India: Government and Politics in a Developing Nation,* Orlando: Harcourt College Publications: 373.
3. Ibid: 377.
4. C. P. Bhambri, (2005). *The Central Government in the Age of Globalization* in Dua D.D and Singh M. P. (eds.), *Indian Federalism in the New Millennium,* New Delhi: Manohar Publications: 328.
5. D.V. Smiley, (1987). *The Federal Condition in Canada Series,* Toronto: McGraw Hill Ryerson Series on Canadian Politics: 2.
6. Lloyd Rudolph and Susanne H Rudolph cited in G. Gopa Kumar (ed.), (2007). *Future of Parliamentary Democracy in India,* New Delhi: Icon Publications: 280.
7. Bhambri, op. cit.: 328.
8. W S Livingston, (1956). *Federalism and Constitutional Change,* London: Oxford University Press: 4.
9. Tremblay R. C, (2005). *Globalization and Indian Federalism* in Dua and Singh, op. cit.: 341.
10. T remblay, op. cit.: 341.
11. T remblay, op. cit.: 341-42.

8

Water, Federalism and International Law

Deepa Karthikeyan

We know more about celestial bodies than soils underfoot. Water is the driving force of all nature. -Leonardo Da Vinci (1452–1519) [1]

"Water has no taste, no colour, no odour; it cannot be defined, art relished while ever mysterious. Not necessary to life, but rather life itself. It fills us with a gratification that exceeds the delight of the senses." – Antoine De Saint-Exupery (1900-1944), Wind, Sand, and Stars, 1939

A Watery Understanding

The significance of water as a vital resource is an established fact that requires little explanation. Nevertheless, while the role played by water in the sustenance of life is undisputable, its complex nature continues to elude man and remains far less understood.

Our understanding of the hydrological cycle and more specifically the terrestrial portion of the hydrological cycle which exhibits considerable spatial variability remains insufficient to formulate generalizations. Added to this predicament is the presence of multiple approaches employed while attempting to understand the hydrological process. Here, instead of sharing a common set of assumptions about its operation, adherents to the various approaches to hydrology view the subject of water from their own vantage points. [2] This creates a patchy understanding of our water reality, thereby contributing to the creation of a number of waters laws, which are often seen to be in blatant defiance of the underlying hydrological unity.

This inconsistency in our understanding of the water reality creates a gap between natural water laws and the complex legal systems that govern the use of the same. Here, lies the dilemma of water governance. Water, while a simple and familiar feature of our daily life remains (on account of wrong approaches, bad policies and misdirected planning) perhaps one of the least governed aspect of our living environment.

This makes water governance and the formulation of water laws a very special process. Interestingly, a glimpse at the evolution of laws on water show that water laws both in the domestic and international spheres evolved in response to specific disputes or crises. The differences in the nature of disputes and the interests of states, contributed to a large body of legal doctrine that seem to have offset the objective of developing our water resources on a sustainable basis. In fact, these divergences between natural and man-made laws on one hand and international and state laws on the other are most manifest in the case of inter-state conflicts on water sharing. This is further complicated in the case of federal or quasi-federal states where the interests of the sub-national governments are also involved while formulating treaties.

These difficulties bring us back to the traditional dilemma of having to explore in greater detail the 'hazy' interfaces between international and national/federal law. Here, the tricky issue of having to define 'where federal law ends and international law begins' occupies the crux of the discourse. In fact this debate attains greater significance in the case of trans-boundary waters, as water despite being far more delimited in space and time vis-à-vis other commons such as air, still cannot be constrained by statistic definitions.

Given the aforementioned premise, this paper seeks to explore the problems that arise when the principles of international law contradict constitutional/domestic law. Here, the fuzzy interfaces between national and international law when it comes to the use and sharing of trans-boundary rivers, is explored in the context of India. In this direction, the paper begins with a brief overview of the evolutionary histories of international and Indian federal law so as to enable one to identify specific divergences that persist between the two.

The Road to Helsinki

At the international level the domain of water laws are restricted to the use and sharing of trans-boundary water sources. The evolution of modern international water laws was the result of a series of dynamic interactions amongst various nation-states on the use and sharing of its trans-boundary waters. In fact, several international and federal cases concerning issues like defining political borders, flood management, reallocating waters for growing populations, diverting river flow for agriculture, and developing new industries defined its (International Water Laws) architecture, relevance and scope. However, while the legal framework governing water changed its shape, form and essence to accommodate changing priorities at various points in time, the essence of international water laws as they exist today continues to be inspired by the civil law traditions (Romano-Germanic) on water.

In the Roman law there was a highly developed law of waters. It was based on the principle of common usage where equal access to the common property water was legally secured. In fact, in ancient Rome, people could obtain temporary usufructary rights on running water, and these rights were independent of land. Roman jurists inspired by Greek philosophy of reason clearly distinguished between the more important, perennial streams and rivers from the less important seasonal water bodies and established the former as a common or public resource to be owned by none and governed by the immutable laws of nature. This made the prohibition to alter the natural watercourse an enforceable legal claim even in ancient times [3] (actio aquae fluviae arvene). [4]

However, with the rise in travel and commerce, many of these communities developed complex rules for the navigation, allocation and use of water, making navigational rules pre-eminent over non-navigational uses. This led to the formulation of a legal doctrine that began to distinctly deviate from the principles as laid down under the Roman legal system. [5] This shift in 'water-use' priorities from the Roman ideal was further strengthened with the advent of the transport, urban and industrial revolutions in the early part of the eighteenth century. Here, the increased demand for water for purposes other than navigation resulted in a lot of legal conflict over water rights resulting in the evolution of a large but unstable body of legal doctrine, specifying strong property rights in flowing water attached to riparian possession, and also limited rights to surface and underground water. [6] Water, thus, slowly came to be seen as a mere usufruct, adjunct to land and confined within geographical and temporal spaces. This approach received greater support on American soil. The principle of absolute territorial sovereignty also popularly called the Harmon doctrine provided legitimate space for the upper riparian states to break the previously accepted principle of no significant harm and deviated substantially from the civil law code.

In fact, until the late 19th Century, water laws retained such a utility-oriented approach (that is there were separate laws dealing with municipal use, river navigation, irrigation, etc.). It was only in the later part of the 20th Century that water laws underwent deep conceptual changes and became resource oriented, encompassing all uses and problems related to water. [7] In this context, the idea of 'equitable appropriation' or the theory of community interests, emerged, which despite its limitations for the first time provided a legal basis for alienating water from land and attached it to the principle of 'beneficial use' anywhere in the basin. [8]

The Helsinki Rules (1966), drafted as a comprehensive code for the use of trans-boundary drainages, attempted to resolve inter-state conflicts based on the aforementioned principle of beneficial use. Applicable to all drainage basins that cross national boundaries, except where other agreement between bordering nations exists, the Helsinki Rules asserted the rights of all bordering nations to an equitable share in the water resources, with reasonable consideration of such factors as past customary usages of the resource and balancing variant needs and demands of the bordering nations. [9] Nevertheless, despite their soundness, the Helsinki Rules and their supplementary declarations received little recognition as official codifications of international water law. Thus, in an attempt to seek greater conformity the United Nations commissioned the International Law Commission in 1970 to draft a set of articles to govern the non-navigational uses of trans-boundary waters. This led to the adoption of the UN Convention on the Law of the Non-Navigational Uses of International Watercourses on the 21st of May 1997.

The 1997 Convention was designed to accommodate the development of more specific bilateral and multilateral agreements related to the use, management, and preservation of trans-boundary water resources. Despite being a fairly more comprehensive and flexible code, its influence as a binding principle in the signing of international water treaties still remains questionable. Voting results showed that 103 countries voted in favour of the text of the Convention [10] while three voted against and 27 states abstained from the voting process. In fact, the countries that voted against the convention were China, Turkey and Burundi, all three of which are primarily upper riparian states and two of which namely China and Turkey are engaged in controversial hydro projects. [11] Despite its limitations, the UN Convention reflects contemporary international thinking on the use and sharing of trans-boundary water resource and has value as the product of a democratic process and may yet serve as a standard for state practice. [12]

Thus, in short, the trend observed in international water

law, increasingly, seems to favour a drainage basin approach where water is managed by reference to the shape or form of the land that forms the catchment of a major river, and its tributaries, from the upper watersheds down to the sea, or other final "terminus" (such as a lake). This approach is entirely logical from a hydrological perspective given that surface water within the basin will naturally flow in a common direction towards that terminus. [13] However, Indian laws on water took a very different path.

Federalism and Water in India

Federalism in India is a by-product of a long history of Colonialism. The unique needs of the Indian republic in the post independence phase resulted in the creation of a very special system of governance as visible in the constitutional provisions of the state. In its zeal to establish a durable democracy under a common banner, the Constitution deliberately designed the devolution of powers in a fashion that ensured a quasi-federal system where power flowed from the top. To this end, the federal legal relations in India had a tendency to structurally delink economic issues from other constituents of spatial relations such as social, political, gender, caste and environment by designating them as state subjects. [14] This tendency is also visible in the formulation of laws on the subject of water within the Indian Constitution.

When it comes to the subject of water, the Indian constitution borrows extensively from British Common Law to regulate and develop the state's water resources. In fact, colonial rule and modern engineering replaced the pre-colonial ways of managing the state's water resources to the extent that 'water-use' came to generally mean irrigation; irrigation meant canals and canals were built and operated by government engineers. [15] Irrigation laws, thus, constitute the most developed part of water laws in India [16] and most of the basic principles of water laws applicable today in India are derived from irrigation acts. [17]

With regard to surface water existing rules still derive their logic from the principle of riparian rights, where the owners have a right to use the water of a stream flowing past their land equally with other riparian owners, to have the water come to them undiminished in flow, quantity or quality. [18] Whereas, when it came to question of groundwater, the almost outdated principle that sees water as being adjunct to land continues to govern water use. While land ownership is critical to both surface water and groundwater, the riparian rights in the case of surface water are usually subject to the doctrine of reasonable use whereas groundwater continues to be governed by the freewheeling rule of capture. [19] This idea was further strengthened by the high court decision to uphold landowner's rights to groundwater in the Plachimada case. [20] Thus, a large component of our domestic water laws continues to remain anachronistic and do not serve the emerging concern of using our waters in a sustainable manner.

In fact, even the current Constitutional scheme on water is largely based on the model of the Government of India act of 1935 as formulated under the British. The three main provisions relevant to water in the Indian Constitution are Entry 17 in the State List, Entry 56 in the Union List and Article 262.

The first provision makes water a state subject but qualified by Entry 56 in the Union List which states that "regulation and development of inter-state rivers and river valleys to the extent to which such regulation and development under the control of the Union is declared by Parliament by law to be expedient in the public interest". Article 262 empowers the centre to intervene and adjudicate disputes relating to waters of inter-state rivers. The two most important legislations relating to inter-state waters in the Indian federal system is the Inter-state Water Disputes Act (1956) and the River Boards Act (1956).

In the case of a water dispute between two or more state governments, the provisions of the Inter-State Water Disputes

Act (ISWDA), 1956 allows the disputing states to request the Central Government to refer the dispute to a tribunal for adjudication. The tribunal shall then investigate the complaint and forward a report to the Central Government known as the order or award of the Tribunal. The Central Government then shall publish the tribunal's decision in the official gazette, when the decision is final and therefore, will be binding on the parties involved in the water dispute. [21] Despite the presence of such an elaborately defined conflict resolution mechanism, thirteen inter-state water disputes remain unresolved. The River Boards Act (1956) similarly aims to provide for the establishment of river boards for the regulation and development of inter-state rivers. This, however, continues to remain a dead letter as not a single river board has been established yet under the act. [22] Moreover, even when established these boards will remain ineffective as their role is constitutionally limited to that of an advisory board. [23]

An overview of the federal constitutional provisions on water governance in India exhibits the presence of several flaws. Firstly, water laws in India continue to retain the framework as set by common law traditions, which is inappropriate, unsustainable and hydrologically unsound. Moreover, the provisions on water as laid down by the constitution exhibit a great degree of ambiguity when it comes to defining the development of micro-and macro-water sheds. This is visible under the head of 'economic and social planning' in Entry 20 of the Concurrent List, where the centre's role on water is brought out through a circuitous route. Here, the development of major and minor irrigation projects, hydropower, flood control and other multipurpose projects are placed under the control of both the centre and the state with the former wielding greater power in the decision-making process. That is development of water resources, despite being a state subject, is often subservient to the interests of the nation.

Thus, even though the centre has not invoked its powers as

defined in Entry 56 in the Union List, it still continues to wield considerable influence on the development of the nation's waters. Here, while large water projects remain a centralized affair, the idea of allowing sub-national units to formulate their own water policies represents a kind of 'nominal decentralization' where states have the freedom to chalk out fancy policies without the financial independence to carry it out. Here, federal legal relations in India as argued by Radha D'souza tend to reproduce an essential feature of colonial rule that places 'development' outside of the authority of states.

Secondly, dams and structural interventions to augment supply of water, still dominate thinking amongst the members of the water establishment in India, and the laws seem to implicitly support this parochial approach by focusing entirely on the development of surface waters such as rivers, lakes, ponds etc without much emphasis on the regulation of other water forms such as groundwater aquifers. This has resulted in the over exploitation and contamination of our aquifers. Currently, out of 4,272 blocks in the country, 231 blocks have been categorized as 'over-exploited' where the stage of groundwater development exceeds the annual replenishable limit and 107 blocks are termed 'dark' where the usage of groundwater development exceeds 85 percent. [24]

Finally, the absence of an umbrella framework at the centre creates a situation of anarchy as different states may adopt different principles on the use and sharing of waters that may often be antagonistic to the interests of neighbouring federal units. For example, in the case of the Cauvery Dispute, while Tamil Nadu continues to emphasize its rights over the Cauvery waters on the basis of 'Prior Appropriation', Karnataka being the upper riparian asserts it's right on the Cauvery waters on the basis of the principle of 'absolute territorial sovereignty'. Here, the absence of a central framework to guide the sharing of trans-boundary waters (such as the one mentioned in the Helsinki Principles of 1966) has emerged as one of the primary causes of the dispute. [25]

Fuzzy Interfaces between International and Domestic Water Law

The super-imposition of the laws of a state over the natural laws of a river have resulted in the evolution of a new kind of developmental conflict located in the interstices of national and international law. [26] A brief glimpse at the evolution of International and Constitutional laws exhibit the presence of a passive hostility between the two. Here, while contemporary international law continues to be strongly influenced by civil law traditions (Romano-Germanic) which upholds the principle of 'equitable apportionment' and 'beneficial use' anywhere in the river as the guiding principle to share water resources, common law traditions that see water as being adjunct to land dominates the legal discourse in India. These passive differences between domestic and international law make the process of formulating and meeting treaty clauses a process entrenched in too many differences and difficulties. This may be illustrated in the case of the Indus Water Treaty signed between India and Pakistan under the auspices of the World Bank in 1960.

The Indus Water Treaty, while often lauded for having sustained three gory wars between India and Pakistan sadly does not entirely conform to the international principles on sharing trans-boundary waters. Here, while the initial aim was to provide for a water sharing formula on the basis of equitable apportionment by accounting the entire river basin as an indivisible and composite whole, the strong opposition to such a sharing formula for almost twelve years by both the disputants resulted in the surgical division of the basin itself into the eastern and western rivers. The partitioning of the six rivers of the Indus on a crudely longitudinal basis was irrational from an ecological point of view and has implicitly accentuated the problem of water sharing.

The inflows to Pakistan depend not just on rainfall and snowmelt in India and China but also on the health of tributaries, streams, nallahs and acquifers as well as groundwater, soil and forest management practices in both the states. [27] By dividing the basin along statist lines, the responsibility of developing the waters of the entire basin in a sustainable manner falls outside the spheres of both states and ruptures the hydrological system. [28] Thus, despite being politically successful in resolving the dispute, the Indus Water Treaty, blatantly deviates from the internationally accepted principle of developing the river basin as an integrated whole. Here, the contradiction between International Law (that advocates the sharing of the beneficial uses of a river as a whole) and federal law (that places riparian rights above equitable apportionment) is visible.

Moreover, in the absence of a comprehensive law to govern the water resources of the federal state, certain practical difficulties emerge while carrying out one's treaty commitments as the interfaces between national and international law in the process of treaty making remain ill-defined and unclear. This may be illustrated with the help of the Ganges Water Sharing Agreement signed between India and Bangladesh in the year 1996.

The Ganges Water Sharing Agreement is often quoted as an example to illustrate the successful resolution of a trans-boundary water conflict based on the guidelines as adopted by the 1997 UN Convention. In an attempt to establish a reasonable framework for the sharing of the Ganges waters, the Treaty of 1996 formulated a water sharing formula, where the proportion of sharing between India and Bangladesh was set at a ratio of 45:55. However, once the clauses of the treaty were operationalized certain discrepancies between the actual volumes of water released at Farakka and the water levels as observed at the Hardinge Bridge were observed and created a lot of discontent amongst the Bangladeshis who suspected Indian involvement in the observed discrepancy in water levels. However, after a lot of finger pointing and a series of heated negotiations, it was discovered that one of the factors that contributed to the fall in water level between Farakka and

Hardinge Bridge was the proliferation in the number of tube wells operating in the region between the two. [29] Here, despite the clauses of the treaty being in compliance with the principles as mentioned in the UN Convention, the absence of a comprehensive domestic law on the regulation and use of groundwater in the region created a lot of misunderstanding between the disputants and came in the way of the state's international commitment.

Apart from the obvious contradiction in the intent of international and domestic law, another interesting and implicit trend is visible in both these aforementioned illustrations. Here, the theoretical relevance or supremacy of international law in governing trans-boundary water conflicts is disputed by the observed domination of state law in the settlement of inter-state water disputes. Theoretically, from the international law vantage, international law prevails over any domestic law while two states come together to formulate a treaty. This point of view finds ample evidence in customary international law. For example Article 27 of the Vienna Convention on the Law of Treaties, provides that "a party may not invoke the provisions of its internal law as justification for its failure to perform a treaty". Here, (according to international law) Constitutions, then, "are merely facts"' that like the rest of national law have no bearing on the responsibilities that a nation undertakes within the international community. However, from the vantage of the domestic legal system, international law has no bearing on the Constitution, which operates as an absolute constraint on how Indian obligations may be observed. [30] This mutually held notion that international law and constitutional law have no bearing on one another are vulnerable at the margins and do not hold well in a world where the borders are becoming increasingly irrelevant.

The presence of such contradictions therefore calls for a re-alignment of our legal structure domestically in a manner consistent with the efficacious principle of international law.

Here, while international law imposes a duty on national governments to pursue the good faith exploitation of national legal institutions, including constitutions, in order to adhere to treaty obligations, conversely constitutional doctrine is expected to episodically encourage legal constructions that permit states to perform its international obligations. [31]

Any effort in this direction, however, must begin with an examination of water laws under the federal framework in the "Indian context" as discussed previously in the paper. One of the first problems faced by Indian laws governing water (as previously discussed in the paper) is that they reflect the concerns of their makers more than half a century ago and are therefore anachronistic and almost irrelevant in today's world. Moreover, our understanding of the science of water has greatly improved over the last fifty years calling for a dynamic revamp of our laws to accommodate the water reality as we understand it today.

Sadly, the legal frameworks in India lack the dynamism required to eliminate irrelevant laws and replace them with new and more enforceable ones. This lethargy is visible in our national water policies where in an attempt to keep with outdated domestic law, the more sound principles of hydro-morphology are sacrificed. For example, the National Water Policy of 2002 while a slight up gradation over the previous policy framework, does not address the complex difficulties involved in water governance and are still primarily concerned with the building of big-projects, transferring water over long distances, and facilitating private investments in such projects. [32] Added to this is the ambiguous nature of our water laws, complemented by the large number of institutions governing aspects to our water policy. This makes the process of legal reform a Herculean task that demands both enormous political will and vision.

Road Ahead

A first step in the direction of revamping our system might

involve the creation of a unifying framework, at the centre to guide various federal units in the development and management of their waters. Here, a special effort must be made to break the common prejudice of looking at water as being synonymous with rivers so as to include all forms of water. This will help us move closer to the internationally accepted standard on water management, thereby reducing the vagueness in the interactions between domestic and international law.

The creation of a unifying framework here however must not be seen as a step against the trend of de-centralization and could work on the lines of the European Union Directives on Water, which commits European Union member states to achieve good qualitative and quantitative status of all water bodies without taking away their autonomy to develop their water resources. It is a framework in the sense that it prescribes steps to reach the common goal rather than adopting the more traditional limit value approach. [33]

A similar approach in the case of India will help reduce the internal differences on the question of water governance (without actually diluting their autonomy) by persuading the states to at least concur on certain basic principles of water management and use. [34] This will go a long way in reducing inter- and intra-state water disputes, thereby indirectly enabling Indian federalism to function more smoothly both in the domestic and International arena.

Currently, mismanagement and conflict dominate the water scene in India. However, this malady traces itself not to the absence of leadership, vision or innovation but rather the lack of political will. Today a series of exceptional individuals such as Anna Hazare, Sarpanch Popat Pawar and organizations such as Dhan (Madurai) [35] are doing wonderful work in the area of water management through the re-invigoration of traditional water management systems. This has helped break the almost mythical grasp that big projects hold on the minds of the people at least at the lower levels in certain areas. An extrapolation of some of these principles at the national level might help the winds of change blow with greater vigour.

Moreover, the verdict delivered in the M.C. Mehta vs. Kamal Nath case where the Supreme Court delivered a verdict supporting the public trust doctrine and making it a part of domestic law represents a step in the right direction and brings out the important role played by the judiciary in interpreting and integrating various efficacious clauses of international law into the domestic one so as to make our legal system more dynamic and comprehensive.

An ancient Chinese saying quite nicely sums up the path that one must take while managing water and goes as follows,' (while) man always aspires higher water flows to the lowest point'. May be we could take our cue from nature and start the reform process at the lowest levels. One way of doing this is perhaps engaging in a social dialogue at the lowest level aimed at enhancing awareness amongst people on the importance of using our waters in a sustainable fashion. Here, federalism might actually emerge as amenable political system where devolution of powers is better defined, and might enable the reconciliation of national laws with international laws through a constructive reform process so that the laws of man go hand in hand with the laws of nature.

End Notes

1. Laurent Pfister et al, (2009). *Leonardo Da vinci's Water Theory: On the Origin and Fate of Water,* IAHS: 7.
2. David N. Collins, Hydrology *and Hydrologist, International Association of Hydrological Science,* No: 171 (1987):93.
3. Karl Weber, (2007). *Who Owns Water?,* Innsbruck: 13.
4. This idea finds relevance in contemporary international law as the 'Doctrine of Public Trust'.
5. Gabriel E. Eckstein, (2002). *Development of International Water Law and the UN Watercourse Convention* , in Anthony Turton & Roland Henwood (eds) *Hydropolitics in the Developing World : A Southern African Perspective,* Pretoria: 82.
6. Joshua Getzler, (2004), *A History of Water Rights at Common Law,* New York:1.

7. Guillermo J Cano, *The Legal and Administrative Implications of the Hydrological Cycle and Water-Related Resources Facing the 21st. Century, Water International,* Vol. 4, No. 4 (1979):20-24.
8. Radha D'Souza, *At the Confluence of Law and Geography: Contextualizing Inter-state Water Disputes in India, Geoforum,* 33 (2002):260.
9. *The Helsinki Rules on the Uses of the Waters of International Rivers, www.wikipedia.com,* < accessed on 13/02/2010.
10. While the Convention was adopted with the support of 103 countries, only 16 countries have ratified it—according to the law, 19 out of the 35 were needed for the law to enter into force.
11. Gabriel E. Eckstein, (2002). *Development of International Water Law and the UN Watercourse Convention* , in Anthony Turton and Roland Henwood (eds.) *Hydropolitics in the Developing World : A Southern African Perspective,* Pretoria: 82.
12. Ibid.
13. S. Hodgson, (2004). *Land and Water: The Rights Interface,* Rome: 30.
14. Radha D 'Souza, op.cit:256.
15. Ra maswamy R. Iyer, (2007). *Towards Water Wisdom: Limits, Justice, Harmony,* New Delhi: Sage: 152.
16. The early Northern India Canal and Drainage Act of 1873 sought for instance to introduce the right of the government to 'use and control for public purposes the water of all rivers and streams flowing in natural channels, and of all lakes. This act was a milestone in the evolution of water law as it exists today as it asserted direct state control over water.
17. Philippe Cullet, (2007). *Water Law in India: Overview of Existing Framework and Proposed Reforms*, IELRC, *Working Paper,* Geneva: 3.
18. Ibid: 4.
19. Sujith Koonan, (2007). *Legal Implications of Plachimada: A Case Study* International Environmental Law Research Centre, *Working Paper:* Geneva: 9.
20. Plachi mada is often cited as a prime example of corporate aggression over natural resources and the consequent denial of the rights of the people. It has also been portrayed as the fight against a multi national corporation by a small section of the local population in order to protect basic human rights, such as

the right to drinking water and the right to livelihood. The Coca Cola Company started their operation in the year 2000 and the people's agitation against the Company began in 2002. Meanwhile, the Kerala legal system underwent a major change in 2002 through the enactment of the Kerala Ground Water (Control and Regulation) Act. But the said Act was not applicable as it was notified only in 2003. In the absence of a specific statutory framework, principles such as the public trust doctrine and the common law rule of uncontrolled right of the landowner over groundwater prevailed in the Plachimada case.

21. The award of the tribunal on various cases is final and in case of continued dissatisfaction, the state can only go back to Tribunal as constitutionally there is no scope for making a counter appeal against the judgment as delivered by the Tribunal with the Supreme Court. However there have been cases where the states have made a counter-appeal against the tribunal's award with the Supreme Court, in spite of the lack of constitutional space to do so. Moreover, the ISWDA does not deal with the question of developing the nation's waters on a sustainable basis, but rather restricts itself to conflict resolution.
22. A s of now river boards exist for particular projects only such as the Betwa River Board and the Brahmaputra Board that were set up under specific Parliamentary enactments.
23. Ala n Richards and Nirvikar Singh, (1996). *Water and Federalism: India's Institutions Governing Inter-State River Waters, Working Paper,* Dept of Economics, University of California :Santa Cruz: 2.
24. Sharad K. Jain et al., (2007). *Hydrology and Water Resources of India,* Netherlands: 325.
25. ISWDA only discusses the manner in which a dispute on the waters flowing across two or more states may be resolved and does not provide any specific guideline on basic, generally accepted principles of water sharing (1956).
26. Radha D 'Souza, op.cit.
27. Siddharth Varadarajan, *Water as the Carrier of Concord with Pakistan, The Hindu,* 25th February, 2010.
28. While article VII of the Indus Water Treaty 'recognises that they (India and Pakistan) have a common interest in the optimum development of the rivers, and to that extent they declare their common intention to cooperate, by mutual agreement, to the

fullest extent', so far, little has been done by either side to develop this mandate.

29. This interesting piece of information was provided to the author by Prof Ramaswamy R. Iyer in a personal conversation.
30. Ed ward T. Swaine, *Does Federalism Constrain the Treaty Power?, Columbia Law Review,* Vol. 103, (Apr 2003):449.
31. Ibid: 44 9-450.
32. Ra maswamy R. Iyer, op.cit. 163.
33. Water Framework directive, *www.wikipedia.com,* < accessed on 15/02/10.
34. This argument is inspired by Prof Ramaswamy R. Iyer, who has been demanding a constitutional declaration on water and a common framework at the centre to guide policy making on water.
35. Ra maswamy R. Iyer, (2007). op.cit: 221.

9

Treaty Power and its Implications for Federalism: The Case of Indo-US Civilian Nuclear Deal

Manu M.R.

Federations worldwide are undergoing a series of changes. The conventional division of powers is being challenged every other day as the federating units are becoming more and more demanding, venturing into new areas and breaking the previous restraints. The new developments like the process of globalization, increasing integration of the markets, the emergence of a knowledge-based society and the increasingly strengthening nature of local identities and urge for local self-governance has left much impact on federations. [1]

The field of foreign policy has witnessed a series of changes in this respect and the role played by constituent units, as they have become more active in respect of interaction with foreign countries, especially in attracting investments for promoting economic growth. [2] Thus, the monopoly enjoyed by the centre, in terms of foreign relations has changed, with states taking up a proactive role, although the freedom which the states enjoy under neo-liberalism remains paradoxical. The shift to a knowledge-based society also meant the emergence of a significant section in the public sphere being interested in questions of foreign policy.

These developments had serious implications for the nation state. First, its monopoly in terms of calling shots in foreign policy has been verily curtailed to a certain extent. The doctrine of external sovereignty where it was held that the centre enjoyed unlimited powers in things external has been witnessing a change in all federations across the world. The nation state itself had to give way to something which is an intermediary setup in which the states also play a role, having direct contact with the foreign nations or their constituent units or with multinational business houses. This definitely means a certain amount of deterioration in the sovereignty of the nation state. [3] Sovereign nation state, losing its paramountacy to various intermediary and contingent configurations, emerging according to the concrete circumstances, has been a notable development in the recent past. The doctrine of external sovereignty for a long time reserved the foreign policy and the conclusion of treaties as monopoly of the states. But the increasing assertion of federating units in foreign policy matters which are of direct concern to them, is a notable factor in world politics.

The federal structure in India has also seen a lot of changes. The collapse of the Congress system, increasing strength of the regional parties, the increasing assertion of lower castes in Indian politics and the emergence of coalition politics has definitely brought some changes in the centre-state relations in India. [4] There have been arguments that the neo-liberal reforms and globalization has helped in advancing the autonomy of the Indian states, bettering their position vis-à-vis the centre. [5] The paper attempts to analyze the Indo-US Nuclear Deal and implications of the debates surrounding it, as it was one of those rare occasions when foreign policy, usually kept away from the popular domain was actively debated in the public sphere. The paper also tries to perceive the debates set off by the Deal as a key to make sense of the changes in Indian federalism.

It has been observed that one party dominant system often undermines the cause of federalism, even if it is constitutionally enshrined. [6] It has been observed that in case of India, under the Congress system where even the limited Constitutional provisions for federalism were in effect, were nullified under the unified party structure. The Congress high command naming the chief ministers of the federating units and the strong control of Delhi on all administrative matters, hardly left any initiative to the state elites, which is detrimental to the federal spirit.

The Indo-US civilian nuclear agreement has been treated as a significant turn in India's foreign policy. The Deal became so much an issue of debate as the opponents of the deal mainly posted the deal against the sovereignty of India. It was not the only nuclear deal the country was signing with a foreign nation as it had previously singed one with France and Russia also. There have been many nuclear contacts with the external world. But the Indo-US Nuclear Deal was seen by its opponents as the strategy of Indian ruling class to move into the US camp sacrificing the sovereignty of the country. [7]

The Indo-US Nuclear Deal comes in the background of federations worldwide going through a number of changes. Before going to the details of the changing trends in treaty power and federalism, I would like to briefly chalk out the different aspects of the debates which were set off by the Indo-US civilian nuclear agreement. The major reasons cited for opposing the Indo-US nuclear deal were, the possibility of US terminating the deal at any time for reason whatsoever; the deal intrinsically being linked with the neo-liberal framework which will only be strengthening the communal forces; and the deal emerging as a challenge to peace, sustainable energy development and consensual democratic policy-making. It was also noted as a shift in the rightward direction. A small minority had opposed the deal on the grounds of nuclear proliferation. Environmental concerns were equally raised. There were concerns about the possibility of the development of thorium as an alternative source of fuel being ignored. The Hyde Act and 123 Agreement were seen as affecting the sovereignty of the country, with the Hyde Act demanding that India must have a foreign policy congruent to that of USA. [8]

The packages which are associated with the nuclear deal, like joint military exercises and knowledge exchange were seen as steps designed to make India a junior partner of the United States of America. The protagonists of the deal argued that the deal was essential for India with their arguments ranging from the notion of energy security, the concept of clean energy and the need for rural electrification. The partnership with US was considered as something which would help us in achieving the world power status. The reorientation in the foreign policy was considered as pragmatic and necessary.

Other arguments which were put forward were the political reasons and the ethical dimensions of India serving as junior partner to US. The opposition hinged on the controversial Hyde Act which was said to empower the US to cancel the deal whenever India's foreign policy will not be streamlined to the US policy. There has been some evidence of India taking positions so as not to offend if not to appease the US establishment as in the case of voting on Iran in IAEA. This has strengthened the allegations that India was bending over the back to retain the favourable disposition of US towards it.

Much criticism has been there on account of the number of other treaties which the government had signed with, like those concerning the knowledge initiatives, joint military exercises and so on. But to the dismay of all those who believe that federal values hold hope for the future world, the Congress led UPA chose to adopt a path which hardly reflected any concern for values of federalism. The government far from consulting the ISC or NDC obsessively resisted even the discussion of the Nuclear Bill in the Parliament. It insisted on its right to conclude treaties on its own and even a no confidence motion moved by the opposition could not force the government to think otherwise.

This is the paradox which we have to think about. Why on one hand, there is increasing freedom enjoyed by the constituent units in terms of actions to attract Multinational Capital, while the same openness is denied in case of crucial aspects of foreign policy?

The protagonists of neo-liberalism have advocated federalism, as it promotes the market. Market preserving federalism insists that there should be decentralization and inter-jurisdictional competition while the centre should police the process for the common market. The state governments should face hard budget constraints and they should have control over the primary economy. The central government has to provide defence as well as a macroeconomic regime for the country. [9]

In India, one can exactly see how this process has been implemented, much in favour of the market and multinational capital. The centre is holding all revenues and economic powers with it while the states are left free to competitively appease the multinational corporations. The degree of decentralization in India is far from satisfactory. The central government still controls the power to introduce new taxes. The recent example is that of the service tax, which the centre appropriated on its own. The Finance Commission which decides on the principles for the allocation of revenue for the states has no state representation. The Planning Commission which chalks out the entire development plans and sets target for growth of the states and the country is completely becoming a product of the Centre.

Executive federalism could not properly take off in India. The bodies like Inter-State Council and National Development Council are not very well known for healthy functioning. Their contribution to the national policy-making has been minimal if not nil. Even those foreign policy matters which can have direct implication for the state governments, the Indian states were emasculated to speak anything about foreign policy despite being direct actors or pro-active partners when it comes to the implementation of market-friendly economic policies.

Legislative federalism is in complete shambles. The Rajya Sabha or the Council of the States expected to voice the opinion of the states in the Union Parliament, continues to be a partisan body with very weak powers, hardly having any significant role in advancing the interests of the states. Its influence is anything but nominal in advancing the cause of federalism. [10] The US Senate, the representative body of the states was able to pass a resolution and an act binding the US presidents to act accordingly while in India, the executive have not had a single thought that consulting the Rajya Sabha is necessary.

Though the Hyde Act with its anti-Indian provisions was the rallying point of the criticism, the crucial difference of the Hyde Act as an intervention of the Senate on behalf of the federating units and the Indian Parliament having no such role was never highlighted .

The post-Deal debates have become all the more interesting as there have been heated debates about the extent to which it could capture popular imagination. Even among the protagonists of parliamentary sovereignty, there have been apprehensions as to how far the Deal could really become an issue in the public domain. In the elections which followed, it could be observed that the issue could not make an electoral impact to the degree it was expected.

Interestingly, the debates on the Indo-US nuclear deal had as their cornerstone, the concept of sovereignty and it might be argued that 'the shakiness' of this key stone had great implications for the political developments which followed.

On the other hand, the entire debate had its focal point on sovereignty which as a concept had a limited potential to capture the changes in federalism. It can be argued that placing sovereignty as the point of debate, in fact, resulted in the silencing of the question of federalism itself. The sovereignty which is invariably linked with the nation state was never critically engaged with to liberate the concept from its unitary connotations. Instead, uncritically the concept of sovereignty closed the debate about federalism in multinational state like India. Thus, what we have seen is a missed opportunity by the political class of the country to make use of the debate as one aiming at bringing up some genuine autonomy to the states.

The notion that there can be an independent foreign policy formulated by the federal government without compromising the interests of the state is a myth. The foreign policy questions necessarily have many implications on the autonomy of the states. The economic restructuring programme undertook by the centre had serious implications for the functioning and nature of the state governments. Any treaty signed by the federal governments has its impact on the state governments. The Indo-US Nuclear Deal signed by the centre will be binging about crucial changes when the resource allocations are made. But the assumption that such questions can be easily resolved by the Centre led to the silencing of that question.

But the most significant aspect of the entire debate was with respect to the federal spirit of the country as to how a contentious issue which divided the country left, right and centre across the political spectrum, should be resolved and the questions, raised by the unilateral moves on the part of the executive using the technical advantage of the constitutional provisions. There is an urgent need to develop political instrumentalities and mechanisms to make foreign policy more responsive to popular concerns and thus, make foreign policy decisions more democratic and representative.

The nuclear imbroglio revealed the paradoxical nature of the development of federalism in India where there is a selective adoption of federal values. In areas of crucial policy formulation, the aspects of federalism are hardly valued even when it has direct impact on the states. The way in which India entered WTO and the way POTA was imposed were all testimony to this selective adoption of autonomy. [11] The entry of India into WTO was strongly opposed by many states like Punjab where Akali Dal made it an electoral issue. [12] The freedom or autonomy which the states of India have received could be seen as being freed against oneself. The freedom to compete and race to the bottom have been the major features of that freedom.

The Deal could not become an electoral issue because it was never presented in the way it would address the federal questions. People of Kashmir might have had something different to say about the Deal but the debate never addressed their voices. The author argues because the debate happened to be anachronistic and lacking in futuristic perspective in terms of framework in which it evolved. There is a need to challenge the very framework and go beyond the limits of it. The entire wide and extensive debates on the Indo-US Nuclear deal demonstrated that the federal values in our political and civil society are weak and the urge for a revamp in the highly asymmetrical centre-state relations is yet to emerge. Though pressures of regionalization of the Indian polity is advancing the cause of Indian Federalism by bringing some more equitable ground in the centre-state relations, the experience of Indo-US Nuclear Deal reveals that this is hardly enough.

There has to be all out attempts to strengthen executive federalism in terms of making the bodies like ISC and NDC relevant and dynamic. There is an urgent need to ensure state representation in bodies like Finance Commission and Planning Commission and substantive measures of fiscal decentralization like giving the power of residual taxation and ensuring larger share of the states in net tax revenue should be adopted. Most importantly, the treaty making power cannot be allowed to remain as the monopoly of the Union Executive. The Executive should be legally bound to get the legislative consent for any international treaty and the states should get a chance to articulate their opinion as far as these deals affect their way of functioning.

To conclude, the Indo-US Nuclear Deal initiated a lot of debates in the public sphere but far away from the real centres of power. Though the ruling coalition was stubborn in its position and the debate about the Deal could not effectively bring the federal questions into the political society, it can be seen an indication that the notions of the foreign policy as the exclusive preserve of executive is going to be increasingly challenged in the future.

End Notes

1. Blindenbacher, (2003). *Proceedings and Plenary Speeches of the International Conference on Federalism 2002*, Raoul and Arnold Koller (Eds.), *Federalism in a Changing World Learning from Each other: Scientific Background,* McGill Queen's University Press.
2. Mahendra P. Singh and Douglas V. Verney, *Challenges to India's Centralized Parliamentary Federalism, Publius,* Vol. 33, No. 4:1-20.
3. David A. Lake, *The New Sovereignty in International Relations, International Studies Review,* Vol. 5, No. 3: Sep. 2003: 303-323.
4. Amaresh Bagchi, *Rethinking Federalism: Changing Power Relations between the Centre and the States*, *Publius,* Vol. 33, No. 4.
5. Rudolph, Lloyd I. and Susanne Hoeber Rudolph, *Iconisation of Chandrababu: Sharing Sovereignty in India's Federal Market Economy*, *Economic and Political Weekly,* Vol. 36, No. 18: 5 May 2001:1541-1552.
6. C.H. Alexandrowicz *Is India a Federation*, *The International and Comparative Law Quarterly,* Vol. 3, No. 3: Jul.1954: 393-403.
7. Prakash Karat, *The Indo-US Nuclear Deal: Struggle to Defend National Sovereignty*, *The Marxist,* Vol. XXIII, No. 3: July to September 2007.
8. Ibid.
9. Amaresh Bagchi, *Rethinking Federalism: Overview of Current Debates with Some Reflections in Indian Context*, *Economic and Political Weekly,* Vol. 35, No. 34: 19 Aug.2000:3025-3036.
10. Dougla s V. Verney, *From Executive to Legislative Federalism? The Transformation of the Political System in Canada and India, The Review of Politics,* Vol. 51, No. 2 :1989:241-263
11. Uj jwal Kumar Singh, *POTA and Federalism*, *Economic and Political Weekly,* Vol. 39, No. 18: 1 May 2004:1793-1797
12. Rob Jenkins, How Federalism Influences India's Domestic Politics of WTO Engagement, *Asian Survey,* Vol. 43, No. 4: July-Aug.2003:598-621.

10

Parliamentary Control over Foreign Policy: Theory and Praxis

Sivakumar M. V.

Our struggle for Independence was not just a movement to achieve freedom from British rule. It was as much a crusade to free ourselves from the various social evils and socio-economic iniquities and discrimination, and to lift the deprived and the downtrodden from the mire of poverty and to give them a stake in the overall transformation of the country. With this objective, in the political system that we have established, pre-eminence has been given to Parliament, the only organ directly representative of the people and as such accountable to them, with extensive powers which should rightly belong to the highest people's forum. Unfortunately, after six decades of Independence, we have come to a stage nowadays when questions are being asked about the utility and relevance of Parliament in our polity and, indeed, about the workability of our democratic set-up based on the parliamentary system. [1] This paper is an attempt to highlight the decreasing role of Parliament in the field of foreign policy.

Foreign policy is the policy of a state in relation to its external interactions with other states in the International Political system. According to Joseph Frankle, foreign policy consists of decisions and actions which involve to some appreciable extent relations between one state and others. [2] Foreign policy is based on the objectives a nation wants to pursue which are determined subject to determinants, capabilities and national interest. Since foreign policy is formulated with reference to internal needs of state, foreign policy is broadly regulated by the domestic institutions and compulsions like the legislature, political parties and public opinion. In brief, foreign policy is concerned with the actions of individual nations and the processes and means through which these actions are determined. [3]

Indian Context

There are three closely interrelated aspects to all societal decisions: the decision itself, the decision maker or makers, and the decision making process, which combine 'information advice and deliberation, leading to the decision'. [4] As far as foreign policy is concerned, India is even more fathomable than any other country. She resembles neither the third world nor the developed world. Her cultural-religious background, level of economic development and political system are distinctive. Besides, the degree of complexity, diversity or even contradiction embedded into her structures is incomparably greater than in either the developing or the developed countries. All these contradictory elements influence on the functioning of the Indian system and they have a bearing on Indian decision making. A host of institutional and human factors also influence the decision making process. These include: (1) Bureaucracy, (2) Political institutions and public opinion, and (3) Personality factors.

Foreign policy of every country is reflective of domestic political, economic and strategic national concerns and interests. The foreign policy of a country cannot have a smooth sailing if domestic politics is sharply polarized in antagonistic camps or ideological blocs. The existence of national consensus on foreign policy of post-Independent India can be explained by looking into the dynamics of party system especially during the 1950s to the middle of 1990s. National politics was dominated by one party and opposition parties after expressing their differences of opinion extended full support to the national foreign policy of India. The replacement and displacement of one party domination system by a system of multi-party and multi-group coalition government at the centre especially beginning from 1998 to 2008 has created a new situation for foreign policy makers because political parties with different ideological persuasions are evaluating foreign policy choices from the perspective of their distinctive ideological concerns.

Prime Minister Manmohan Singh while referring to differences among parties about his government's foreign policy stated on February 15, 2008, that "the things that we do and the things that we do not do will have a profound consequence on our ability to emerge as a truly global power. An internally divided and divisive society cannot project an external image of strength and power. And I think this is the guideline which should guide the acts of all political parties'. [5] The statement of Prime Minister clearly shows that serious 'political divisions' have emerged among political parties on issues concerning foreign policy.

Constitutional Provisions

Theoretically, Parliament in India is expected to influence the formulation of foreign policy in a variety of ways. Its resolutions, either supporting or opposing policies proposed by government, or by suggesting or forcing upon the government new policies, whether of a broad or of a specific nature, are expected to influence the broad orientation, detailed formulation and implementation of foreign policy. It can also influence specific aspects of foreign policy through its power to sanction appropriations, by cutting down or increasing the budget (or specific item) of the Ministries of External Affairs, Defence and allied ministries. Moreover, Parliament has the power to set up by legislation new machinery and governmental institutions for the making of foreign policy.

Article 246 of the Indian Constitution empowers parliament to legislate on all aspects of foreign affairs which are defined as 'all matters which bring the Union into relation with any foreign country'. This include diplomatic, consular and trade representatives, the UNO and international conferences, international agreements, war and peace, foreign jurisdiction, emigration, passports, visas etc.

Under Article 253, Parliament also has the exclusive authority to legislate for implementation of international treaties, agreements and conventions and decisions arrived at international conferences. Such Parliamentary institutions as the Public Accounts Committee and Estimates Committee are in a position to influence foreign policy marginally, through financial control over external affairs and other related ministries.

Parliament's rules of procedure theoretically provide for considerable parliamentary control over foreign policy. Its authority to give or withhold assent to government bills can theoretically be a powerful instrument of control in the practically improbable event of the government choosing to legislate on foreign policy, Members can table motions for discussion or for consideration of specific issues under Rule 184 and Rule 342 respectively. Adjournment motions and no-confidence motions, short discussions under Rule 193, half an hour discussion under Rule 55, and questions during Question Hour offer considerable opportunities for Parliament in theory to keep the government under control with regard to both foreign and domestic policy.

Functional Aspects

In the operational aspect of foreign policy, we can see a clear dichotomy in theory and practice. According to Article 73 of the Indian Constitution, the executive power of the Union shall extend to all matters with respect to which Parliament has power to make laws. Article 74 says that there shall be a Council of Ministers to aid and advice the President who shall act according to such advice. The Council of Ministers is collectively responsible to the House of the People (Article 75, Clause 3). So, legally Parliament is supreme in law-making and controls the administration through responsible ministers.

In the domestic administration, Parliamentary control is effective to a certain extent. But in the field of foreign policy, irrespective of the party in power, governments have tended to ignore Parliament since the time of Jawaharlal Nehru. In recent times, this neglect has assumed the shape of challenges and clashes between legislature and executive as revealed by the Indo-American Nuclear Agreement and Indo-ASEAN Free Trade Agreement.

An important institutional link between Parliament and foreign policy is the Consultative Committee of Parliament on External Affairs. Informal Consultative Committees were created for the first time in 1954 for the various ministries/departments of the Government of India. In 1969, the prefix "informal" was dropped, and the following "guide lines" were issued by the Department of Parliamentary Affairs."

1. The deliberations of these Committees would remain informal and no reference to the discussion held in the meeting thereof would make on the floor of the House.
2. The Minister concerned with each Ministry/Department shall preside over the meeting of the Consultative Committee attached to his Ministry.
3. These meetings would be attended by the Senior Officers of the Ministries. The Committee would not have the right to summon any witness, to send for or demand the production of any files, or to examine any official records.
4. Brief record of discussions in the meetings on specific matters for which adequate notice had been given, will be circulated to the members. Where there is unanimity of view in the Committee, Government will normally accept the view subject to the following exceptions, viz.:

- Any view having any financial implications;
- Any view concerning security, defence, external affairs and atomic energy; and
- Any matter falling within the purview of an autonomous corporation.

In case of non-acceptance, reason thereof will be given to the Committee.

5. At these Committees, Members of Parliament are free to discuss any matter which can appropriately be discussed in Parliament.

From the very guide lines itself, it can be easily understood that the Committee is not expected to perform any significant role. It has no real powers and to a certain extent it was only a deliberative body. In effect, the Committee was a mere transmission belt between the Foreign Minister and Parliament for the conveyance of official foreign policy. [6] The neglect of the Committee by the Government, though with varying degree, continued unabated.

The twenty-year Indo-Soviet Treaty of Friendship and Co-operation was signed in August 1971. Although this treaty was in many ways a landmark in India's foreign policy, there was no meeting of the Consultative Committee for External Affairs either immediately before or immediately after the sighing of the treaty. The Indian military intervention took place in Bangladesh on December 4 and the Pakistani army surrendered on December 16, 1971. But the Consultative Committee did not meet between October 1971 and April 1972. Negotiations regarding the Simla Agreement took place with Pakistan through June 1972; Agreement was reached on July 2, 1972, and the Agreement was formally ratified by India, in an unprecedented move on July 28, 1972. The Consultative Committee did not meet between April and July 1972. Similarly, the Committee was not associated with the Government's decision regarding the merger of Sikkim in India in 1976.

The neglect continued by the succeeding governments. According to M.C. Chagla, who was Foreign Minister under Indira Gandhi, the Consultative Committee of Parliament for External Affairs was "more of an agency for getting policies accepted and muting criticism than for influencing foreign policy". [7] The role of the Consultative Committee of

Parliament on External Affairs in the making of foreign policy appears to have declined even further in more recent years.

The Standing Committee of Parliament for External Affairs was created in 1991 with somewhat different functions. This includes:

1. To scrutinize the demand for grants of the Ministry of External Affairs.
2. To examine and report on proposed legislation related to the Ministry of External Affairs, if the proposed legislation concerned is referred to the Standing Committee by the Speaker or the Chairman.
3. To review the Annual Report of the Ministry of External Affairs.
4. To review the policy statement read by the Minister of External Affairs, if it is referred to it by the Speaker or the Chairman.

Standing Committee can summon officers, including Foreign Secretary as witnesses. Moreover, at the time of scrutinizing the demand for grants of the Ministry of External Affairs, the Standing Committee discusses the overall foreign policy and offers its suggestions. According to J.N. Dixit, the Standing Committee of Parliament on External Affairs has been more effective, since its inception, than the Consultative Committee in influencing the foreign policy. [8]

However, governments generally tended to ignore parliament before making major foreign policy decisions during the Nehru era as well as the post-Nehru era. Among the important treaties and agreements signed by India during the first 25 years after independence were the Indo-Bhutanese treaty of 1949, the Indo-Sikkimese Treaty of 1950, the Nehru-Liaquat Agreement of 1950, the Indo-Nepalese-Treaty of 1951, the India-China Agreement of 1954, the Nehru-Noon Agreement of 1958, the Tashkent Agreement of 1965, the Indo-Soviet of Treaty of 1971, the Indo-Bangladesh Treaty of 1972, Simla Agreement of 1972, and the Indo-Soviet Trade Agreement of 1971. In none of these cases, were the treaties or agreements discussed or debated in parliament in advance. [9]

The same trend of neglecting the parliament in decision making with regard to foreign policy continued also during 1980s, i.e. during the second Indira Gandhi era (1980-84) and the Rajiv Gandhi era (1984-89). For instance, there was a demand in parliament for some strong action in Sri Lanka in 1986-87 on account of what was perceived as brutal oppression and genocide of the ethnic Tamil population of that country. But when the Rajiv-Jayewardene Agreement of 1987 was signed, neither the terms of the agreement nor the dispatch of the IPKF to Sri Lanka had the approval of the parliament.

Even more blatant was the neglect of parliament by the BJP and NDA Government under Atal Bihari Vajpayee after 1998. For instance, after the second Pokhran nuclear test the BJP leader, Jaswant Singh, who was then Deputy Chairman of the Planning Commission and not a member of either house of Parliament, carried out a series of negotiations with the US Government regarding India's sighing of the CTBT in complete secrecy. There were repeated demands in parliament for details of Singh's parleys, but the Government failed to respond positively. On February 24 1999, the US Secretary of State, Madeleine Albright, stated in the Foreign Relations Committee of the US Congress that India had agreed to sign the CTBT. Challenged in the Lok Sabha, Singh denied the truth of Albright's statement. This led to a furore in the Lok Sabha on February 26, and members urged the Singh to "come clean". But still the Government refused to disclose even the broad outlines of Singh's negotiations with Albright to the Parliament. [10]

An even more serious situation developed during the Kargil crisis. There was a persistent demand from all non-BJP parties and the press for summoning the Rajya Sabha into session, since Lok Sabha had been dissolved in preparation for the general elections. But the Prime Minister categorically stated that he would not call such a session. On July 2 1999, the President of India wrote a two page letter to the Prime

Minister suggesting the calling of the Rajya Sabha into session. But the Prime Minister refused to yield.

The latest episode in the blatant abuse of parliament came in the form of Indo-American Nuclear Agreement. During the issue the Government had purposefully tried to cheat the Parliament. For example, on November 28, 2007, Indian Prime Minister and External Affairs Minister asserted in Parliament that "the Hyde Act is not binding India but the provisions of the 123 agreement are" and at the same time top US executives kept asserting that "any 123 Agreement to be implemented by "USA has to be in a manner fully consistent with the Hyde Act."

Do we have democracy? This question has become most relevant after the Nuclear Deal. Indian government is taking the stand that executive has the power to enter into deals, treaties and agreements with foreign governments and organizations, without the approval of and without even reference to the legislature and people. The government's contention is that it has inherent powers to administer the country's affairs with the foreign governments and bodies, which are independent of the legislature, the people and the constitution. According to this view, external administration is beyond democracy.

It is clear that the Government of India has taken refuge in the technical aspect of the Constitution which does not require parliamentary sanction for international agreements. The Government had survived the confidence vote and the general election which followed but the inherent tenets of parliamentary democracy suffered grievously. 'The current developments added another chapter in weakening the foundation of our most cherished institution. When that happens, a large risk to the rest of the institutions looms large'. [11] From the above discussion it is clear that in spite of the Constitutional provision of Parliamentary sovereignty, executive domination in the field of foreign policy is complete. Both the Executive and Legislature and the changed international atmosphere are responsible for this pathetic situation.

In the wake of September 11 attack on US World Trade Centre, President Bush and his supporters articulated the doctrine of conditional sovereignty. This means that respect for sovereignty of a nation state could be suspended if that state was deemed to be either sponsoring terrorism or developing weapons of mass destruction that might challenge US. American military domination is unchallenged for the time being and to a certain extent, international policy makers recognize this. 'While ascribing a major role to the nation state, policy makers reserve absolute sovereignty for America and give conditional sovereignty to other nations'. [12]

This doctrine of conditional sovereignty had its impact in India also. As illustrated by the Indo-American Civilian Nuclear Agreement, Government of India has adopted a pro-American foreign policy as part of its liberalization policy. Naturally the Government of India also, to some extent, accepted the doctrine of conditional sovereignty. According to this doctrine, all nation states are not equally sovereign in international system, which is increasingly becoming unipolar. Once this doctrine is accepted domestic policy also should be adjusted accordingly. That is, domestic democracy should be made a limited one. In other words, foreign policy should be kept above domestic politics because policy decisions should be taken in conformity with the international goals of the state having sovereign power. With this objective, during the turmoil on Indo-American Nuclear Deal, the Government gave a clear notice in public that it was not concerned with Parliament and asserted that Cabinet approval to the agreement was final and irrevocable.

Irresponsible behaviour of members also contributes to the erosion of powers of Parliament. Democracy offers the most accountable system of governance. Among the different varieties, parliamentary system scores the highest. Parliamentary system offers daily accountability whereas others only periodical. The implication of the system is that representatives imbibe the values of this system and act by it for the system to move towards further maturity. What had happened was just the opposite. This has led the Speaker of the Lok Sabha to suggest that recall of members needs to be introduced in the system. [13]

Conclusion

Because of the competitive and confrontational politics that has overtaken the country today, Parliament cannot appropriately discharge its essential functions. Debates and discussions, the hallmarks of democracy, have been overshadowed by disruptions, confrontations and other non-democratic alternatives, which had made the institution itself a subject of ridicule. 'A recent survey indicated that in the first three years of the 14th Lok Sabha, 26 percent of parliamentary time had been lost due to disruptions. During the Budget Session in 2007, the Lok Sabha lost 73 hours (34 percent of its time) due to disorder. Only 11 of the slotted 25 Bills were passed in the Monsoon Session (2007). In that Session, the Lok Sabha lost 40 percent of its time due to adjournments and Rajya Sabha lost 49 percent. Four Bills were passed without discussion in the Lok Sabha. If Lok Sabha worked 124 hours in the Monsoon Session of 2006, it worked only 65 hours in the Monsoon Session of 2007. Each minute of parliamentary time costs the public exchequer to the tune of about ₹ 26,000. [14]

We have to accept that, to a certain extent, Parliament and parliamentarians themselves are responsible for this pathetic situation. Of course, there is no Constitutional provision for parliamentary veto in foreign policy but at the same time, there is no Constitutional prohibition for the emergence of strong parliamentary conventions which will ensure the dignity of Parliament itself. Such healthy parliamentary conventions alone will be able to rescue our democracy. We can conclude with an advice from our former Speaker, Som Nath Chatterjee, 'all stake holders in our democracy have to unitedly work with dedication, commitment, cooperation and self-discipline to find lasting solutions to safeguard parliamentary democracy from thc tremendous strains experienced today and to strengthen it'. [15]

End Notes

1. Chatterjee Som Nath, *Parliamentary Democracy: Challenges. Yojana* March 2008:51.
2. Frankle Joseph, (1968). *The Making of foreign Policy: An Analysis of Decision-Making,* London: Oxford University Press: 1.
3. Kamath P M, (1990). *Foreign Policy Making and International Politics,* New Delhi: Radiant Publishers: 10.
4. Roseanau, J.N,(1969). *Linkage Politics,* New York: FreePress: 235.
5. *The Indian Express,* New Delhi: 16 February 2008:3.
6. Bandyopadhyaya J., (2003). *The Making of India's Foreign Policy,* (Third Edition), New Delhi: Allied Publishers Private Limited: 100.
7. Brecher Michael, (1968). *India and World Politics: Krishna Menon's View of the World,* London: Oxford University Press: 265.
8. Dixit J.N., (1996). *My South Block Years: Memories of a Foreign Secretary,* New Delhi: WBSPD: 431.
9. Bandyopadhyaya. J, op. cit: 107.
10. Ibid: 113.
11. Prasad Kamala, *Nuclear Shadow over Democracy, Mainstream,* Vol. XLV, No. 44, October 2007:10.
12. G. Narottam, *America Crowning the Unipolar: An Incursion into Sovereignty and Independence of States like India, India Quarterly,* vol.65 No.2, April-June 2009:134.
13. Prasad Kamala,op.cit: 10.
14. Chat terjee Som Nath, op.cit:.52.
15. Ibid: 53 .

11

New Dimensions in the Indian Foreign Policy in a Multilateral Environment

T. Krishna Kanth and K. Lalitha Kumari

India's foreign policy has been showing the dynamic nature of the policy elite due to the changing nature of international relations. From the very beginning, India's foreign policy was simply confined to a few countries such as US, Russia, Britain, France and some West Asian countries. However, India's importance in the present international system has altered everything. The UPA government has been following the age-old tradition of keeping the continuity and build upon the basic tenets of India's independent foreign policy–a foreign policy of peace, non-alignment and autonomous choice based on national self-interest and the expansion of India's strategic autonomy and capability. [1] The fundamental tenets of India's foreign policy have remained steadfast and unaltered despite the changing world order and successive governments have reinforced these guiding principles. At the core is our independence in decision-making on foreign policy issues. The principles of *Panchsheel*, enunciated by India's first Prime Minister are still relevant and we have, over the years, on every occasion, reiterated our commitment to an independent foreign policy– and the strengthening of multilateral mechanisms and institutions.

In an international situation marked by simultaneous competition and co-operation among the major powers, and of unprecedented interdependence created by globalization, representing both a threat and an opportunity for developing countries, the government has steadily improved India's relations with all major powers. India is recognized in today's world as an independent minded nation. In fact, India's national interests require that it should maintain this while simultaneously cultivating close ties with key global players and playing a key role in global affairs–whether trade or security or climate change issues. India today has strategic dialogues with Brazil, China, France, Germany, Iran, Indonesia, Japan, Russia, South Africa, the United Kingdom, United States of America and Vietnam. [2]

In its interaction with the other major powers and the EU, India believes that multilateral and multi-polar solutions are the need of the hour for the world's major issues. The challenges viz. terrorism, proliferation of weapons of mass destruction, climate change, energy security and food security–cut across borders and demand broad-based multilateral co-operation among nations and groups of nations. Our international friends and partners recognize our commitment to pursue an independent foreign policy. They understand that a country like India cannot be persuaded to follow a course in its foreign policy which does not pass the litmus test of meeting our interests. If India could exercise autonomy in its decision-making during the Cold War period, there is no reason to believe that today, when our strength as a global power is recognized, we can be coerced into following a foreign policy dictated by another country. As the world moves into a more complicated environment of interdependence and competition, multilateral solutions to international problems become even more necessary. The UPA Government has strengthened India's contribution and role in international organizations such as UN and added meaningful content to other multilateral groupings in which India participates, such as IBSA, India-China-Russia Multilateral Forum and other such forums. [3]

India's foreign policy, adapting to the new challenges of globalization has now become a principal national objective. The change in the national economic strategy in 1991 inevitably produced abundant new options on the foreign policy front. Implicit in this was the second transition, from the past emphasis on politics to a new stress on economics in the making of foreign policy. India began to realize in the 1990s how far behind it had fallen the rest of Asia, including China, in economic development. With the socialist strait jacket gone, and the pressures to compete with other emerging markets, Indian diplomacy has now entered uncharted waters. In the past, foreign aid was very symbolic to Indian diplomacy that sought to meet the government's external financing requirements as well as developmental needs. India is now seeking foreign direct investment and access to markets in the developed world.

After years of promoting idealistic slogans such as universal disarmament, India by the late 1990s recognized the importance of becoming a declared nuclear weapon power. Despite the steady nuclearization of its security environment over the decades, India remained ambiguous about its attitudes to its own national nuclear weapons programme. Even as it tested a nuclear device in 1974, India refused to follow through with the nuclear weapons project. By the late 1990s, though, India found it necessary to make itself an unambiguous nuclear power. The economic growth of the decade gave it the self-confidence that it could ride through the inevitable international reaction to it. India was also right it betting that a country of its size and economic potential could not be sanctioned and isolated for too long. More importantly, India sensed that there might bc diplomatic opportunities for getting the great powers acknowledge if not legitimize its nuclear weapons programme and remove the high technology sanctions against it. Within seven years after its second round of nuclear testing in 1998, India signed the historic nuclear deal with the Bush Administration in July 2005 under which the US agreed to change its domestic non-proliferation law and revise the international guidelines on nuclear cooperation in favour of India. [4]

Another area of transformation was India's relations with

the great powers. The end of the Cold War and the collapse of the Soviet Union, allowed India to pursue, without the political inhibitions of the past, simultaneous expansion of relations with all the major powers. Injecting political and economic substance into the long emaciated relationship with the United States, now the lone super power became the principal national strategic objective. At the same time, India was unwilling to let its old ties with the Soviet Union, now a weakened Russia, wither away. Since the end of the Cold War, Russia has remained an important source of arms and a strategic partner. Meanwhile, India's ties with Europe, China and Japan have all become far more weighty and diversified. The upgradation of the relations with China since the early 1990s has been one of the biggest achievements of India's new foreign policy. The once wary relationship with China has now blossomed into a strategic partnership for peace and development. China is now all set to emerge as India's single largest trading partner. India and Japan, which drifted apart from the Cold War, have steadily expanded the basis for political co-operation in recent years and have proclaimed a strategic partnership in 2005.

Most Indians agree that its first Prime Minister Jawaharlal Nehru had defined a unique foreign policy for India at the very dawn of its Independence. Despite many critics of his world view, a broad national consensus had emerged around Nehru's ideas on independent foreign policy, non-alignment, and third world solidarity. Since the 1990s, the challenge for the Indian leaders has been to reinterpret Nehru's ideas to suit the new political context that had confronted it. [5] The new Indian leaders could neither denounce Nehru nor formally reject Nehru's ideas, for that would invite serious political trouble. Yet they had to continually improvise and refashion India's foreign policy to suit the new requirements. This has not been easy.

The tension between the imperative of the new and the resistance of the old ideas on how to conduct foreign policy is real and is unlikely to end in the near future. The fear of the new and fondness for the old continue to be reflected in all aspects of Indian diplomacy, from engaging the United States to an optimal strategy towards the smallest of the neighbours. The "new" foreign policy of India is indeed work in progress.

Yet, it is not difficult to see that the direction of Indian diplomacy has changed substantially since the end of the Cold War amidst internal and external impulses. Structural changes in India's current foreign policy strategy are a set of important transitions in India's world view. Not all of these were articulated self-consciously or clearly by the Indian political leadership. A few of those changes stand out and are unlikely to be reversed. The first was the transition from the national consensus on building a "socialist society" to building a "modern capitalist" one. The socialist ideal, with its roots in the national movement, had so dominated the Indian political discourse by the early 1970s that a Constitutional amendment was passed in 1976 to make the nation into a "socialist republic". But 1991 saw the collapse of the Soviet Union, the veritable symbol of socialism, and the edifice of India's state-socialism began to crumble.

US-India Relations: India as a New Global Power

An Action Agenda for the United States proposes the transformation of relations between the United States and India with major implications for the future balance of power in Asia. Carnegie senior associate, Ashley J. Tellis, a leading expert on US-South Asia relations, offers this detailed plan for successfully implementing the Bush Administration's new decision to assist India in becoming a major world power in the twenty-first Century. The major observations made in the earlier paper by the author were: India's strategic and foreign policy establishment must recognize that India's management of its strategic partnerships, both existing and evolving must be adroitly done. India's strategic stances must not generate reverberations from other global power centres, until India reaches the culminating stage of emerging as an independent power centre in the world. Since a substantive India-US Strategic Partnership has the potential to alter the global strategic balance and so also the Asian strategic balance, the evolving Indo-US Strategic Partnership has been under intense scrutiny by China and Russia. In particular, India's participation in the strategic geometries sponsored in East Asia by the United States has raised strategic concerns in China and Russia and their reverberations have not been long in coming in a subtle manner. [6]

In the Indian strategic calculus, China and Russia cannot be discounted for a number of good reasons. China figures in Indian threat perceptions in a major way because of past armed conflicts and the chronic unsettled boundary disputes. While India and China are today engaged in transforming their relationship from one of mutual suspicions to that of mutual trust, both countries cannot ignore their national security interests and strategic priorities. In China's threat perceptions, a substantive India-US Strategic Partnership carries with it, the potential of initiatives for Indo-US containment of China and use of Tibet as a strategic pressure point. Russia's strategic sensitivities in relation to India's future strategic moves need to be paid due respect as the Indo-Russian strategic partnership is a time tested one. Unlike United States and China which have resorted to creation of spoiler states like Pakistan, to checkmate India, Russia has not resorted to such policies against India.

Strategic reverberations from Russia and China do create strategic implications for India. Some may like to be dismissive of the manifested strategic reverberations from Russia and China on the India-US strategic partnership emerging contours on the grounds that these are inconsequential. But what must not be forgotten in strategic analysis is that the inconsequentials are the first indicators of a trend-in-the-making. What is at issue here is the persistence of both India on one hand to indulge in a monochromatic strategic partnership with US and on the rebound the persistence of Russia and China to raise the profile and stakes of their strategic reverberations against India. In terms of strategic implications for India arising from the issues under discussion, the following factors need to be considered by India's strategic and foreign policy establishment. Just as India cannot become a global key player in confrontation with US, so also India cannot become a global key player by impinging on the strategic sensitivities of Russia and China, especially those which intersect with US.

As an emerging global power, India cannot be strategically type-casted as an alliance partner of one or the other powers. Strategically, India would have to be even-handed and maintain an autonomous strategic posture. Russia enjoys strategic leverages over India in terms of India's predominantly Russian-origin military inventories. This cannot be wished away overnight. If India can participate in strategic geometries in East Asia along side US, it can also participate in the strategic geometries of heartland Asia alongside the Shanghai Co-operation Organization (SCO), a global power in the making that should have much of strategic autonomy. The absence of India's present Prime Minister avoiding attendance of SCO summit meetings is noticeable. The Indian Prime Minister's absence indicates a strategic tilt towards the US.

To emerge as a key global play, India would have to first carve a niche in the Asian strategic pecking order and the Asian security calculus. This cannot emerge in opposition to the strategic interests and sensitivities of Russia and China. [7] Lastly, India's security problems can be compounded should Russia and China, singly or in conjunction with each other attempt to counter India's strategic tilt towards the United States.

Effective Multilateralism

India and the EU believe that a multilateral approach, in which the UN plays a central role, is the best way to address global challenges such as development which is economically, socially and environmentally sustainable; effective management of globalisation; terrorism; drug trafficking; organised crime; natural disasters; pandemics; and energy security. Accordingly, we will:

- Work closely to promote effective multilateralism;
- Continue to hold regular consultations on thematic issues prior to the UN General Assembly (UNGA), and work together on negotiation and implementation of the outcome of major international conferences and summits on security, trade, environment, development and human rights;
- Exchange views on the issues raised by the Secretary General of the United Nations in his comprehensive report entitled 'In Larger Freedom: Towards Development, Security, and Human Rights for All'; and
- Endeavour to invite each other reciprocally for conferences sponsored by either side where the other is, or can be, a participant.

Peace-Keeping, Peace-Building and Post-Conflict Assistance

India and the EU have a common interest in UN peace-keeping and in post-conflict political and economic rehabilitation and reconstruction. [8] We propose to work together in the first instance in the following areas:

1. Consultation before major UN debates on peace-keeping and peace-building and in the preparation of major peace conferences;
2. Establishing a dialogue at official level on UN peace-keeping and peace-building to exchange perspectives on conceptual and operational aspects of peace-keeping operations, including post-conflict reconstruction and rehabilitation, in order to identify and develop specific areas of co-operation in the following sectors:

- Training for military and civilian components of peace-keeping missions, including police and other security forces;

- Exchange of trainees and instructors between Peace-keeping Training Centres of India and EU Member States;
- Joint support of UN peace-keeping and peace-building efforts, including as regards improved analytical capacities and greater co-operation between EU and Indian components of UN peace-keeping missions;
- Trade and development in peace-building;
- Post-conflict and confidence building projects in other regions of the world; and
- Seminars and other activities designed to facilitate post-conflict management.

Disarmament and Non-Proliferation of WMD and Security Dialogue

India and the EU have a shared interest in working towards achieving the goals and objectives of universal disarmament and non-proliferation of weapons of mass destruction and their means of delivery. The proliferation of weapons of mass destruction and its linkages with terrorism poses a threat to international peace and security. In this context, we resolve to enhance collective action to fight the proliferation of WMD as well as their means of delivery. We believe that our response to proliferation challenges require strengthened multilateral consultations and the pooling of all efforts and resources. We agree that effective export control measures for dual use goods can play an important role in preventing proliferation, and at the same time, such measures should not hamper international co-operation in materials, equipment and technology for peaceful purposes. We will establish a bilateral India-EU Security Dialogue at senior official level which will include regular consultations on global and regional security issues, disarmament and non-proliferation to increase mutual understanding and identify possible areas of co-operation. [9]

Fight against Terrorism and Organized Crime

India and the EU recognize the fact that terrorism constitutes one of the most serious threats to international peace and security, and reaffirm their condemnation of all acts of terrorism as criminal and unjustifiable, irrespective of their motivations, forms and manifestations. Both India and EU propose to work together to strengthen our co-operation in counter-terrorism efforts in accordance with the UN Charter and applicable principles of international law. Both agree to:

1. Support the work of the UN to ensure universal respect for and full implementation of all relevant UN Security Council Resolutions (UNSCRs), UN Conventions on terrorism and related protocols;
2. Co-operate in the fight against terrorism and establish contacts between the Indian and EU Counter-terrorism Co-ordinators;
3. Co-operate in the fight against trafficking in drugs and psychotropic substances, and the diversion of chemical precursors related to their production;
4. Work closely to promote the early entry into force of the International Convention for Suppression of Acts of Nuclear Terrorism and for the early conclusion of the Comprehensive Convention on International Terrorism;
5. Work together to reduce terrorist access to financing and to fight money-laundering, and monitor suspicious transactions, taking into account international standards adopted by the Financial Action Task Force (FATF);
6. Exchange views on how to develop the comprehensive United Nations counter-terrorism strategy based upon the recommendations in the Secretary General's report "In Larger Freedom";
7. Expand the EU-India dialogue to include the link between drug trafficking and terrorism, document security, illicit arms trafficking and cyber-terrorism;
8. Promote co-operation between Europol on the EU side and the Central Bureau of Investigation (CBI) on the Indian

side; and

9. Establish an Indian contact point in India for Euro just.

World Trade Organization (WTO)/Doha Development Agenda (DDA)

India and EU are committed to a successful outcome of the Hong Kong Ministerial Declaration in December 2005 and agree to move forward the Doha Development Agenda (DDA) negotiations to a successful conclusion as a matter of priority. In this respect, both parties agree to continue their dialogue with a view to greater convergence in areas of mutual interest. To this end, India and EU agree to strengthen their dialogue on the DDA negotiations which *interalia* include agriculture, Non-Agricultural Market Access (NAMA), services, trade facilitation, anti-dumping, geographical indications, special and differential treatment, and implementation, including as regards the relationship between Trade-related Intellectual Property Rights (TRIPs) and the Biodiversity Convention. [10]

The Triangle and the Deal

How significant are the US and Indian decisions to shape a deal that would allow trade in civilian nuclear technology? It certainly violates the spirit if not the letter of the non-proliferation treaty. Whatever one's view of the merits of that Treaty, an explicit initiative to work around the intentions of one of the major co-operative security treaties of the post-World War II period represents a major event in international affairs. Should the Deal go through, and US public law be amended to permit the transfer of militarily significant high technology to India, this will also represent a significant change in as much as no non-NATO state or state that does not have US troops based on its soil (such as Japan or South Korea) who have enjoyed such a relationship with the US. Add to this, the fact that India is a nuclear weapons state. This is a clear signal that the US fears no long-term threat from India. Taken together, the changes that will be wrought by the Indo-

US Nuclear Deal certainly represent a major perturbation in global politics.

Beyond this immediate perturbation, however, lies the question of what such a deal means for strategic interaction within the US-India-China triangle. The most obvious implication is that the US is trying to recruit India to help the balance against rising Chinese power. India, wishing to balance against the threat of a neighbouring Chinese single-party state, that is intruding in "India's region" and proliferating nuclear, when taken together with the Iraq war and Bush Administration's efforts to work around the Anti-Ballistic Missile Treaty (again regardless of one's view of the merits of that agreement today), the job of anyone trying to present the US as a status quo power and China as the potential revisionist, becomes much harder and missile technology to its enemy Pakistan, may wish to bandwagon with the lone superpower.

The cue for airing the India-as-a-China-balancer argument in public policy consideration beyond the pages of academic journals and editorial columns was the July 2005 Indo-US Nuclear Deal. Some applauded the willingness of the US to court India as a balance against China. For a time in the spring of 2006 (as the tide of debate was swayed by non-proliferation concerns) it looked as though using the Deal to balance China with India might become the most compelling US public policy talking point in favour of the Deal. The venues for this airing were congressional and parliamentary hearing rooms in Washington and New Delhi, the White House briefing room and the press.

Long Term Implications

The innovations in India's foreign policy strategy since the early 1990s has resulted in the happy situation of simultaneous expansion of relations with all the major powers, growing weight in Asia and the Indian Ocean region, and the prospect of improved relations with important neighbours. Given its impending relative rise in the international system, India is bound to be confronted by a number of challenges. First, the new focus on the importance of power is not without problems. Despite being marginalized in recent years, the imperatives of idealism and moralism have not completely disappeared from India's foreign policy. Since 1991, India has moved from its traditional emphasis on the "power of the argument" to a new stress on the "argument of power". Given its noisy democracy, India cannot build domestic political support to foreign policy initiatives purely on the argument of power. It would continue to need a set of values and norms to justify its actions on the world stage. As a consequence, the tension between "power and principle" would remain an enduring one in India's foreign policy strategy.

Second, increased power potential will mean that India would have to take positions on major international issues and regional conflicts. In recent years, New Delhi has either avoided or merely substituted them with generalized slogans. Just as Beijing is being pressed to become a "stake-holder" in the international system, New Delhi too would come under greater pressure to stop being a "free rider". In other words, India would have to often find ways to limit the pursuit of "national interest" in order to contribute to "collective interests" of the international system. [11]

Third, as India emerges as an important element of future balance of power in the world, it would be pressed to make choices in favour of one or the other great powers at least on specific issues. The absence of great power confrontation in the last few years has allowed India the luxury of converting the slogan of "non-alignment" into an "independent" foreign policy. But amidst potential new rivalries among the US, China, Europe, Russia, and Japan, New Delhi would be compelled to make often wrenching political choices. While India making potential alliances with one or other major powers cannot be ruled out in the future, as a large country, India would remain loath to limit its freedom of action through formal alliances.

Fourth, the demands on India to contribute to order and stability in its immediate and extended neighbourhood would dramatically increase in the coming decades. This would in turn draw India deeper into great power rivalries in various regions and the internal conflicts of smaller countries. Use of military force, either unilaterally or under multilateral mechanisms, could also become frequent. Meanwhile, India, like China, is increasingly turning towards other developing countries for stable supply of energy and mineral resources, giving growing amounts of economic assistance, providing arms and military training, and seeking long-term naval access arrangements. A rising India would, then, be no longer remain immune to the many tragedies of great power politics. [12] Finally, India, like other great powers before it, is also in the danger of falling a victim to ultra-nationalism and an over-determination of national interest. [13] Tempering nationalism and balancing ends and means are two challenges that come inseparably with a rising power potential on the world stage.

End Notes

1. Baldev Raj Nayar and T.V. Paul, (2002). *India in the World Order: Searching for Major-Power Status,* Cambridge: Cambridge University Press: 18.
2. Sumit Ganguly, *Introduction to India as an Emerging Power, Journal of Strategic Studies* December, (2002): 1-5.
3. Krishan Mathur D., (1996) *Conduct of India's Foreign Policy,* New Delhi: South Asian Publishers: 14, 25-30.
4. Ashley J. Tellis, (2009). *India's Emerging Nuclear Posture: An Action Agenda for United States,* Carnegie Publications: 12-18.
5. Gupta K. R. and Vatsala Shukla, (2009). *Foreign Policy of India,* New Delhi, Atlantic Publishers: 21-24.
6. C. Raja Mohan, *India and the Balance of Power*, *Foreign Affairs* vol.85, no. 4, (2006). 26-42.
7. Sumit Ganguly, op.cit: 34.
8. Surya Narain Yadav and Baghel Indu, (2009). *India's Foreign Policy: Opportunities and Obstacles in the Post-Cold War Era,* Manohar Books: 43-46.

9. Ashley J. Tellis, op.cit:16.
10. Ra meshan P, (2008). *WTO, India And Emerging Areas Of Trade: Challenges And Strategies,* Excel Publishers: 24.
11. A shley J. Tellis, (2001). *The United States and Asia: Toward a New U.S. Strategy and Force Posture,* Santa Monica: RAND: 47.
12. Srivas tava B. K., *Indo-American Relations: Search for a New Equation, International Studies,* vol.30, no.2, Apr-Jun, 221.
13. Rajiv Sikri, (2009). *Challenge and Strategy: Rethinking India's Foreign Policy,* New Delhi: Sage: 317.

12

Reorienting Non-alignment: Indian Foreign Policy in the New World Order [1]

K.S. Pavithran

A marked feature of international relations in the post-Cold War era is the attenuation in the ideological confrontations between the East and West. In the post Soviet international system, economics began to dominate the foreign policy agendas of most of the states including that of India. The fact is that 'the economic struggle had taken primacy over the political struggle' [Dutt, 1999:15]. Accordingly, in 1991 India under the former Prime Minister P.V. Narasimha Rao, launched the economic liberalization programme and began to change the substance and style of her foreign policy. The National Democratic Alliance (NDA)-1994-99 and United Progressive Alliance (UPA) governments followed and still following same economic and foreign policies initiated by the Rao government. The impact of these new measures on the direction and nature of the Indian foreign Policy in many respects is the negation of the Nehruvian legacy of an independent foreign policy. However, the impact of economic liberalization and globalization on Indian foreign policy cannot be properly understood without an adequate understanding of the basic principles of India's policy of Non-alignment. The present paper is largely an attempt to conceptualize Non-Aligned Movement (NAM) and analyze the impact of post-Cold War international environment in re-orienting the Indian foreign policy in the New Global Order.

Emergence of India's Policy of Non-alignment

Non-alignment was the natural outcome of a process that could well prove disastrous to the sustenance of the new nations. With the end of Second World War, the dominant nations of the world grouped into two power blocs under the United States and the USSR. Emerging from the nightmare of global war, the world found itself on the threshold of an era of escalating international tensions and Cold War politics. It was against this background of a rapidly deteriorating international situation, contributed by Cold War rivalries, that a number of nations of Asia and Africa became independent. The newly independent states vibrating with nationalist spirit were eagerly looking forward for their rightful and honoured position in the community of nations. The aim of the Asian-African nations was a progressive revision of international order and the internal set up. They saw the Cold War as a struggle for power between two super powers for world domination. Non-alignment as an idea was a concerned appeal to the nations of the world for a retreat to peace and security. The initiative came from the three nations-India, Yugoslavia and Egypt, respectively represented by the three statesmen Jawaharlal Nehru, Josip Broz Tito and Gamal Abdel Nassar. [2] From its modest beginnings at the Belgrade Conference in 1961 with a participation of 25 nations the NAM has expanded to include 119 members in the fifteenth NAM Summit Conference at the Sharm El Sheik (Egypt) in July 2009.

Originally as projected in India's foreign policy, Non-alignment implied a country not joining any of the Cold War power alignments while trying to maintain friendly relations with all kinds of nations and helping the preservation of world peace. Historically, the foreign policy of India to a certain extent emanated from the past legacy of India her national urges and objectives, her way of life and cultural heritage. The Indian National Movement which draws its inspiration from the Indian Renaissance of the 19th Century was a national experience successfully wrested independence from Britain and exemplified the political tradition of the country which is an important constituent of the country's foreign policy. The Non-aligned policy symbolises the Indian national ethos, sporadically springing out our struggle for freedom. Thus it appears that non-alignment imparted to the foreign policy of India the character of a national policy.

Besides these factors, the public opinion in India did not show any special enthusiasm for any one of the ideologies-capitalism or socialism. Public opinion at the base and at the higher level of leadership was to be largely conservative. No doubt Nehru was the undisputed leader, with leaning to the left yet his authority over the Indian National Congress was no means unquestioned. In the centre of the spectrum of public opinion were the dominant section of the Congress, Praja Socialist Party and Socialists, the Jan Sangh and the Swatantra parties were on the right, the communists were on the left. Naturally the foreign policy of India cannot ignore the views of the middle sectors of which obviously have no special affection for any of the super powers. Non-alignment was the only credible and viable alternative for India after Independence.

Furthermore, the question of stability of foreign policy of India can be seen in contexts like the gigantic social problems after the partition during 1946-54 and the tensions expressed themselves through linguism, provincialism and communalism during 1956-62. Another important factor that influenced the shaping of India's foreign policy was her perceptibly precarious economic situation. The British had ravaged Indian economy and when they left there was rampant poverty and misery; the social and economic system had lost its vitality and viability and life for the common man had become almost stagnant. India had been watching the simmering international situation in which conflicting ideologies, confrontationist ambitions, economic self-interest and a host territorial, racial and religious disputes posed a danger to world peace. It was in the midst of this unsetting and unstable environment that India had to adjust herself with the power blocs without any way compromising her fundamental policy objectives. It is an undeniable truth that the economic imperatives of independent India had pre-determined the colour of her foreign policy.

It is in the early phase of non-alignment that the fundamental objectives of the India's foreign policy were determined. These are to maintain national identity in world politics instead of becoming cogs in the wheels of great power politics, to help the preservation of world peace and promotion of international co-operation antithetically to the Cold War for the sake of a pluralistic and just world order; to seek the liquidation of colonialism racialism in international politics; to promote disarmament, conventional as well as nuclear, to work for riddance from economic backwardness by putting the pressure of persuasion on the advanced nations for economic and technical aid and for relaxed trade terms; to promote and help sustain egalitarian and democratic trends in world politics against hegemonistics ones. The idea is that, non-alignment seldom if ever means isolationism or neutralism. It signifies not a way of withdrawing from world politics, but of avoiding permanent or certainly onerous prior and continuing commitments to a particular multinational military team led by a super power.

Jawaharlal Nehru elaborated the idea while replying to the debate on foreign affairs in the Lok Sabha on December 9, 1958. He said:

"When we say our policy is one of Non-alignment, obviously we mean Non-alignment with military blocs. It is not a negative policy. It is a positive one". He further said ".... we do not align ourselves with either bloc....the policy itself can only be a policy of acting according to our best judgment, and furthering the principal objectives and ideals that we have." ([Nehru, 1955-1963:381]

Nehru's concern after attaining Independence was peace and economic development. He described non-alignment as a policy which is nationally profitable for any country. Nehru successfully emphasized that non-alignment is an instrument for catering national interests and every non-aligned nation is certainly guided in whatever it does by the considerations of its national interests. In this respect, it is important however that enhancing the prospects of world peace and international co-operation has come to them as something akin to their common interest of gaining political and economic stability. At the same instance, non-alignment as a universal movement, directed towards universal democratization of international relations or as Marshall Tito said "Active Non-alignment means an increasingly broad and active participation in the struggle for the triumph of the principles of the United Nations" (Schou and Brundtland, 1971:103).

Elucidating the opposition of Non-alignment to imperialism and colonialism Nehru asserted:

"Where there is continued domination, whether it is in Asia and Africa, there will be no peace either there or in the people's minds elsewhere, there will be a continuous conflict going on, continuous suspicion of Europe in the minds of Asia and therefore the friendly relationship which should exist between Asia and Europe will not come about easily. It is therefore important that all these areas of colonial dominations should be freed and they should be able to function as free countries" (Nehru, 196:44-48).

India gave its lead further, in elaborating the concept of Non-alignment and in causing the evolution of its new dimensions by working out with People's Republic of China, the five principles of peaceful co-existence [3] governing bilateral relations between two sovereign countries following different social ideologies and political systems. These principles were first enunciated in the Sino-Indian agreement on Tibet and then in the Joint Statement by the Prime Ministers of India and People's Republic of China in 1954. Both India and China had credit of giving birth to '*Panchsheel*' or the five principles of peaceful co-existence.

In this context Michael Brecher, one of Nehru's

biographers wrote in the 1950's that "Non-alignment is considered essential to the fulfilment of India's economic revolution and avoids alienation of India's two powerful neighbours China and Russia. Beyond that is the conviction that it contribute to the maintenance of peace and relaxation of tension. Indeed, the possibility of total destruction and international balance of power impose a moral as well as practical obligation on India to remain uncommitted" [Brecher, 1969:266-68].

In an address to the United Nations General Assembly on November 3, 1948, Nehru said "I should like to the state in this General Assembly on behalf of my people and my government, that we adhere completely and absolutely to the principles and purposes of the United Nations Charter and that we shall try, to the best of our ability, to work for the realization of these principles and purposes" [Nehru, 1946-49, 1958:323]. Thus by challenging the monopoly of the United States and USSR and their blocs in the world organization, the Non aligned Movement made an important contribution to preserving the universal nature of the United Nations [Jevremovic, 1996:293].

The contours of India's foreign policy of non-alignment was succinctly summarized by K.R. Narayanan as " it [India's foreign policy] is really an alchemy or shall I say a chemical combination of certain attitudes, the thirst for Independence, the determination to be independent, the desire to safeguard our national interest, the desire to pursue peace and cooperation in our environment and in the world as a whole and if I may put it more simply, it is a chemical combination between Nationalism and internationalism and this is where the uniqueness of Non Alignment comes in the manner in which these two considerations are combined and project in our interest and the interest of the world as whole..."[Narayanan, 1986:23]

Non-alignment and Changing Manifestations of Imperialism

The disintegration of the USSR and the end of the Cold War has radically changed the international environment. The United States became the dominant power in restructuring the international political and economic order. The dominant position of USA and the continued tendencies of political and military expansion demonstrated by the United States and its Western allies, in different parts of the world stands in sharp contrast to world trends characterized by the strengthening of multilateralism and of open, mutually beneficial international co-operation. Then there is the interface between global and regional organizations in the context of globalization. Some times these accounts are concerned with the implications for sovereignty of the increasing permeability of national boarders, a symptom of globalization, with what are seen to be transnational systems of accountability and authority [Taylor, 2006:25]. In this largely chaotic situation, international relations have become extremely complex and unpredictable due to the new distribution of military and political might, the domination of United States in the global order as well as the emergence of many countries, varying in size and strength, which do not try to conceal their ambitions to create their own respective spheres of influence.

While direct political imperialism is by and large only past experience, economic and cultural imperialism practiced by the same imperialist powers is an obnoxious contemporary reality. The process of globalization, the use of World Trade Organization (WTO) for forcing developing countries to reduce tariff walls and observe labour standards, while continuing to protect the economies of developed countries by tariff barriers and other no-tariff measures, is another case in point. Joseph E. Stiglitz, once chief economist of the World Bank, in his critique of globalization has observed that the financial institutions [World Bank and the International Monetary Fund (IMF)] have pushed a particular ideology–

market fundamentalism–that is both bad economics and bad politics; it is based on premises concerning how markets work that do not hold even for developed countries much less for developing countries. The IMF has pushed these economic policies without a broader vision of society or the role of economics within society. And it has pushed these policies in ways that have undermined emerging democracies (Stiglitz, 2002:0114). Consequently, globalization itself has been disadvantageous to developing countries, especially the poor within those countries [Loomba, 2007:221].

The fact is that the collapse of the bi-polar system and emergence of uni-polarity in political, economic and military terms is leading to further inequality and injustice and hence, the role of non-alignment becomes much more important as a counterforce to unilateral military and economic coercion [Dutt, 2001:62). Po litically, as Ngaire Woods suggests, the impact of globalization differs not just according to the sector of the economy being examined but also according to the character of each state. Strong states have not only influenced the nature and pace of globalization, but, equally, have controlled their own integration into the world economy. Their sovereignty may well be qualitatively changing, but it is surely not being eroded. Weak states by contrast risk being further weakened by globalization.

At the same time however, globalization is opening up new kinds of governance (such as regional institutions) and adding new actors to the process (such as non-governmental organizations and transnational arbiters and regulators) [Woods, 2000: 2-3]. This is because capitalisms globalizing tendencies have been substantially realized in particular historical context, and this has been the political project of a tangentially transnational–if also US led historic bloc comprised of particular fractions of the capitalist class, state managers and international bureaucrats, journalists and mainstream labour leaders [Rupert, 2003:190]. The fact is that Neo-liberal globalism envisages global ascendancy of non state actors like markets and transnational corporations. Neo-liberal globalists argue for the separation of economy and politics (markets and states) and the end of political control over economy. The global assertion of economic interests at the expense of political freedom and democratic aspirations of the people is the most significant characteristic of neo-liberal globalism. It is curious that in this period of neo-liberal globalist ascendancy the state it self tries to introduce and promote an idea and practice that undermines the primacy of politics.

The above naturally reminds us of the 'World System' theory of Wallerstein which means in a nut shell, the following: Capitalist accumulation (and its attendant exploitation) has created global inequalities based on the domination of the core capitalist states of the West over non-western peripheral countries. [4] This surge of inequality especially in the conditions of extreme economic instability such as those created by the global free market in the 1990's is the root of the major social and political tensions of the new century. In so far as international inequalities may be under pressure from the rise of the new Asian economies, both the threat to the relatively astronomic standards of living of the peoples of the old north and the practical impossibility of achieving anything like it for the vast populations of such countries as India and China, will produce its own domestic and international tensions [Hobsbawm, 2007:3].

In the absence of countervailing forces which existed in bi-polar world, the Allied forces under the hegemony of United States using unrestrained force in Afghanistan, in Iraq or in Kosava, underlined the need for restraining the use of military power to settle disputes. There are still many areas of conflict- in Angola, Bosnia, the Democratic Republic of Congo, Rwanda, Sudan and Somalia. The NAM does not appear to be doing anything to settle these disputes. In all these cases, armed intervention has come from US-led coalitions. This proves that the international system is potentially unstable and the disintegration of the USSR and the East European communist models increased this instability. It is evident that uni polar domination is what the US imperial project is all about. Ceasing, post-9/11 to disguise its hegemonic intent is an "emollient cream of tact", divisions between the sole superpower and a world that doesn't recognize its manifest destiny are emerging" [Eric Hobsbawn, 2004:9].The American ambition is not the creation of a global equilibrium through power balancing but the establishment of its global hegemony through a world wide system of alliances that would accept its undisputed and indisputable leadership. Behind the rhetoric of wanting to help India become 'major power in the world' lays this crystal clear ambition [Achin Vinayak, 2005:3583].

On the surface it does seem logical that with the disappearance of bloc divisions and rivalry between the two nuclear super powers, there was no longer any reason for countries wishing to stay away from these divisions to remain together hence the relevance of non-aligned movement. It may seem paradoxical that the first serious dilemmas concerning the future of the NAM were voices, both within and outside it, as detente evolved between United States and USSR. It was said in various quarters that the Non-aligned Movement has become superfluous. Now, it is alleged that during its decades of existence Non-alignment has proved to be ineffective. However, at the same time NAM maintained its regular schedule of periodic summit meetings, while increasing its number of member countries. However, one should note that the existing contradictions making the non-aligned movement itself, which could be to a great extent reduced to a discrepancy between theory and practice, between declared goals and behaviour in practice-weaken the capacity of NAM to carry out more successfully its historical mission.

In the present context of the collapse of east bloc led by Soviet Union and the consequent globalizing capitalism and neo-imperialism, the notion of non-alignment appears more problematic. However, the Movement constitutes an integral part of the profound changes in the structure of contemporary international relations. The only way to strengthen the role of Non-aligned Movement as the greatest independent and biggest peace movement in the world is to reinforce the non-aligned countries unity. The basis of such an approach can be cited in the idea of democratization of international relations as an imperative necessity of our times, which will lead to the realization of the unfettered development and genuine independence of all states. Democracy then requires the collective public regulation of these activities responsible for our social reproduction, which in most parts of the world are currently affected through the capitalist market [Colas, 2003: 97]. This means that the uni-dimensional and unipolar versions of the new international system need to be contested by the NAM as a whole. Unity and solidarity among the non-aligned countries are all the more necessary in the present crisis in international relations.

It is difficult to discern the future political profile of the Non-aligned Movement in the turbulent present day world. Not withstanding, all the development occurred in the international arena with the last decade of the 20th Century, the world situation is still in a state of transition. It is, therefore, incumbent on the Non-aligned Movement to ensure its full participation in the building of the new world order, the more so because a new international order has proven to be elusive and what transpired to date is little more than a new international realignment.

One of the greatest living historians of the world, Eric Hobsbawm, poignantly prophetic in stating "that the US has failed and will inevitably fail, to impose a new world order (of any kind) by unilateral force, however much power relations are skewed in its favour at present, and even if it is backed by an (inevitably short-lived) alliance. The international system will remain multi-lateral and its regulation will depend on the ability of several major units to agree with one another, even though none of these states enjoys military predominance.

How far international military action taken by the US is dependent on the negotiated agreement of other states is already clear....The era of wars ending with unconditional surrender will not return in the foreseeable future [Hobsbawn, 2007:27]. It is, therefore, imperative for the NAM to play its role in defining and shaping the international realities, to adapt to change and to articulate and implement appropriate strategies and approaches in the new millennium.

Post-Cold War Indian Foreign Policy

As India tries to carve out its place in the New Global Order, its relationship with the United States and Israel has undergone major shifts. An important catalyst in the Indo-US relations was the liberalization of the Indian economy and India's policy of inviting more and more foreign direct investment in industry and development projects. The United States has been very appreciative of the economic liberalization programme, initiated in 1985 by the Rajiv Gandhi regime, but vigorously pursued since 1991 by the P. V. Narasimha Rao government. The five nuclear tests conducted on March 11-13 annoyed the US. However, in March 2000 with President Bill Clinton's visit to India, India and US brought out a joint statement known as "India-US Relations : A Vision for the 21st Century" in which the two countries resolved to build a dynamic political partnership and "work together for strategic stability in Asia and beyond". Prime Minister Vajpayee visited US in September that year. However, differences existed in their perceptions and policies. The United States believes that India should forgo nuclear weapons; India believes that it needs to maintain a credible minimum nuclear deterrent in keeping with its own assessment of its security needs. Thus, India took very strong and independent on the question of signing of Comprehensive Test Ban Treaty (CTBT) in 1996 first at Geneva Conference on Disarmament and later in the UN General Assembly. Nonetheless, India and US are prepared to work together to prevent the proliferation of nuclear weapons and their means of delivery" [Government of US 2000].

In September 2003, India received the Prime Minister of Israel, Ariel Sharon. This was the first ever visit of an Israeli Prime Minister since India established diplomatic relations with that country. It was during the period of P. V. Narasimha Rao government that India established normal relations with Israel in 1992. India has already become one of Israel's strongest trading partners in Asia. India and Israel decided to co-operate in space research and defence. The US welcomed this friendship and expressed willingness to constructively work with both India and Israel. Home Minister L. K. Advani and external affairs minister Jaswant Singh also visited Israel.

With the replacement of the BJP-led NDA regime with the Congress-led UPA government, no significant change has taken place in the neo-liberal economic policies and foreign policy behaviour. The present leadership in the Congress has few foreign policy differences with the BJP. The ideological fervour that lay behind the BJP's desire for alignment with Israel is missing but commitment of the congress to strategic partnership with United States and to sustaining the relationship with Israel remains intact, despite Left pressure. India's decision to vote against Iran at the International Atomic Energy Agency [IAEA] meeting on 24 September is an instance of the fact that the India-US civil nuclear deal has altered New Delhi's foreign policy perceptions. India which has championed the non-aligned cause for long, did not find itself in the company of South Africa and Malaysia at the IAEA governing board meeting in the Vienna.

The process that was initiated by Clinton and Vajpayee was carried forward by Prime Minister Manmohan Singh and President George W. Bush. The two leaders met in Washington D.C. in July 2005 and in March 2006 in Delhi and resolved to transform the relations of the US and India "to establish a Global Partnership". They also resolved to strengthen energy security. In this respect, one of the major initiatives of the congress led United Progressive Alliance (UPA) government has been to put India's relations with the United States of America on a new footing [Bajpai, 2005:3577]. On June 28 2005, defence minister Pranab Mukherjee and the US defence secretary Donald Rumsfeld signed an agreement titled "New Framework for the US-India Defence Relationship" and on July 18, 2005 during Prime Minister Manmohan Singh's visit to the US, the two countries issued a document called the "India-US Joint Statement" and the signing of the 123 Agreement to separate India's civil and military nuclear facilities.

The Deal was approved by the US Congress (subject to the provisions of the Hyde Act) in November 2006 but it did not fully address India's concern. Even defence analysts and scientists expressed concern at the deal. On the other hand, India's relations with its neighbours are under stress. Rapid Developments in the Indo-US military to military relations have been the most visible aspect of the transformed by the bilateral relationship since 2000 [Malik, 2006:100]. Prime Minister Manmohan Singh following his meeting with Bush remarked that "best is yet to come" in terms of Indo-US relationship [Chaudhry, 2006:199]. The whole saga of the nuclear agreement with the U.S., currently developing in to a bill [5] that caps the liability of suppliers and operators at ₹ 300 crore, whereas a Chernobyl like development could impose unimaginable costs on the current and future costs often appears like a black comedy in the making [Bagchi, 2010]. "Any such move to limit compensation will be in defiance of Supreme Court judgments and will be contrary to the interest of people of India and their fundamental rights under Article 21 of the Constitution [Sorabjee, 2010]. However, the Government is keen to get the bill passed because it is crucial to operationalize India-US Civil Nuclear Agreement and allow the entry of private US companies which have already been assigned land for a nuclear park.

The UPA's (2004-09) common minimum programme

commits the government to pursue an independent foreign policy– "the policy will seek to promote multipolarity in world relations and oppose all attempts at multilateralism". Such a framework also goes against the grain of foreign policy initiatives such as the Russia-China-India-Brazil-South Africa forum. The emergence of multipolarity therefore requires a very substantial political and strategic weakening of the United States. The US needs to be politically defeated in places like Iraq, in Central and West Asia, and elsewhere, in Latin America where resistance to neo liberalism is strongest and where Venezuela is proving to be growing irritant. In the new situation with issues of military occupations, human rights, new dimensions of North-South conflicts, restructuring of the United Nations and nuclear disarmament, it falls on the NAM to survive meaningfully and not just ceremonially as a movement. This would require a newer unifying rationale [Vanaik, 5047] to strengthen the United Nations to ensure security of smaller states, to settle disputes among the member states and to defeat the Neo-con ambitions globally.

The Iran vote underlines the fact that Indian foreign policy suffers from insecurity, a poor understanding of the realities of the international situation, a lack of confidence in the nation's strategic weight, and an absence of belief in, or commitment to, genuine independence and non-alignment. The downward trajectory initiated by the NDA government in dealings with the United States, signalled by the support of all things to 'star wars' has hit a new low [The Hindu, 2005, September 26]. In fact some influential policy makers in the present government are of the view that the NDA government's cosying up with Washington and Tel Aviv when it was in power was only a continuation of the foreign policy initiated by the Congress in the 1990's after the end of the Cold War [Cherian, 2005:14].

The new defence agreement and nuclear accord are proof enough of that. With the vote against Iran on September 24, the UPA government has taken a major step which adversely affects India's independent foreign policy and its status in the non-aligned movement. This proves that India cannot expect to be a beneficiary of the nuclear agreement unless it meets the US concerns about Iran and China. The irony of the India capitulation on Iran is that its display of political weakness comes at a time when the US has finally aware of India's strategic weight and significance and is attempting desperately to harness these for its own ends. There seems little doubt that India's eagerness to get a membership in the UN Security Council and the civilian nuclear deal between India and the US has begun talking a toll of New Delhi's "independent foreign policy".

It was no secret that Bush administration regarded China as a long term threat to the US and India appeared as a possible counterweight or balance [Cohen, 2005:117]. India's geopolitical impotence for the US lies southwards and eastwards towards Indian Ocean and as a junior partner in strategic perspectives concerning the possible containment of China. While India should not be a reluctant to accept Americans support to become a major player in Asia and beyond, it needs to ensure that it retains the space to be able to carve out its own equation with China, Iran and other countries.

The situation calls for a strategy from Indian Foreign Policy makers to deal with the crisis of the international system and to adjust the terms of its dialogue for the global negotiations to the new conditions, integrating the security and economic aspects for the development of the country and for world peace. It is obvious from the current developments in world affairs that there is a dialectical relationship between the imperialist economic order and imperialism, and the Third World can never hope to alter the one without the other. In this era of global change, old alignments are yielding to new arrangements that may not be always palatable but their appraisal and understanding has to be the first task before Indian foreign policy.

In a situation where the IMF and World Bank prescriptions

are further tightening the noose, it is imperative to work to release us from debt traps and economic degenerations. Priority should also be given to consolidate and update India's cooperative relations with the neighbours. Any kind of military and strategic partnership with the United States will create unnecessary complications in our relations with our neighbours. This is because as K.R. Narayanan has succinctly remarked, "That politics is the soul of the movement (NAM) and even when you are following questions of global economics or elimination of economic disparities, it is this political attitude, which is propelling, which is giving vital life to this movement even though the problem has taken an economic shape" [Narayanan, 1986:20]. Hence, the battle for a new economic order is the battle against neo-imperialism.

There are four possible strategic perspectives that a state can pursue through appropriate diplomacy and statecraft when faced with an aspiring hegemon like the US. It can seek to balance against it. It can bandwagon on it. It can try to hide i.e., be neutral. It can try to transcend i.e. insist on abiding by international laws so as to excuse, itself from not aligning with the hegemon [Vinayak, ibid]. What the Indian state is currently doing is precisely bandwagoning and therefore exactly what the United States wants.

However, India is also pretending to itself that is in its national interest. The end result is that India merely pays lip service to the striving for multipolarity and does not at all see the contradiction in what it is doing and in what it says it ultimately wants. With so many forecasts of a multipolar world, it should have been the clear that India would have a significant place in it. But little analytical work has been done on the emerging poles and even less on the potential relations among them [Delpech, 1998-99:57]. There is a profound disjunction at the level of diplomacy and foreign policy behaviour between the claimed strategic goals that it believes it must pursue because it would give it greatest relative autonomy and authority in the system of nation states-promoting multi-polarity and its actual practice of statecraft as embodied in the policies and diplomatic stances it pursues and adopts.

Conclusion

India's policy of non-alignment was against the status quo situation in international relations that meant opposition to colonialism, imperialism and racial discrimination. It advocates sovereign equality of all states. However, with the break down of Soviet Union and rapid opening up of Indian economy, globalization and India's acquisition of nuclear weapons–because of its potential of market in India and for its policy of containment of China–US changed its attitude towards India. This stance has been encouraged by Indian governments even in the matter of US's arms supply, joint military exercises and other exchange of delicate information. This was totally against multilateralism in international politics and the proclaimed objectives of Indian foreign policy. In the wake of 9/11 and consequent war on terror, the neo-conservatives in the US have embarked upon a programme of action and international behaviour wedded to the sole objective of how best it will serve US's interests even by causing damage to world peace [Sachar, 2006:13]. However, in the post Cold War context, in many respects the Indo-US relationship is evolving in response to the changing role of India as a regional power.

With the "New Frame work for the US-India Defence Relations" and the 123 agreement on India-American Civil Nuclear Co-operation and the India's votes against Iran in the IAEA, India has become the something more than a 'major non- NATO ally' of America. It has joined the 'free world'. It has gone from being a victim of nuclear discrimination to a 'beneficiary'. While 'non-proliferation' concerns figure in 'the Joint Statement, the UPA government has regrettably failed to show the slightest interest in returning to India's traditional policy of promoting nuclear disarmament on the world stage.

By aligning so closely with United States, Prime Minister Manmohan Singh has ensured that terms such as "multipolarity" and democratization of international relations" spouted often by Indian leaders in the past–have little or no meaning left. Dr. Singh has raised the political stakes, preferred the 'economic advantages' over the military, and even sold a bit of national pride. There remains the unsolved question of how under the globalist agenda to avoid the hegemony and domination of a strongest power over the rest of the world. Reminicensing the words of Jawaharlal Nehru (1947) "ultimately foreign policy is the out come of the economic policy and until India has properly evolved her economic policy the foreign policy will be rather vague, rather inchoate and will be groping" [Nehru, 1961: 21-32]. Indian foreign policy has undergone noticeable transformation in the post-Cold War era.

The language of India's foreign policy shifted from an ideological orientation of non-alignment in the Cold War period to what is very often referred to as 'pragmatic' policy in the 1990s. In the political realm, the Soviet Union and East European Socialist Systems and military and political rise of American Power and in the economic realm the exacerbation of the dependence of Indian economy on international financial institutions and global capital, contributed to the changes in India's foreign policy. The unmistakable tilt towards the United States and Western bloc in the name of enhancing national strength is a deliberate move away from non-alignment and external independence. This kind of an approach is profoundly inimical to the people's interests and damaging to national strength. It is certainly unworthy of a country that is widely seen as a rising power on the international stage.

End Notes

1. The idea of a 'New World Order' was camouflaged by president Bush as "a new era, free from the threat of terror, stronger in the pursuit of justice, and more secure in the quest for peace, an era

in which the nations of the world can prosper and live in harmony". For full text of *president George Bush's statement of 11 September 1990* see, US Department of State, (1990), *Current policy Documents,* No. 1298, Washington D.C.

2. Non-alignment first sprang into popular use with V.K. Krishna Menon, while articulating the aspirations of the newly independent countries in the United Nations. see, Peter Lyon, *Non–alignment at the Summits: From Belgrade 1961 to Havana 1979- a Perspective View, Indian Journal of Political Science,* Vol. 41, No. 1, March 1980:149, also see K.R. Narayanan, *Relevance of Non-alignment, Kerala Journal of Political studies,* Vol. 1, No. 1, January 1986,16.
3. The five principles as they originated in the sino-Indian Agreement on Tibet were: 1. Mutual respect for each others territorial integrity and sovereignty; 2. Mutual Non-aggression; 3. Mutual non-interference in each others internal affairs; 4. Equality and mutual benefit; and 5.peaceful co-existence.
4. For a detailed analysis see, Immanuel Wallerstein, (1979). *The Capitalist World Economy,* Cambridge University Press, Cambridge.
5. The *Civil Liability for Nuclear Damage Bill,* limiting the liability in amount and in time has been sought by US for its nuclear- exporting firms like Westinghouse and General Electric, to forestall law suits filed against American suppliers in US courts by victims of a nuclear catastrophe. Washington has also pressed for exclusive jurisdiction for Indian Courts so that there will be no repeat of what happened after the Bhopal gas disaster. The bill essentially seeks to give foreign reactor builders a free ride at the Indian tax payers' expense. India is under no international obligation to pass such a law. The BJP and the Left parties have resolved to oppose the bill. For details see Brahma Chellancy, *A Radio Active Bill Fraught with big Risks, The Hindu,* 13 March 2010.

References

1. Bagchi, Amya Kumar, *Vision 2010: A Dangerous Myopia, The Hindu,* 10 March 2010.
2. Bandyopadhyaya J., *The Non–aligned Movement and International Relations, India Quarterly,* Vol. XXXII, No. 2, April- June 1977.

3. Brecher Michael, (1969). Nehru: A Political Biography, 2nd edition, Deep and Deep Publications.
4. Chellaney Braham, *A Radio Active Bill Fraught with Big Risks, The Hindu,* 13 March 2010.
5. Colas Alejandro, (2003). *The Power of Representation: Democratic Politics and Global Governance*, in David Armstrong, Theo Farrell and Bice Maiguashca (eds.), *Governance and Resistance in World Politics,* Cambridge: Cambridge University Press.
6. Chaudhry Shantonu, (2006). *The Future of Indo- US Co-operation in Multilateral and Bilateral Peace Keeping Operations* in Sumit Ganguly, Brian Shoup and Andrew Scobell (eds.), *US-Indian Strategic Co-operation in the 21st Century: More than Words,* London: Routledge.
7. Dutt Ruddar, (2001). *NAM–Its Relevance in the Unipolar World,* in Pramila Srivastava (ed.), *Non-aligned Movement: Extending Frontiers,* New Delhi: Kanishka Publications.
8. Dutt V.P, (1999). *India's Foreign Policy in a Changing World,* New Delhi: Vikas Publishing House.
9. Government of US: *Official visit of Prime Minister Vajpayee to United States, September 13-17, 2000*, Public Affairs Section, Embassy of the United States of America, New Delhi.
10. Hobsba wm Eric, (2007). *Globalization, Democracy and Terrorism,* London: Little Brown.
11. Jevre movic Pavle, *Nonaligned Movement: The End or a New Beginning?, International Studies,* Vol. 33 (3), July-September 1996.
12. *Jawaharlal Nehru's Speeches: September 1955-April 1963,* Vol. 4 (1964), Delhi: Government of India, Publications Division.
13. Loo mba Ania, (2007). *Colonialism/Post-Colonialism,* London: Routledge.
14. Malik V.P, (2006). *Indo-US Defence and Military Relations: From "Estrangement" to "Strategic Partnership*, in Sumit Ganguly et.al (ed.), *US-Indian Strategic Co-operation into the 21st Century: More than Words,* New York: Routledge.
15. Narang A.S., (2001). *NAM in the New Millennium: Challenges and Issues*, Pramila Srivastava (ed.), *Non-aligned Movement: Extending Frontiers,* New Delhi: Kanishka Publications.
16. Nara yanan K.R., *Relevance of Non-alignment, Kerala Journal of Political Studies,* Vol. 1, (1), January 1986.

17. Nehru Jawaharlal, (1961). *India's Foreign Policy,* Publications Division: Government of India.
18. Rupert Mark, (2003). *Globalising Common Sense: a Marxian Gramscian (re-) vision of the Politics of Governance/ Resistance*, in David Armstrong et al; (ed.), *Governance and Resistance in World Politics,* Cambridge: Cambridge University Press.
19. Sachar Rajindar, (2006). *India's Foreign Policy* in V.D. Chopra (ed.), *India's Foreign Policy in the 21st Century,* Delhi: Kalpaz Publication.
20. Schou August and Arne Olav Brundtland (eds.), (1971). *Small States in International Relations,* New York: Wiley Interscience Division.
21. Sorabjee Soli. Quoted in *The Hindu,* 15 March 2010.
22. Stigl itz, Joseph E., *Globalism's Discontents, American Prospect,* 12 January 2002, accessed at: *http:// www. Globalpolicy.org/globalitz/econ/2002/0114 Stiglitz.htm* on November 24, 2004.
23. Taylor Paul, (2006). *International Organization in the Age of Globalisation,* London: Viva Continuum Edition.
24. Vanai k Achin, *National Interest: A Flawed Notion, Indian Foreign Policy Since 1991, Economic and Political Weekly,* Vol. XLI (49), 9 December 2006: 5045-5049.
25. Vanai k Achin, *Post Cold War Indian Foreign Policy, Seminar,* No.581, June 2008.
26. Woods Ngaire, (2000). *The Political Economy of Globalisation,* New York: St. Martin's Press.

13

Violence in West Asia: Implications for India's Federalism and Security

A.K. Pasha

In contemporary West Asia, terrorism normally brings to our mind Palestinian suicide attacks in Israel and growing violent resistance to US invasion and occupation of Iraq and Afghanistan. A number of countries since the end of Second World War have been hit by violence or terrorist attacks such as Provisional Irish Republican Army in United Kingdom, Liberation Tigers of Tamil Eelam (LTTE) in Sri Lanka, Maoists in Nepal, Chechnya in Russia, Al Qaed a in USA, National Liberation Front (FLN) in Algeria, and for India, Pak sponsored groups, especially in Kashmir among many other countries. Little earlier it would have meant Palestine Liberation Organization (PLO) led by Chairman Yasser Arafat or Popular Front for the Liberation of Palestine (PFLP) led by a Christian physician George Habash's, killings in Munich (Germany) of Israeli athletes playing at the Olympics or hijacking of civilian aircrafts by Palestinian groups in late 1960's and early 1970's. It also brings us memories of Palestinian attacks against Israel from Southern Lebanon until recently when Israel decided to unilaterally withdraw mainly due to global pressures as also due to mounting losses–both men and material.

The military attacks launched by Hezbollah, Islamic Jihad from South of Lebanon and occupied Palestinian territories (Hamas-zeal) also played a crucial role in Israeli pull-out from Lebanon. Many condemned terrorist attacks on US and French marines in Lebanon in the early 1980's when peace keeping forces from these and other countries were stationed in and around Beirut soon after the Israeli invasion of Lebanon in June 1982. Lebanese President Basher Jamayil and Lebanese Minister Elias Hobeika and others were killed in 1980's and more recently Rafik Harriri former Lebanese Prime Minister and many Lebanese journalists and leaders. [1] Other important leaders in West Asia like UN Representative Count Bernadette, King Abdullah of Jordan, King Feisal of Saudi Arabia, Anwar Sadat of Egypt and Yitzhak Rabin of Israel have also been victims of terrorist violence.

Many such violent attacks targeting prominent people and large number of innocent civilians can be cited as evidence for prevalence of terrorism in West Asia. All or most of all the above instances of violence or terrorism are linked to Israel, Palestinians, Islamic groups and the eternal struggle over the occupied Arab lands in and around Palestine. PLO leader Yasser Arafat was also accused of organizing several terrorist acts. On this issue one can also go back to the terrorism unleashed by the Jewish groups like Haganah, Irgun, and Stern Gang against the British, UN and Palestinians. Leaders like Menachem Begin (Israeli Prime Minister from 1977-1983), Yitzhak Shamir, Ariel Sharon and others were associated with terrorist violence. In fact, many historians argue that the Jews established Israel through terrorism, expulsion of Palestinians, violence, assassinations and war. Since its establishment in 1948 and especially since 1967 Israel has targeted Palestinians killing them in the region especially in Gaza, West Bank, Lebanon, and Tunisia and also in Europe. [2]

In the context of contemporary West Asia, the fundamental reason for violence has been the gradual take-over of Palestinian lands and resources by Israel especially after 1967 i.e. in West Bank in clear violation of UN resolutions and international law. The Palestinians responded by attacking the Jewish settlements and other Israeli assets. To this Israel mounted disproportionate violence which it termed as legitimate and this soon became the focal point of world media. Thus, one has to honestly address the legitimate anger and genuine political despair which provide fertile ground for terrorists to exploit. US double standards in West Asia especially due to blind US support to Israel which has been consistently rejecting UN Resolutions on the issue of withdrawal from occupied Arab lands and expecting full compliance or strict implementation of UN resolution by Iraq, Iran and other Arab states as also threat of unilateral military action for any defiance. A leading West Asia expert from India says: "the case of the US appears to be a typical in that almost all terrorist acts directed against it in recent years are by-products of its interventionist policies abroad, especially in the West Asian region. And its response to these acts is therefore conditioned by its vision of a global role rather than by domestic developments". Undoubtedly, the US military posture in the region is creating instability which is fertile ground for the spread of terrorism. It should also be noted that "the ability of the US to persuade peoples and governments in West Asia to effectively reject terrorism has been significantly undermined" (Thelhami 2002).

The 1993 Oslo Accords gave Palestinians and others a ray of hope but Israeli and US aggressive policies are creating fertile ground for the emergence of new terrorists. To throw more light on this issue one has to look at the recent past history of the region and recall that the West perceived Arab (secular) nationalist movement (Nasserism) in the 1950's and 1960's "as the primary destabilizing political force in the region (West Asia) and viewed Islamic groups, especially those supported by friendly governments as more desirable and more stabilizing". [3] Moreover, Israel viewed PLO as a threat to its security and encouraged Islamic groups in Gaza and West Bank which led to the emergence of Hamas and Islamic Jihad, which have used violence on a bigger scale compared to the PLO. Many in West Asia, however, see the operations of Hamas, Hezbollah and Islamic Jihad not as terrorism but as acts of national liberation.

The aim of the Palestinian groups is viewed as legitimate

i.e. liberation from Israeli occupation, especially from the clutches of an enemy which has vast military capability. Thus, suicide bombings and terrorism is seen as a powerful weapon of the weak, desperate, and helpless facing a far stronger and vicious enemy. One should also recall Israeli invasions of Egypt in 1956 along with France and Britain, Israeli invasion of Egypt, Jordan and Syria in 1967, Israeli invasion of Lebanon in 1982, and Palestinian territories in 2002 and later. Now Israel wants the US to invade Iran after creating the mess in Iraq. Moreover Raanan Gissin spokesman for the former Israeli Prime Minister Ariel Sharon said "thank God, Israel has the means at its disposal to bring about the downfall of this extremist regime in Iran. There will be no second 'final solution". The suicide bombings as a method of political violence in Palestine did not materialize at the push of a button. It took several years before it was put to frequent use. Its genesis can be traced to the failure to get the Israeli military to redeploy its military forces stationed in Palestinian territories–a key failure of the 1993 Oslo Accords.

The Palestinian Authority's failure to secure the redeployment and to guarantee Israel's security demands led to political factions opposed to negotiations and disposed towards suicide bombings gaining popularity. Under Article 8 of the Oslo Accords, the Palestinian Authority was allowed to establish "a strong police force", while Israel would continue to carry "the responsibility for overall security of Israelis for the purpose of safeguarding their internal security and public order". [4] Although the sharing of security responsibilities between Israel and the Palestinian Authority was working well with minor problems until Ariel Sharon of the Likud Party became Israeli Prime Minister in February 2001, but faced with mounting problems even the US Central Intelligence Agency intervention couldn't make the mechanism work. The creation of the Palestinian security services under the Oslo Accords, with a mandate in Palestinian populated area (Area A) of the West Bank has been irrevocably undermined.

Similarly, the territorial division of the West Bank that resulted from the Oslo process–the creation of Areas A, B and C–is no longer relevant to the reality in the West Bank and Gaza. So, today the "Oslo map become meaningless", as one US official admitted.

The government of Ariel Sharon systematically and effectively destroyed the principle feature of the Oslo peace process by ending Israel's consent to recognize the security responsibilities of the PA in Area A-covering the principal Palestinian towns in the West Bank. As Amir Oren of *Ha'aretz* wrote on April 5, 2002, "The Israel Defence Forces is doing as it pleases in all (Areas A, B, C) of them." Thus, there is only one area and that area is controlled by the Israel Defence Forces without Palestinian intermediaries. The Sharon government was determined that Yasser Arafat and the structures he represented–PLO and the Palestinian Authority - were no longer diplomatic or security partners. Arafat failed to play the role outlined for him, and soon he was no longer "relevant" to Israeli designs and had to go. Arafat's security services, nurtured and paid for by the CIA, had failed to enhance Israeli security and were therefore decimated. Israel's unprecedented military operation in the Palestinian territories was not only to deploy the Israel Defence Forces in Palestinian cities in West Bank and Gaza but also in the security zones in the Jordan valley and in the region east of the Green line separating Israel from the West Bank. As *Haaretz* reported on 14 April 2002, "the logic of Sharon's plan was this "a military defeat would convince the Palestinians and the international community to leave these security zones, including major population centres, under effective Israeli control for many years."

The establishment and expansion of Jewish settlements led to spread of violence against the settlers. Since the Oslo Accords, successive Israeli governments continued to build new Jewish settlements and expand existing ones where the number of Jewish settlers doubled since 1993. The 20 largest settlements in West Bank and Gaza in 2002 had 138,660 settlers. Also the 20 smallest settlements in 2002 had 2,261 settlers. By 1993 there were 32,750 housing units in the Jewish settlements completed since 1967 when Israel captured these Palestinians lands from Egypt and Jordan. Since the Oslo Accords, according to one study 20,371 new housing units have been constructed representing a 62 percent increase in eight years from what had been built over roughly a quarter century. About 4 lakh Israeli settlers now live in some 200 settlements that dot the occupied Palestinian lands and are linked to one another by means of 450 kilometres of highway and "bypass" roads which also serve to isolate Palestinian population centres from one another turning them into Bantustan- like little islands.

The rapidly increasing Jewish settler colonies in Occupied Arab Territories (OAT's) strengthened the political power of those Palestinians who rejected the Oslo Accords. As the number of Palestinian opponents of the Oslo Accords increased, the work of the Palestinian security forces became more and more difficult. Israel expected full cooperation from PA irrespective of their colonial or expansionist policies and what effect these negative policies were having on popular Palestinian support for PA. Whereas the Clinton Administration was willing to devote enough time to resolve the thorny Palestinian-Israeli dispute, the Bush administration since 2001 adopted a 'hands-off' approach and wanted both the parties to resolve their problems bilaterally. But there was a crucial difference. Whereas Clinton would talk to Yasser Arafat and other Palestinian leaders' along with the Israeli leaders, George W Bush ignored Arafat and built up close ties with Israeli Prime Minister Ariel Sharon. "More importantly, the Bush administration seemed receptive to the Sharon line that Yasser Arafat is a terrorist, that the Palestinian Authority is a terrorist entity, and that they should be treated as such." The Bush administration appeared to side with Sharon who argued that Israel would not talk to the Palestinian Authority until there is a "complete cessation of violence". According to one writer the US Vice President Dick Cheney went as far as to justify in public, Israel's policy of assassinating Palestinian activists suspected of orchestrating the violence.

The September 11, 2001 attacks on World Trade Centre and the Pentagon gave Israeli leaders a unique chance to win US support for their war against the Palestinians. The Israeli Prime Minister Ariel Sharon is reported to have said to US Secretary of State Colin Powell, "Everyone has his own bin Laden and Arafat is ours." Sharon was hopeful that he would make Israel a partner with the US in the war against international terrorism. The US administration very quickly realized that Israeli Prime Minister Sharon tried to take advantage of the September 11 events to push forward his own agenda against the Palestinians. Colin Powell made it clear that "Israel will not be part of any anti- terror military action" against Afghanistan or elsewhere. Israeli attempts to paint Arafat in dark colours as a terrorist also backfired. The US administration realized the significance of Arab support in its war against terrorism.

To win over the Arab world and the Palestinians, the then US President Bush called for the establishment of a Palestinian state with East Jerusalem as its capital in September 2001. This was bad news to Sharon who was determined to keep the entire Jerusalem and large chunks of Gaza, West Bank under Israeli control. More and more Israeli leaders began to fear that the US is getting closer with the Arab states and the Palestinians in the anti-terror war with Israel being seen as a burden or ignored. Sharon warned Bush: "Do not try to appease the Arabs at our expense. Israel will not be Czechoslovakia. Israel will fight terrorism." This prompted Ari Fleischer, White House spokesman to say: "The Prime Minister's comments are unacceptable", and reminded Sharon that "Israel has no stronger friend and ally in the world than the US. President Bush has been an especially close friend of Israel". This led to a brief strain in US-Israeli ties and ultimately Sharon had to express regret for provoking this public row. [5]

In August 2001 Israel had killed a prominent Popular Front for the Liberation of Palestine (PFLP) leader Abu Ali Mustafa thereby stoking the fires of war. In retaliation the PFLP killed the Israeli Tourism Minister Rehavam Zeevi in Jerusalem on October 17, 2001. Israel wanted Yasser Arafat to hand over the assassins and without waiting for a reply, he sent IDF to reoccupy Palestinian cities under Palestinian Authority's control under the Oslo accords. To be sure (the Palestinian Authority) Arafat's judicial authorities did take action against the PFLP killers but this was seen by the Israeli's as slow and insufficient. Sharon's war against the Palestinians brought sharp US criticism as the fragile coalition against Taliban and Al Qaeda leader Osama bin Laden was under strain. For Osama bin Laden, Sharon's attack on the defenceless Palestinians came as a God sent opportunity to expose the US and its allies in the region. He said: "Israeli tanks are wreaking havoc in Palestine – in Jenin, Ramallah, Rafah, and Beit Jala and other parts of the land of Islam, but no one raises his voice or baits an eyelid." Elsewhere bin Laden said which stirred many: "It is what we instigated, for a while in self defence...And it was in revenge of our people killed in Palestine and Iraq...So, if avenging the killing of our people is terrorism, let history be a witness that we are terrorists...Every time they kill us, we kill them, so the balance of terror is achieved."

However, it was Israeli invasion of Lebanon in 1982 and large-scale destruction which followed that Osama bin Laden brought about a change in his outlook. This is clear from the following extract from Osama's videotaped message to US voters on the eve of 2004 presidential elections: "The events that influenced me directly trace back to 1982 and subsequent events when the US gave permission to the Israelis to invade Lebanon, with the aid of the Sixth Fleet. At those difficult moments, many meanings that are hard to describe went on in my mind. However, these meanings produced an overwhelming feeling to reject injustice and generated a strong determination to punish the unjust ones. While I was looking at those destroyed towers in Lebanon, it occurred to me to punish the unjust ones in a similar manner by destroying towers in the US so that it would feel some of what we felt and be deterred from killing children and women". [6]

His statements not only exposed the Arab states friendly to the US as also other Arabs states in the region, but the greatest impact was made on the Arab and Islamic peoples who saw their rulers as puppets of the US, when bin Laden declared that the Americans would not live in peace as long as Palestine did not get freedom from Israeli occupation, he succeeded in setting the agenda for Arab demands on Palestine.

More and more Arab people clearly saw US double standards as one applied to Israel and another to the Palestinians. No wonder people in the Islamic world were lukewarm in their response to US led war against terrorism, because it did not satisfy the reasonable Arab demands on Israeli withdrawal from occupied Palestinian lands, return of refugees and sharing of the city of Jerusalem. Whereas Bush invoked international justice to justify the war in Afghanistan but the same standard of justice to the Palestinians was not applied. Whereas the US kept silent on Israeli nuclear capability but used the pretext of nuclear weapons to illegally invade Iraq and went on to effect regime change and occupy the country. Iraqi resistance initially to US occupation was mainly local but soon Al Qaeda was attracted due to large-scale destruction of one of the most developed Arab country. It is very clear that Arab rage is not against Americans but against their "policies". Al Qaeda targets America for what it does, not what it is". [7]

Even though Yasser Arafat was the first Arab leader to denounce the September 11 attacks but when Arafat faced Israeli attacks the US squarely blamed the PLO leader for his predicament as "largely of his own making" and openly ignored/sidelined him and called for the election of new Palestinian leadership. By doing this the US was clearly undermining its own moral authority. As a result, its Arab allies in West Asia find their ability to delegitimize terrorism undermined. More and more people in the region view US allies as puppets and servants of America and in the face of daily Israeli killings or destruction of the Palestinians, their call for an end of Palestinian terrorism further delegitimizes themselves rather than terrorism. [8]

As we have seen earlier, soon after the September 11 events the US led a global campaign against terrorism and especially the Al Qaeda net work with its invasion of Afghanistan. Although Al Qaeda appears to have been disrupted as its members were either killed, imprisoned or they fled to safer places, but terrorists means have increasingly become legitimate and popular in the perceptions of most people in West Asia. It is interesting to note that those carrying out terrorist acts in West Asia and elsewhere (not just Al Qaeda) are claiming to do it in the name of Islam. If seen objectively Islam is not central to the terror issue, although one cannot say that religion plays no role. Some groups in the West Asian region may be dangerous not because of their Islamic character but due to their violent methods and intolerant ends. The actions of a few (misguided) radical Muslims should not be seen as a general phenomenon flowing from Islamic faith.

It is interesting to note that Hezbollah, Hamas and Islamic Jihad were treated by the US as local movements fighting against occupation, and not as part of the global terrorist networks like the Al Qaeda and so not included in the list of 27 terrorist organizations whose assets were frozen by the US Congress. No wonder Arafat and most secular Palestinians distanced themselves from Al Qaeda and even Saddam Hussein. Bin Laden's struggle against the West is essentially a religious war whereas the Palestinian struggle against Israel is a national liberation movement. While the former uses mindless violence and terrorism the Palestinians resort to violence in self defence. Much of the world sees Israeli violence against Palestinians as violation of international law, Geneva conventions, UN Resolutions and hence illegitimate because the Israeli goal is to continue its occupation of Palestinian land and the Palestinians have a legitimate and globally accepted right to resist Israeli occupation (Kepel 2002).

The Israeli Gaza military action in the summer of 2002 and continued occupation of Palestinian territories generates an ever deepening pool of Palestinians ready to fight and die for an independent Palestine state. Israeli repression is increasingly becoming counterproductive. Palestinian groups opposed to Israel and willing to launch attacks on Israel are growing and they are totally decentralized as the Palestinian infrastructure is being gradually but systematically destroyed by Israel. Palestinians will not break further because they are already broken as government, and the attacks are seen as individualized acts of patriotism. Terror is a tactic used by those struggling people who do not possess planes, tanks and trained infantry. Israel has tried to be a model occupier since the 1967 war but no people in modern times will ever for long submit to the indignity of occupation and military repression. Ending the Israeli military occupation and atrocities on Palestinians alone will perhaps end all forms of violence in most parts of West Asia. Palestinians are fighting for their very survival as a people and a nation and Israel against universal opposition wishes to control and suppress them. Israel is aware of a new culture where Palestinian suicide bombers are valued and praised–where they bring distinction and some money to a family that has little of either.

There is no doubt that the suicide bombers are frustrated Palestinians fighting for their liberation from Israeli control. It is their chief weapon and moreover it has been working well. It is quite likely that this state of affairs would persist until the Palestinians get a state of their own which involves Israeli withdrawal from Occupied Arab Territory's. The Palestinians have little or no motive to halt their increasingly effective guerrilla (terrorist for some) campaign if they do not get-statehood. Palestine Liberation Organization leader Yasser Arafat in an article at the beginning of February 2002 in *New York Times* condemned terrorism, underlining it by stating that violence against Israeli civilians was indeed terrorism. He equally condemned Israeli state terrorism against Palestinian civilians. Each time Israel bulldozes more Palestinian homes and each time Israel kills Palestinians and their hope, it creates more Palestinian suicide bombers and terrorists.

Israel's policy of territorial expansionism did not end the confrontation but actually increased terrorism in Palestine and in other parts of the region and elsewhere and people would get inspiration from these activities. Early resolution of the Israeli-Palestinian issue is crucial to avoid the spectre of terrorism spreading worldwide (Gunaratna 2003). Here, it must be mentioned that US State Department reports had identified that West Asia was not the leading region in the number of terrorist incidents throughout the 1990's. It was also not the leading area as far as the number of attacks against US targets was concerned. Five years before the September 11 incident, terrorism in West Asia had significantly declined every year and by 2000 West Asia had emerged as a region with the fewest terrorist attacks of any around the world except North America. This global trend must be kept in mind to counter the mindless attempt to link Islam with terrorism.

The recent phenomenon of suicide attacks and its effectiveness especially by Hamas, Islamic Jihad, Hezbollah, Al Qaeda and others began to be emulated by the secular Palestinian groups due to Israeli repression and unbearable conditions under Israeli occupation of West Bank and Gaza. Since the secular groups could not recruit the number of members as the Islamic groups did, no wonder they began to emulate the suicide method. "The suicide bombing phenomenon has thus become secularized". This is born out of the hopelessness and humiliation at the hands of Israeli and other oppressors. Since the Islamic doctrine prohibits suicide, the perpetrators and their sympathizers may have used religion to suit their ends.

It must also be stressed that suicide bombings are not confined to Islamic groups in West Asia. One might recall the label given to Palestinian fighters as fedayeen–self sacrifices. Suicide bombings have been effectively used as an instrument of violence by the Japanese in the Second World War and by the Tamil Tigers in Sri Lanka and elsewhere. Although many Israeli civilians have fallen victims to Palestinian violence inside Israel and Occupied Arab Territory's but over 8000 Palestinians have been killed by Israeli military forces, 50,000 injured and over 80,000 permanently crippled in recent attacks. Thousands have been arrested and kept in Israeli jails without any charges. Many have called Israeli attacks against innocent Palestinian civilians as savage, barbaric and state sponsored terrorism.

Several human rights groups worldwide have condemned Israeli use of excessive violence against Palestinians in clear violations of international law, Geneva Conventions, United Nations Security Council Resolution's and other global conventions. Moreover, the rate of unemployment in the West Bank has risen to 40 percent and in Gaza to 80 percent. More than half of the Palestinian population lives below poverty line of $2 a day. Israel has cancelled work permits to a large majority of Palestinians who worked in Israel, uprooted crops from thousands of hectares of orchards and imposed curfew for weeks which prevents people even from going to hospitals and places of work.

The Palestinian infrastructure is in very bad shape due to constant Israeli military attacks and the Israeli military out posts have multiplied on Palestinian lands with military check points humiliating Palestinian men, women and children everyday in their own land especially since Ariel Sharon became Israeli Prime Minister and now under Benjamin

Netanyahu. The mounting Palestinian casualties due to excessive and disproportionate violence by the Israeli forces caused much anguish and anxiety to America's faithful allies in the region like Egypt, Saudi Arabia, Jordan, other Gulf Cooperation Council states and others.

As one writer put it, "They had been shamed and discredited in the eyes of their own people by their inability to help the Palestinians or to modify the United States blatant partiality towards Israel". [9] Saudi Arabia after the Pentagon attack despite accusations that 15 out of 19 pilots who crashed with aircraft's at World Trade Centre and Pentagon were Saudi nationals, has managed to keep its pro-American image but has been "staunchly anti-Zionist," despite Abdullah's peace plan to resolve Arab-Israeli conflict which was endorsed by the Arab summit in early 2002. He advised the US to examine the roots of terrorism: "We see Palestine children being shot at, buildings being destroyed, trees uprooted, people encircled, and territories closed and women killed, unborn babies delivered at check points. They are very painful images. And when we worry about the future, and we worry about the causes that lead people to become violent, the reasons that lead people to become violent, the reasons that lead people to become suicide bombers, these are the reasons they do so".

One must recall here that Osama bin Laden is largely a creation of the US. The need to expel the USSR from Afghanistan in 1980's propelled the US to cultivate Islamic groups worldwide. The US mobilized Muslim fighters in the name of Jihad or holy Islamic struggle against Communism. Saudi Arabia, Egypt, Sudan and others were pressurized to send fanatically religious people like Osama bin Laden who is also a wealthy person. Bin Laden was very much part of the Saudi establishment. His point of departure came when he objected to the presence of American troops on Saudi soil. Osama bin Laden focused his attention on expelling US forces from Saudi Arabia and creating an Islamic political order across the Muslim World.

Even though Saudi Arabia is an Islamic state with most of the laws based on the shariah, it has still become a target of Osama bin Laden who began to highlight Islamic issues that resonate with the public especially the Palestine issue and sanctions against Iraq. Osama bin Laden said, "Let there be no two religions in Saudi Arabia"–based on a Hadith. According to one writer in a classified survey, it was found that 95 percent of the Saudi's agreed with bin Laden on the presence of American troops in Saudi Arabia. US war on terror is seen as a substitute for cold war. As former British Foreign Secretary Robin Cook said: "The spirit of the cold war lives on in the minds of those who cannot let go fear and who need an enemy to buttress their own identity. Hence, the vacuum left by the Cold war has been filled by George Bush's global war on terror. It is tragically true that terrorism, partly as a result, is now a worse threat than before". Dilip Hiro in his new book *War without End* says the on-going war on terrorism "is a war without end".

He emphasizes the need to go to the root cause of terrorism, and argues that US threats to Iraq – an established government amounts to terror. According to him, "Americans always blame others, never themselves. Whatever happens to America, it was their own fault. Americans won't like to hear that. This war on terrorism will go on because of the definition Bush has put on it. He himself is threatening established governments:" so long as anybody is terrorizing established governments, there needs to be a war" (Findlay 2002).

If anti-Americanism sentiments sweeping the Islamic world are not neutralized soon by way of full US withdrawal from Iraq and Afghanistan, then the US invasion and occupation undoubtedly seen as illegal, unjust and unnecessary would fuel deeper anti-US feelings and would lead to wider complications for the US. Due to the non resolution of the Palestinian-Israeli conflict, the US could become target of suicide attacks and terrorism on a much larger scale. Many analysts believe US double standards with war on Iraq and soft approach towards Israeli occupation and repression on the Palestinians would hurt US interests both in the long and short term. Although Ex-British Prime Minister Tony Blair and Foreign Secretary Jack Straw accepted "double standards" on Palestine and understood Arab concern about what he described as "injustice against the Palestinians", but only quick progress towards establishing a Palestine state and an end to Israeli oppression is wanted. Straw said, "There is a real concern too that the West has been guilty of double standards– on the one hand saying the UN Security Council Resolution's on Iraq must be implemented, on the other hand, sometimes appearing rather quixotic over the implementation of resolutions about Israel and Palestine". Asked if he would plead guilty to double standards, Straw said, "To a degree yes… and we're going to deal with it".

It is our responsibility, yes, to deal with Iraq but also, yes, to deal with the Israel-Palestine crisis", Straw said, citing UN resolutions calling for two independent states. He said he felt "angry and upset" at the Israelis. Britain, he told the BBC is "100 percent committed" to the establishment of a viable Palestinian state with its capital in Jerusalem, based on United Nations Security Council Resolution's Article 242, the 1967 borders, the end of Jewish settlements, and a solution of the Palestinian refugee problem. The Israeli-Palestine Peace Road-map prepared by the so-called "Quartet", the UN, European Union, USA and Russia call for a phased peace plan which stipulates the creation of an independent Palestinian state by 2005. But due to Israeli pressure the US repeatedly postponed the publication of the Road Map. Israel's supporters raised four objections to the plan. Firstly they opposed the notion of "simultaneous steps" and called for sequential, with Palestinians first full filling all of their requirements, and only then would Israelis be required to act. Secondly, they objected to the roadmap's mandates and time tables.

Israel wants the stipulation that the roadmap's call for a provisional Palestinian state be based not on a mandate but on

Israeli–Palestinian negotiation and the completion of an Israeli-Palestinian treaty. Thirdly, they want to eliminate the mention of Saudi Abdullah's peace initiative since it speaks of Israel's' return to the June 1967 borders. Finally, they wanted the roadmap to specifically call for Palestinian acceptance of Israel as a Jewish state, meaning that Palestinian should agree upfront to relinquish the right to return. They are also opposed to the deployment of international observers to implement the plan. The Israelis also have to freeze Jewish settlements and the Palestinians have to reform the Palestinian Authority.

What is important is not the roadmap as there are several plans starting from UN Security Council Resolution's Articles 242 and 338, Oslo plan, Mitchell and Tenet plan so on. There has to be a clear mechanism established to implement what is agreed upon. Israel has always refused to implement the agreed provisions as it desires to retain West Bank and East Jerusalem. If the US or UK continue to express lack of seriousness on this issue and like before tolerate Israel's massacre of Palestinians, wholesale destruction of every vestige of Palestinian statehood, targeted murders, house demolitions, settlements building, by pass roads, closures, curfews and daily humiliation of Palestinians, the world would call for sanctions on Israel like the UN did on Iraq, Iran, Libya, South Korea, South Africa among others.

The US policy makers had hoped to achieve quick victory over Iraq to boost the flagging US economy with cheap Iraqi oil and then to reorder the strategic map in the strategically important Gulf region, but due to mounting opposition in Iraq, from Syria, Iran, Saudi Arabia and other countries in the world, the US could face new and entirely unexpected challenges to its objectives. And surmounting those hurdles could drag the US deeper and deeper into the Arabian deserts or quagmire. The US had unique and unprecedented goodwill after the 11 September 2001 attacks on World Trade Centre and Pentagon throughout the world including most Islamic states, but anger and hatred due to its double standards and dubious policies; this has been dissipated fairly quickly. The short-sighted Bush administration with its war mongers led by Dick Cheney was in no mood to listen to saner voices from any quarter. Only the American people can save the USA and the rest of the world from what is fast becoming a dangerous situation.

The world has seen the awesome power of the US and most are frightened. But surely peoples, societies, nations are also working hard to prepare strategies to challenge, to resist, to preserve their lives, cultures, values, and self prestige. It may be America's call now, but every Iraqi, Palestinian, Afghan killed, injured and suffered would one day wake up and when he musters courage, he will find out the truth. US invasion of Iraq and Afghanistan and Israeli invasions of Palestinian lands is a wake up call for the struggling people as it's a short term gain for the US and Israel. In the final analysis the oppressed will take their destiny in their own hands sooner than later.

US support to Arab authoritarian states like Saudi Arabia, Egypt and other despotic states has also been breeding religious extremism. These rulers are seen as puppets of the USA merely to protect US interests. Such Arab states merely use rhetoric on the Palestinian issue and the US also does not take them seriously. More and more people in West Asia now believe that their governments due to the authoritarian nature of the political system and also under US influence cannot do anything to relieve their humiliation and improve their lot–hence, the emergence of more radical Islamic groups which employ suicide bombings. Moreover, the secular groups also follow this strategy under popular support. According to one writer, "suicide bombings take root because they free the desperate from the need to rely on governments. Rather than being sponsored by states, this form of violence challenges states." Al Qaeda and other terrorist groups in West Asia may be ultimately defeated but newer groups would emerge and may follow their Al Qaeda's methods. [10]

Undoubtedly, movement towards democratic reforms, new innovative methods for economic cooperation and even-handed policies on the Arab-Israeli conflict and towards the West Asian region as a whole would go a long way to turn people away from terrorism and violence as it will inspire hope for a better future as the region has witnessed several wars, unprecedented violence, insecurity, revolutions and instability for several decades due to external interventions and internal mismanagement or despotism. In the end, it must be pointed out that initially the Palestinians reacted to the several extremely harsh Israeli measures by throwing stones at Israeli soldiers, who retaliated by sending armoured personnel carriers and began targeted assassinations of prominent Palestinians. As Israeli attacks multiplied on Palestinians, the latter resorted to suicide bombings and to kill themselves. Many asked–"when it is normal and legal for Israel to kill Palestinians with an Apache helicopter, why is it not normal to kill an Israeli by myself?" It an Israeli kills a Palestinian wearing military uniform, it is not terror but if a Palestinian in civilian clothes kills an Israeli, it is terror". Hence, state terrorism and counter-terrorism have become vicious cycle with action and reaction before Israel and the Palestinians and also unfortunately gradually spreading to other parts of the world. [11]

Indian Interests in West Asia

Jawaharlal Nehru's bold initiative to organize the first Asian Relations Conference in Delhi at Indian Council of World Affairs, Sapru House in March 1947 signalled his determination to make India a major global player. In the inaugural speech, he fervently pleaded for Asian unity, coöperation, solidarity and identity. Nehru said: "We stand at the end of an era and on the threshold of a new period of history...we can look back on our long past, and look forward to the future that is taking shape before our eyes...Asia...has suddenly become important again in world affairs...the time has come for us, peoples of Asia, to meet together, to hold together and to advance together. It was not only a vague desire, but a compulsion…". With considerable clarity, he pinpointed the strategic role of Asia in global politics in, what he called, the 'atomic age'. "In this atomic age Asia will have to function effectively…Indeed, there can be no peace unless Asia plays her part. There is today conflict in many countries, and all of us in Asia are full of our own problems. Nevertheless, the emergence of Asia in world affairs could be a powerful influence for world peace".

Nehru, therefore, pleaded for a 'close union of countries bordering on the Indian Ocean, both for defence and trade purposes', a system of defence, stretching from the West to Southeast Asia in which 'India because of her intrinsic importance and her strategic position was to play a significant role'. For Nehru India "is the natural centre and focal point of the many forces at work in Asia. Because of this, the history of India is a long history of her relations with other countries of Asia". He desired that 'the coordination of various countries in Middle East, India and the Southeast Asia is not only possible, but undoubtedly certain in the future.' He rejected the idea of a pan-Islamic bloc and said: "Some people, living in a world of their own creation, imagine that there is a pan-Islamic block which may threaten India. This is pure fancy. Every one of the Islamic countries is developing on intensely national lines and there is absolutely no room in them for an external policy based on religion. Indeed, even their domestic policy has little to do with religious dogmas.

The interests of these countries are and will continue to be our interests". He also indicated that the question of 'Asiatic Federation' was necessary, both for defence and trade purposes. The gathering of such large number of Asian leaders in Delhi and the conference call for Asian unity "announced the arrival of Asia on the world stage". Later Nehru declared "…the world is something bigger than Europe…Asia counts in World Affairs. Tomorrow it will count much more than today." Thus, the underpinnings of India's foreign policy were laid during the freedom struggle as also anti-colonial struggle and in the initial decades of nation building. All of this gave rise to non-alignment. [12]

Soon Nehru came to support Egypt's Nasser during the Suez crisis in 1956 when UK, France and Israel attacked Egypt to regain the Suez Canal and overthrow the Nasser regime. Nehru publicly branded Israeli aggression as a case of "clear, naked aggression". Through his support to Nasser in the Suez Crisis a much closer rapport between the two leaders was established. Whatever little sympathy was left for Israel in Nehru's heart vanished due to its aggression on Egypt and its alignment with Anglo-French military attack. Nehru concurred with Nasser on Israel, which was seen as an outpost of western imperial interests and as a country that did not have any links in the area. India's close ties with Egypt to some extent neutralized the Pakistani campaign against India in the Arab world, especially over the Kashmir issue.

Egypt went to the extent of declaring that Kashmir was an integral part of India and that "Suez is as dear to Egypt as Kashmir is to India". Pakistan was branded as the "number one enemy of Cairo and Arabs". Pakistan's membership in the Baghdad Pact led to its isolation in the Arab world with even Saudi Arabia clearly denouncing the Pakistani decision. King Saud was astonished to find that the "Islamic state of Pakistan should accede to those who have joined hands with the Zionist Jews" and called the Baghdad Pact as a "Stab in the heart of the Arab and Muslim states", and urged it "to return to the right path", by withdrawing from the widely unpopular western military pact. The secession of Syria from the United Arab Republic in 1961, Egypt's intervention in North Yemen after the 1962 revolution, US decision to supply offensive weapons to Israel under President Johnson, emergence of Faisal as Saudi King and his emphasis on Pan-Islamism to counter Nasser's Arab nationalism, all these were major issues which impacted India's West Asia policy which had come to be identified as Cairo-centric.

In order to contain Nasser, the US encouraged a Saudi-Iranian-Pak-Turkish alliance since 1964. Soon Riyadh termed India as an aggressor in the 1965 Indo-Pak war and warned New Delhi not to take undue advantage of its close ties with the Arabs. Egypt's defeat in the 1967 war with Israel and Nasser's death in September 1970 pushed Riyadh as the leading Arab State influencing the politics and foreign policies of several Arab states. Soon they took interest in the establishment of the Organization of the Islamic Conference in May 1971. For India the 1969 Rabat Islamic conference over Al Aqsa mosque in Jerusalem gave a jolt to Indian diplomacy in the Arab world. After having been officially invited to participate in the conference at Saudi intervention, Pakistan staged a walk out from the conference due to the presence of the Indian delegation. This event evoked sharp criticism from several political parties in India. For India it had become obvious that Pakistan would use the Islamic gatherings to denounce India and raise the issue of Kashmir, along with its declaration of world Islamic solidarity. So far India had come to establish close ties with secular nationalist Arab states like Egypt, Algeria, Syria, Iraq, Libya and Palestinians. In the light of new regional developments, India had to reorient its policy from one of heavy reliance on Cairo to other power centres which had emerged in the Gulf area. [13]

Israel's refusal to withdraw from occupied Arab lands pushed Egypt and Syria to launch the 1973 October war. India supported the Arab military initiative and declared that the cause of tension in the area is due to Israeli aggression and refusal to vacate lands occupied by armed force. India joined other countries in demanding immediate implementation by Israel of UN Security Council Resolution's Articles 242 and 338. Israel's refusal to withdraw from Arab lands made several of Israeli supporters to abandon it just before and after the 1973 Arab-Israeli Conflict and the subsequent oil embargo by the Arabs against USA and other supporters of Israel. India did not have to make such utterly opportunistic changes in its policy towards the Arabs for the sake of oil. The Arab states due to India's unequivocal support for the Arab and Palestinian causes assured New Delhi uninterrupted supply of oil and treated India as a "friend". Thus, India due to its consistent support to the Arab causes was assured abundant oil supply.

Moreover, India's policy opened significant possibilities for Indian exports. It soon led to a large presence of Indian workers in the Gulf area. So far India's economic ties were mainly with Egypt, Iraq and Sudan and at a low key with other Arab States. However, after 1973, India's economic, political contacts widened with the oil rich Arab Gulf States. This partly alleviated India's balance of payment situation caused due to increase in oil prices.

The 70's and 80's saw India's ties growing with Gulf states as India began to import its oil requirements from them, growing remittances from Indian workers, exports and investments became important. All these issues brought India and the Gulf States closer. The outcome of the 1973 war convinced Sadat that in the prevailing international situation a limited success in the war was the maximum that Arabs could achieve and he visualized that only through diplomacy the Arab Israel Conflict could be solved. He calculated that the US alone could compel Israel to vacate Arab lands hence his famous saying that 99 percent of the cards in the Arab Israel Conflict are with the US. This led to peace treaty with Israel in March 1979 ending thirty years of armed confrontation with Israel. India's response to the Camp David accords war "uncritical but guarded". In fact, New Delhi did not openly endorse or condemn the accords. One reason cited for the incoherent Indian response was the Egyptian factor. Although India wanted to steer clear out of any intra-Arab disputes but New Delhi still valued friendship with Cairo and all efforts were directed towards preventing Egypt's suspension from Non-Alignment Movement at Havana NAM Summit. Earlier the emergence of Janata party in 1977 raised the question of a review in India's Arab policy. This was mainly due to A. B. Vajpayee of the Jan Sangh becoming the Minister of External Affairs, who had been a vocal critic of India's support to the "Arabs and who advocated close ties with Israel".

It was during this period that Israeli leader Moshe Dayan paid a secret visit to India in August 1977. Unfortunately for Israel Dayan achieved nothing concrete as Prime Minister Morarji Desai refused to establish diplomatic ties with Israel unless the latter withdrew from all Arab lands. He told Dayan that if he establishes ties, his government would collapse. To the surprise of Israelis, A.B. Vajpayee reiterated India's traditional policy towards Arabs when he said: "there is no change in India's stand. Israel must vacate all occupied Arab territories and the legitimate rights of the Palestinian people must be restored".

Since then up to 1992 successive Indian governments highlighted the absence of ties with Israel as an indication of support to the Arabs. The outbreak of war between two major NAM members Iran and Iraq in September 1980 was a cause for deep concern to India. Of particular significance to India was the fact that both were New Delhi's major suppliers of crude oil supplying about 75 percent of Indian oil imports. In addition many Indians were working in several projects sending remittances. Indian policy makers feared major powers involvement in yet another conflict in the Gulf area where developments related to security and instability had a direct bearing on India's security. India as Chairman of NAM did try hard to find a solution of the Iran-Iraq war but without success. Non-involvement in internal or intra-regional disputes has been an integral part of India's West Asia policy and it applied to Iran-Iraq as well, though in fact both sought India's support against the adversary which India found hard to provide.

On surface, India was strictly neutral but friendly ties with Iraq gave a certain tilt towards Baghdad. India's inability to mediate in the war exposed the inadequacy of Indian diplomacy in the region. Much to the dismay of India, towards the end of the Gulf war, great power naval presence substantially increased in the Gulf area and in seas surrounding India which assumed large dimensions in the wake of the 1990-91 Iraq-Kuwait crisis. The Soviet withdrawal from Afghanistan and the disintegration of USSR together with the end of the Cold War and the emergence of Pax Americana in West Asia initiated a gradual but necessary change in India's policy towards the region while at the same time continuing its basic policy. It can be said that it is now much more realistic as well as practical in terms of its objectives. In the wake of the 1990-91 Kuwait crises and the Madrid Peace Conference which was held in October 1991, India decided to establish diplomatic ties with Israel on 29 January 1992 under the Congress government led by P.V. Narasimha Rao.

Things changed dramatically after 1991 when Arabs and Israelis decided to sit down and negotiate their problems. With this new development India was encouraged to break the ice with Israel, the Jewish state was no more a pariah as before. There were also major changes as far as Palestine Liberation Organization was concerned. After Arafat appeared before the UN in 1974 and Palestine Liberation Organization was recognized by Arab states at Rabat, the Palestine Liberation Organization went on a peace offensive under Egyptian influence after it moved to Tunis in 1982-83 when Israel invaded Lebanon. In 1988 Arafat accepted UN Security Council Resolution's Article 242 and renounced violence and recognized Israel. After the 1991 Madrid conference and the Oslo Peace accords of September 1993 many expected Israel to withdraw from Arab lands leading to final peace between Israel and its neighbours and the formation of a Palestinian state.

However, the assassination of Israeli Prime Minister Rabin in November 4, 1995 and the emergence of Netanyahu and Sharon led to the collapse of peace with Israel. Many have accused Arafat of rejecting Israeli peace offers at Camp David (July 2000). Although Arafat was willing to concede 77 percent of historic Palestine and wanted Israel to withdraw from the 23 percent of Palestine i.e. Gaza, West Bank and East Jerusalem, Israel only offered Gaza and parts of West Bank and refused to remove the Jewish settlements, rejected the right to return of the Palestinian refugees and reiterated its stand that Jerusalem will remain the eternal and undivided capital of Israel. Moreover, it continued the building of its apartheid security wall in West Bank and said its control over water resources in West Bank will remain absolute. Meanwhile, Israel reoccupied Palestinian lands in March 2002 carried out indiscriminate arrests, killings, curfew, house demolitions humiliating check points so on.

The result has been that deprivation, destruction and death rained on the Palestinians. Palestinian suicide bombings against Israelis and the Jewish state's excessive use of force continued. Arafat was seen as an obstacle to peace and Israel painted him in the darkest colours since the Al Aqsa intifada in September 2000. The result was US President Bush and his neo-con dominated team refused to meet and deal with Arafat whom he described as an obstacle to peace. If Arafat had accepted US-Israeli proposals at Camp David he would have become the hero eligible for another Nobel Prize. But Arafat avoided violent end to his life by rejecting the proposals and remained largely popular among the Palestinians. Soon Sharon projected Arafat as a terrorist. Under the circumstances the US and UK were telling others that the road to peace in Palestine runs through Baghdad. Iraqi Weapons of Mass Destruction's and the toppling of Saddam regime became priority for Bush. The result was US invasion of Iraq in March 2003.

Israel had bombed Iraqi nuclear reactor in May 1981 and since then Israeli policy had been to destroy Baathist Iraq which was perceived as a threat to Israeli security. Soon after the US invasion and occupation of Iraq, the Quartet–the US,

European Union, UN and Russia announced the Roadmap for Peace between Israel and Palestine calling for a "Viable and independent Palestine". Sharon raised 14 objections to the plan and the US insisted on political reforms in the Palestinian Authority. Arafat appointed Mahmoud Abbas and subsequently Ahmed Qoreai as Prime Minister but Israel continued its policy of relentless killings of Palestinians in the Gaza and West Bank, demolition of houses, confiscation of land and construction of Jewish settlements on Palestinian land. Hamas and Islamic Jihad and young Palestinians took to violence in the aftermath of such an Israeli attitude. The death of Arafat in November 2004 and the election of Mahmoud Abbas as Palestine Authority's President on January 9, 2005, together with heavy resistance in Iraq to US occupation, growing anti-Americanism sweeping the Arab-Muslim world, should have made the US put pressure on Israel to implement the Road Map for peace. Unfortunately, until the very end the Bush administration supported Israel and showed its utter helplessness in forcing Israel to implement the UN Resolutions and the several peace plans to alleviate the sufferings of the Palestinians. In the face of universal support to the Palestinians the US remains the only major power to support Israel's military occupation and monstrous policies towards them (Pasha, 1999).

To sum up, even though India opposed the partition of Palestine by the UN in 1947 but Nehru recognized Israel in September 1950. But ever since India's decision to establish diplomatic ties with Israel in 1992, Indo-Israeli ties in military, intelligence and economic spheres have improved quite rapidly, especially during the BJP-led National Democratic Alliance when there was even talk of a strategic alliance with the Jewish state. The common "war on terror' and great deal of talk about Hindu-Jewish common values and ancient ties gave Indo-Israeli collaboration under the BJP a distinct ideological and communal direction. No wonder Israel has become India's largest supplier of arms and one of its largest trading partners in Asia. Moreover, Israeli Prime Minister Ariel Sharon visited India on September 9, 2003 and talked about his determination to act against terror and called for greater Indian support to Israel in UN and NAM for Iraqi Weapons of Mass Destruction. Although India was keen to join the Arab-Israeli peace process after the Madrid (1991) Peace Conference but this did not survive for long. India more recently was also excluded from the 2003 Road Map of the Quartet.

Mahmood Abbas has visited India several times since May 2005 and India has given over ₹ 65 crore in aid for infrastructure projects in Palestine including the building of a library-cum-activity centre at the Palestinian Technical College at Deir al Balah and one at the Al Azhar University in Gaza. India has been offering scholarships to Palestinian students for studies in Indian universities through the Indian Council for Cultural Relations (ICCR) as well as giving training in security to Palestinian police officers. Medicine and other humanitarian aid has also been going regularly to the Palestinians. India has reiterated its support to the Palestinian struggle for self-determination and also called for an end to violence.

Fully aware that the UPA (United Progressive Alliance) government led by the Congress Party is as keen as the NDA to consolidate its ties with Israel, cemented by a steady stream of ministerial visits and growing arms purchases, Abbas confirmed that India's ties with Israel were its own bilateral affair. Nonetheless the visits of Abbas and other Palestinian leaders could have been used to expose Israeli policies against Palestinians and a firm call issued to end Israeli occupation in a time bound schedule. Notwithstanding the so-called "enlightened self-interest", India's *de facto* support for continued Israeli occupation is perceived as not in harmony with its widely acclaimed anti-colonial policy of the past. Israeli policies especially the construction of settler-only (Jewish-only) by-pass roads on the West Bank is nothing short of what the South African racist and apartheid regime pursued.

India cannot and should not maintain silence over such monstrous Israeli policies. There is no doubt that the Palestine issue remains widely popular in India with overwhelming support from all sections of Indians for an early end to the misery and sufferings of the Palestinians. Many Indians see the continuing violence in Palestine mainly due to the oppressive Israeli policies. Although India is keen to join the Arab-Israeli peace process but it has become imperative to coordinate its efforts with Russia, China and the regional states like Egypt, Turkey, Saudi Arabia and others. But with India taking a "less strident position against Israel in the UN forums much to the chagrin of the Palestinians" and having "made considerable attempts to moderate anti-Israeli resolutions" at the NAM meetings in Durban, South Africa and elsewhere, it is obvious that the expectations of many especially in the Arab and Islamic world that the Congress led UPA government would restore the balance it had pursued in its policy towards West Asia earlier remains largely elusive.

Any contention that Israel is a major arms supplier to India and hence the government should soft pedal any firm stand against Israel will affect India's credibility not only in the Islamic world but also on the global stage. As an urgent humanitarian task India should work to lift the Israeli boycott or seigeof Gaza and the unfair financial sanctions by the US and Israel on the Palestinians who are being deprived of the basic necessities of life. India in order to regain genuine global respect must not only continue to support wholeheartedly the Palestine cause and work with other interested states to bring about complete end to Israeli occupation but also ensure justice is given to the Palestinians.

Actually one wonders what prevents India from taking the diplomatic initiative along with like-minded states in resolving this conflict especially when it has good relations with both the US and Israel. Surely India can take the initiative with Russia, China and the European Union in opposing Israel's illegal settlements and Apartheid Wall and jointly take a forthright position that would surely make it much more difficult for Israel to avoid reaching an acceptable and just solution based on UN and other relevant resolutions. This should be done sooner than later as any delay in resolving the Palestinian-Israeli issue will positively lead to more violence and instability in a crucial area where Indian interests are growing especially economic energy. The US occupation of Iraq and Afghanistan and the fierce resistance will only make these two states the magnet and training ground for Islamists from all over the world.

It might become a more dangerous place than Somalia. Since Iraqi oil is going to last at least for 50 years and with growing US demand for oil, Iraqi oil is indispensable for the US. So far the US used to get its job done in the Arab world through Israel, now both Israel and the US have decided to work in tandem to rearrange the whole West Asian region according to their strategic needs. As Lord Curzon said, which ever states dominates the Arab world or West Asia it will be in a position to influence India is coming true. Pax Americana and Israeli domination of the region should be a wake up call for India to devise new policies to prevent fragmentation, violence, wars, instability and terrorism which is spreading fast in the Arab world and whose impact will be surely felt in India and broader South Asia as well. [14]

West Asia and Oil Crisis

West Asia in general and Gulf region in particular has seen over the last thirty plus years several wars and perpetual instability. The implications flowing from the 1973 Arab Israeli war and the oil embargo imposed by Organization of Arab Petroleum Exporting Countries (OAPEC) on US and its allies to force Israel to withdraw from Arab lands captured in the 1967 war are still being felt. The oil shortage and sudden price increase led to supply disruptions. The Arab oil embargo lasted for nearly six months and the loss of oil supplies was estimated at 4.4 million barrel per day. Barely had the world recovered oil supplies were again disrupted due to the 1979 Iranian revolution for about six months with a loss of about 3.7.million barrels per day. The subsequent Iran-Iraq war which continued for eight long years not only disrupted oil supplies from two major oil producers but also pushed oil prices from US$ 14 to 35 per barrel. Then followed the Iraqi invasion of Kuwait in August 1990, and soon UN embargo was imposed on Iraqi oil supplies. Of course, Kuwait was able to resume its oil supplies soon after its liberation in early 1991, but the invasion, war and UN sanctions pushed oil prices to record levels.

All the above crises in the Gulf region which disrupted oil supplies and led to increase in oil prices were related to US policies in the region especially linked to its support to Israel and the Arab autocratic regimes. The 1973 oil crisis pushed India's oil bill by over fifty percent. The Iranian revolution and the Iran-Iraq war also affected India's economy both by disruption of oil supplies and hike in oil prices. During 1990, Kuwait had agreed to sell India about 1.5 million tones of oil and Iraq 6.25 million tones, which included about 4.5 million tones that Iraq was transferring to India on behalf of the USSR against rupee payment. Before Iraqi invasion of Kuwait, India had received only half the oil from the total of about 7.75 million tones and it's was difficult for India to procure the rest. Moreover, increase in oil prices in the international spot market increased from about US$ 16-17 per barrel in July 1990 to over US$ 35 per barrel which upset India's economy. According to one estimate the direct overall adverse impact of the 1990 Iraq-Kuwait crisis on India's balance of payments was estimated at ₹ 5,180 crore.

According to another conservative estimate, India lost nearly US$ 3 billion in foreign exchange alone. This includes US$ 2.36 billion as extra import of oil; US$ 200 million to evacuate Indians from Gulf; US$ 200 million as loss of exports to Iraq and Kuwait and about US$ 200 million as loss of remittances sent by Indian workers from both the countries.

India (for 2002-2003) has needed about 110 million tones of oil of which only about 32 million tones was produced domestically. India imports oil from about 30 countries, but it imports about 75 percent from five countries; Saudi Arabia, Nigeria, UAE, Kuwait and Iran. India imports over 72 percent of its oil needs from the Gulf region alone. India's oil demand is expected to grow by over five percent annually from 2.4 million barrels per day in 2003 to 6 million barrels/day in 2025. India's Planning Commission's estimates are that oil import dependence could go up to between 90-93 percent of oil demand in 2031-32 from the current level. As seen before India's domestic oil production is gradually declining. India's import of oil and products costs the economy over ₹ One lakh crore and imports from Gulf Cooperation Council countries alone is over US$ 20 billion. As seen above any disruption of oil supplies or increase in oil prices due to uncertain situation in the Gulf region will adversely affect Indian economy both in the short and long term. Nearly five million Indians are gainfully employed in the Gulf Cooperation Council states alone who send over US$ 28 billion annually as remittances.

Not only this foreign exchange is important but the safety and security of Indian workers is of uppermost concern for Indian governments. The minority government of V.P. Singh in 1990 was mainly concerned with the evacuation of more than lakh Indian citizens from Kuwait and about 25,000 from Iraq. Mounting public pressure as also the decision of Members of Parliament from Kerala to sit on hunger strike at the Parliament House on 16 August 1990 to protest against the "inaction of the government regarding the plight of Indians" in both the Gulf states also forced the V.P. Singh government to accord the safe evacuation of Indians top priority.

This was one of the crucial reasons why India did not condemn the Iraqi invasion and occupation of Kuwait as it could have adversely affected the evacuation of Indians from the Gulf. US-Israeli policies in the West Asian region and more particularly US support to authoritarian regimes has, allowed Islamic groups to grow but this is also allowing these groups to use the Palestine issue to resort to greater violence. Growing US military presence in the region as also control of oil resources and blind US support to Israel is leading to religious extremism and most resort to terror not only against the US but also against US allies in the region. Since bulk of the Indian workers live and work in GCC states which are slow in initiating genuine democratic reforms and where US influence is predominant, hence some Indians are likely to be influenced due to mounting religious extremism preached by religious groups thereby impacting India's secular domestic stability.

The Gulf region is equally important to India in terms of trade especially exports (about 16 percent of India's total valued at over US$ 100 billion) which fetch us valuable foreign exchange. Investments from the Gulf-both official and private are also significant for the Indian economy. US domination of the Gulf region is slowly elbowing India out from the region as witnessed by sanctions(and now chaos) in Iraq, Iran, so on which has led to reduced trade, winding up of joint ventures, return of Indian workers, and declining investments from the region. India should actively encourage the process of political change and modernization because once the Gulf regimes become democratic and responsive to popular demands, not only their legitimacy would be enhanced but their absolute and abject dependence on US would be reduced.

This would lead to reduction in US military presence and thereby maintain security and stability so very essential to protect India's vital interests as also contain the growing violence in this volatile region from spreading to India in future. But in India there is growing concern about the religious extremist groups in the Gulf Cooperation Council states targeting Indian workers due to developments in Iraq and elsewhere in the region as also due to India's close proximity to the United States and Israel and now strain in

Indo-Iranian ties due to India's votes against Iran at the IAEA (International Atomic Energy Agency) on the nuclear issue. This has divided the country's public and the UPA government is under pressure to support Iran due to India's energy predicament. All the efforts towards Iran-India-Pakistan gas pipeline appear to have been undermined. Undoubtedly, US opposition to the above pipeline due to its hostile policy towards Iran and massive presence in the Gulf region are contributory reasons. [15]

As seen earlier in certain Arab countries, Islamic parties have gained substantial seats in legislature or come to share power through democratic process but such groups have also learnt how to be responsible and accountable. It is far easier to control terrorism and religious extremism in liberal democratic political systems which have high level of legitimacy and strong domestic control than the present political set up where the rulers want to remain in total control of all state affairs. The long over due change has now become inevitable but if its not coming soon internal and regional violence may be directed against such autocratic regimes unwilling or unable to initiate meaningful reforms. Instability, religious extremism and terrorism could spill over into South Asia as security and stability in both the regions are mutually interlinked through a number of factors. The most credible option to tackle this twin menace which is posing a new challenge to India's composite culture, liberal democratic structures and also national security is to adopt a political course that prevents alienation of any segment of the population especially religious minorities-so that they do not take recourse to unlawful activities or violence.

Thus, instability, religious extremism, border conflicts, Arab-Israeli tension over Palestine, authoritarian regimes in control of affairs and US support to them is complicating factors for India's energy security. In the States, democracy has become a victim of a political process in which legitimacy and consensus politics are truly wanting. Under such circumstances dissent is seen as unacceptable. The concept of a loyal opposition is not even known in Gulf Cooperation Council states. Suspicion, paranoia, fear of assassination and of being overthrown are leading to expulsion, assassination, repression, incarceration, including torture and in some cases execution of dissenters under fake trials. To a very large extent this sad state of affairs is also due to the ongoing Arab-Israeli conflict. More and more people in the Gulf now believe that their governments due to the authoritarian nature of the political system and also under US influence cannot do anything to relieve their humiliation and improve their lot. Hence, the emergence of Islamic groups which employ violence and suicide bombings.

Moreover the secular groups also follow this strategy under popular support. One writer says, "suicide bombings take root because they free the desperate from the need to rely on governments. Rather than being sponsored by states, this form of violence challenges states." Al Qaeda and other religious groups may be ultimately contained but newer groups would emerge and may follow their methods. Lack of democracy and suppression of political opposition invariably drives people to join Islamic groups and repression alone cannot eliminate terrorism. "Any successful counter-terrorism strategy must thus address both the opportunities available to militants and the level of their motivation"(Pasha, 2000, 1995).

The External and Regional Factors

There is clearly no doubt US-Israeli policies in the West Asia are undermining peace, security and stability leading to periodic threats of military intervention or wars or to prop up threatened fragile regimes against their own population who are demanding political participation. US invasion and occupation of Iraq and the continued instability or the fear of split in many parts of Iraq, in addition to US accusations of Iranian interference in Iraqi affairs is used by the US to put pressure on Iran to cease its ideas and programs. This has also put pressure on Indo-Iranian ties. US attempts to reshape Afghan affairs to increase Pakistani influence also strains Indo-Pak and Indo-Iranian ties. US determination to stay in Iraq and its attempts to put pressure on Iran for regime change is partly linked to help project its power into Central Asia, due to the oil and gas reserves.

From the Indian perspective increasing bilateral ties with West Asian states is not only important due to trade, oil and gas, but also due to the unique proximity of these states to events in Afghanistan, Central Asia, and the Gulf region. The common political and strategic concerns of India and these states will reinforce and strengthen mutual cooperation. Some perceive that if India in cooperation with the US, reassures the Gulf Cooperation Council states of its desire to work for peace, security and stability in the region, outside interference could be contained, which many perceive to be the root cause of much of the problems which India and the Gulf Cooperation Council states face. 1990s saw the reassertion of regional identities in the face of external interference. The critical space is widening and it is in this context that India and Gulf Cooperation Council states can create opportunities for mutual benefit and jointly prepare to meet emerging domestic and external challenges in the Gulf region. Instability in the region poses a greater threat than ever before, as India's reliance on Gulf oil is growing. Although the issue of terrorism is also important and imported arms from Israel are vital for India's security, there is no need for India to place undue emphasis on bilateral relations between India and Israel as the National Democratic Alliance leadership did.

The United Progressive Alliance (UPA) government's Common Minimum Program stated that it will maintain the independence of India's foreign policy stance on all regional and global issues even as it pursues closer strategic and economic engagement with the US. But the reality is that in the context of Gulf, US policy is actually affecting India. Pax-Americana in West Asia has serious implications for India. US control of Gulf oil may in the future affect our quest for energy security, especially as India imports over 70 percent of its oil from outside especially the Gulf. US support to undemocratic regimes in the region is encouraging the Islamic groups to use violence in the face of reluctance of the rulers to initiate political reforms. The security and future of Indian workers in the region in the wake of continued wars and instability has become an issue of concern. Peace, security and stability in the region are crucial for India's own security and prosperity and these calls for new initiatives, dynamism and recognition of the traditionally close historical relationship with the Islamic world. India's economic ties are unlikely to suffer with these states in the immediate future, but one needs to be cautious in developing closer ties with Israel until the process of reconciliation gets under way between the Arabs, especially Palestinians and Israelis. The UPA coalition should attempt to balance the traditionally close ties with the West Asian states with Israel.

Security and stability in the region is linked with early resolution of the Iraq crisis, (withdrawal of US forces) establishment of a viable Palestinian state and encouraging political reforms and democratization which alone can contain the growing slide towards religious resurgence, violence and terrorism leading to instability in the region. But what we witnessed recently are record oil prices of over US$ 150 per barrel. US policies to put pressure on Syria and Iran and the 2006 Israeli invasion of Lebanon and Gaza 2008-09 have made the situation much worse. Although oil prices have come down lately but undoubtedly the region is gradually sliding towards religious extremism, ethnic hatred and growing sectarian animosities which are bound to affect peace, security, stability in the entire West Asian region. [16]

New Challenges from West Asia

Any disruption of oil supplies or increase in oil price due to uncertain situation in the Gulf will adversely affect not only the Indian economy but global economy both in the short and long term. US-Israeli policies in the wake of occupation of Iraq and attacks on Lebanon and more particularly US support to authoritarian regimes has, allowed Islamic groups to grow but this is also allowing these groups to use the Palestine issue in order to resort to greater violence. US talk of further fragmentation of the area into smaller states based on sectarianism and ethnicity and the emergence of so-called Shia crescent is likely to further destabilize the already volatile region. India should help the Gulf Cooperation Council states in establishing the elections commissions, train officials for elections, help in drafting electoral laws, preparing constituencies, and prepare mechanism to resolve electoral disputes, supply stationery for elections so on. Also there are a number of rules and regulations needed to initiate the electoral process and India can assist the Gulf Cooperation Council states. The fact that these are essentially Islamic states and 'Sharia' has to be complied, needs to be kept in mind while devising electoral support structures.

This would lead to reduction in US military presence and thereby maintain security and stability so very essential to protect India's vital interests as also contain the growing violence in this volatile region from spreading to India in future. The big question is: Are the Gulf Cooperation Council monarchies willing to share power with their own people and reduce their dependence on US? The other question is: will the US allow them to become truly democratic and independent from US influence. The area of armed resistance to US-Israeli policies has only widened with violence spreading to new areas in the region. US and Israel would like to tackle the peripheral groups first before launching all-out attacks on Iran and Syria-two states still holding out in West Asia-a region which has largely been subjugated to US-Israeli domination. The developments in Iraq especially growing violence and sectarianism are pushing the country (until recently secular) towards religious chaos and perhaps fragmentation. US pressure on Iran may lead to greater violence in Iraq. If US or Israel attacks Iran, Tehran may retaliate on oil tankers in the Gulf or Strait of Hormouz. Oil terminals, platforms may also become vulnerable thereby pushing oil prices. If violence spreads in the Gulf region, Indian workers in the Gulf Cooperation Council states may have to be evacuated from some places. India should prepare contingency plans to move the workers to nearby safe places.

In this effort India may need Iran's assistance. India must also keep an eye of the impact of religious groups preaching extremism on Indian workers. US ability to dictate terms to India on our energy security like its doing in the case of Iran and Syria are bound to increase in future. As the US pressure on Iran mounts, Tehran will urge the Gulf Cooperation Council states to remove or reduce US presence like bases and troops. India need not share Iran's view on this issue entirely but actively work to have autonomy for Iran and the Gulf Cooperation Council states. India's energy needs are growing and everything possible has to be done to have the closest ties with oil producers in West Asia. This has become vital for India's growth and prosperity. Of course India must have good ties with the US but her policy in West Asia should be autonomous of US and not subservient to the dictates of the dominant power in the region. After 9/11, it has become obvious that some countries in West Asia are looking to the East especially Saudi Arabia and they find India an attractive partner in some areas. India should extend support to such countries which are willing to stand up to US hegemony as the US doctrine of pre-emption is likely to destabilize the region still further. US domination is clearly restricting the role of India and the room for autonomous engagements is narrowing. Under the notion of unlimited war on terror the US is justifying its military intervention to contain terrorism.

All of this is mounting pressure on the states in the region as also on India. Not only the West Asian rulers have become nervous due to US incited developments but despair and discontent among the unemployed youth in the region is also mounting. India should quietly urge the leaders in the region to move ahead with democratic reforms leading to political participation in the decision making process, thereby enhancing regime legitimacy. This will help reduce the Arab regime's dependence on outside powers, and tackle the dependency syndrome. It is clear that most regimes are going through severe loss of sovereignty and threat of disintegration, civil war and identity crisis. While continuing the fight against terror, problems like Israeli occupation of Arab lands and ending US occupation of Iraq and other local concerns need to be urgently addressed. [17]

Adoption of India's Proactive Approach

Is there need for greater Indian interest and initiative in the Gulf area so as to ensure peace, security and stability in the region? Indian interests in the Gulf include safety and security of Indian migrant workers residing in the Gulf Cooperation Council states, and continued supply of oil and gas from the region. Besides, political stability is a precondition to ensure mutual cooperation through trade, aid and investment opportunities in the region. From the strategic point of view both India and Iran can work towards reducing the role of non-regional states whose policies, especially those of the US and Israel, are undermining peace, security and stability leading to periodic threats of military intervention or to prop up threatened fragile regimes against their own population who are demanding political participation. US occupation of Iraq and the continued instability in many parts of Iraq, and US pressure on Iran are putting pressure on Indo-Iranian ties. US determination to stay in Iraq and its attempts to put pressure on Iran for regime change is partly linked to help project its power into Central Asia for energy and to contain Russia and China. Gulf Cooperation Council states and India face the menace of terrorism and religious extremism and the need to combat such forces has assumed urgency.

A modest beginning has been made for cooperation in the field of security with some of the Gulf Cooperation Council states like Qatar and Saudi Arabia, which has a rich potential field ahead. Many also emphasize the need to fulfil the growing aspirations of the Gulf people to play a greater role in the sphere of political participation and decision making process. Political systems which allow more space for civil society and work for enhancing their legitimacy would prove to be more enduring as also develop stake in peace and stability. Of course, outside support will continue to be a major factor in Gulf politics but it is internal support which will eventually decide the final outcome especially major issues concerning peace, security and stability. So far Indian diplomacy has been fairly successful in containing the negative impact flowing from domestic issues on India's relations with the Gulf Cooperation Council states but things are rapidly changing in the region. Lest we become complacent, there is urgent need to do hard thinking how best to keep our house in order and not give others the chance/opportunity to harm our interests. It would be foolhardy to assume that things would remain the same despite serious developments domestically and that any disturbance of status quo would hurt the Gulf Cooperation Council more than India.

We must be vigilant and not allow domestic developments in India to get out of hand due to electoral politics and posturing and allow outsiders to interfere in our domestic affairs. The key factor driving its policy is India's quest for energy security. Despite global search for oil/gas resources, the focus remains on the Gulf region to ensure adequate supplies to sustain its high economic growth. As seen earlier, this region has become an important foreign exchange earning zone from the standpoint of growing trade, workers remittances, and investment opportunities and tourism. One can notice numerous steps being taken both by India and the Gulf Cooperation Council to strengthen bilateral ties in all of these areas. All the Gulf Cooperation Council states have security agreements with the United States and some NATO members and with their consent the presence of United State troops and a huge naval fleet in the region. As new threats emerge in the Gulf region which would destabilize the area it is imperative for India to further engage all the states in the region on a regular basis and at a much broader level. It would be in the long term interest of India to have a balanced relationship with all the Gulf States. Any over-identification with one group of states is not in our long term interest. Of course there are bound to be pulls and pressures between US and Gulf Cooperation Council and Iran and India.

However, an independent Indian approach has much greater chance to broaden and deepen our relationship with the Gulf States. In this connection India should quietly but forcefully urge the leaders in the Gulf region to move ahead with gradual but meaningful democratic reforms leading to political participation. At the same time India must also keep in touch with some of the civil groups advocating democratization in the Gulf Cooperation Council states. We must keep in mind European Union's example of allowing groups from the Gulf which propagate democratization of the Gulf Cooperation Council regimes. It is obvious that most Gulf Cooperation Council regimes are going through severe loss of sovereignty and some even threat of disintegration, civil war and identity crisis. Outside support to religious minorities, ethnic groups and to members of former ruling families is becoming sharper in the Gulf region. Should India be unaware of these momentous developments which have a direct bearing on its future interaction with this vital region? While continuing the fight against terror, and focusing on problems like ending Israeli occupation of Arab lands and US occupation of Iraq among many other local concerns, we need to constantly review our policies emerging from a strategic and volatile area and explore new ways of overcoming the mounting constraints which need to be addressed with a sense of urgency. [18]

Due to its duplicitous policy in the region the US stands accused of fomenting wars leading to instability and insecurity. Shielding Israel, with its nuclear arsenal and targeting Iran will raise several crucial issues. US-Israeli policies of invasions, assassinations, bombings, massacres, torture are creating fertile ground for extremist's violence and growth of religious groups and terrorism. US-Israeli occupations in Palestine, Afghanistan and Iraq have to be ended soon so as to spare the region from more suicide attacks, bloodshed and destruction with obvious implications on India. Instead of making amends to its policy, the US plans to stay in Iraq for long years. Growing corporate interests will compel the US not to abandon Iraq, despite sharp rise in the world price of oil. Also the US appears in a strange way to be preparing to say that whatever needs to be done should be done on Iraqi terms to bring order to a chaotic state. To conclude, we need to keep in mind three facts.

Firstly, despite US pressure on India not to go ahead with the gas pipeline project with Iran via Pakistan, India should not give up this important energy security project. India failed to support Mossadeq in 1953 and we have seen the consequences in the Gulf since 1979 when the Shah was toppled. India should do everything to prevent an invasion or attack on Iran either by the US or Israel. In future Iran could be very useful to our interests in Central Asia, Afghanistan, Gulf and even Pakistan. As the Iranian Ambassador to India said: "any Israeli attack on nuclear facilities of Iran would be devastate countries of the west region as well. India's relationship with Iran is also vital for Iraq and stability in the Gulf region. President Mubarak of Egypt was awarded the 1995 Nehru Award for International Understanding in 1997 but he could visit India only in 2008 to take the award. Why? The answer probably lies in India's pro-Israeli tilt which has become a burden and its high time India pursues a more vigorous policy to strengthen its relations with the Arabs in Gulf and West Asia in general. Peace, security and stability in West Asia are crucial for India's own security and prosperity and these calls for new initiatives, dynamism and recognition of the traditionally close historical relationship with the Islamic world.

Secondly, many expected the Congress led UPA government to follow a balanced policy between Israel and the Muslim states. Contrary to this, not only defence, security ties with Israel are growing but India by launching an Israeli spy satellite to track activities in Iran and the region is perceived differently and negatively by the Iranians and Arabs. Moreover as the CPI (M) mentioned UPA's "collaboration" and "shameful silence" over Israeli "criminal" blockade of Gaza strip is harmful to India's interests.

Lastly, Indian Ambassador Ronen Sen to US is right when he said India and US cannot be "allies in the traditional military sense" and are more of "strategic partners" given their cooperation in diverse areas. India's purchase of six C-130 J Hercules planes for $ 1 billion will be useful to evacuate Indian workers from the Gulf Cooperation Council states in emergency. India's PM has visited some Gulf Cooperation Council states like Oman, Qatar and Saudi Arabia to further strengthen ties with them. From the Indian perspective increasing bilateral ties with Gulf States is not only important due to trade, oil and gas, but also due to the unique proximity of these states to events in the wider West Asia-North Africa (WANA) region. The common political and strategic concerns of India and these Gulf states will reinforce and strengthen mutual cooperation. Given the close Gulf Cooperation Council -US relations as also growing Indo-US ties, if India in cooperation with the US and others vitally interested in Gulf security, works out a harmonious approach which reassures the Gulf states of the need to work for peace, security and stability in the region, outside interference could be contained, which many perceive to be the root cause of much of the problems which India and the Gulf Cooperation Council states face. 1990s saw the reassertion of regional identities in the face of external interference. The critical space is widening and it is in this context that India and Gulf Cooperation Council can create opportunities for mutual benefit and jointly prepare to meet emerging domestic and external challenges in the Gulf region. [19]

Dealing with Iraq Repercussions

The developments in Iraq especially growing violence and sectarianism are pushing the country towards religious chaos and perhaps fragmentation. US pressure on Iran is leading to greater violence in Iraq. Together with the lack of infrastructure, growth of religious groups and their militias and US inability to handle the developments, the implications flowing from Iraq are likely to impact the region as a whole if not beyond. Shia-Sunni tensions are raising in the Gulf Cooperation Council states especially Saudi Arabia, Bahrain and Kuwait, in view of developments in Iraq. India's former special envoy to West Asia Ambassador CR Ghare Khan has already spoken on the spill over of Shia–Sunni acrimony into India. If the US or Israel or both attack Iran on the nuclear issue, Tehran may retaliate by attacking US ships or oil tankers in the Gulf or Strait of Hormouz. Oil terminals and platforms may also become vulnerable thereby leading to oil shortage and which would be pushing oil prices still higher. As the US pressure on Iran mounts, Tehran may redouble its efforts to get Weapons of Mass destruction. [20]

Due to its unique location India has been a central part of the vast net work of ports and harbours and her commercial, maritime, cultural and other links with Indian Ocean region have been intimate and vibrant. As regional groupings increase and free trade areas or customs union multiply there is substantial room to enhance the level of economic interaction, trade, investment and technological flows. As arrangements increase to promote trade and investment and as markets increase, they are creating a growth multiplier effect. It has particularly given a boost to tourism and movement of persons involved as service providers. All of this has meant phenomenal increase in the number of ships, ports, harbours, and maritime traffic. Just to take one example in South East Asia which sits aside some of the world's most critical sea lanes, it is estimated that more than US$ 1.5 trillion worth merchandise trade passed through the narrow Straits of Malacca in 2000, which was nearly half of world's trade, including crucial oil supplies from the Gulf to East Asia. No wonder it is called the international choke point. The other two important international choke points are the Straits of Hormouz at the month of the Gulf from where bulk of the world's oil supplies pass through as also hundreds of cargo ships every day. Bab El Mandeb at the month of the Red Sea is also another significant choke point from where oil tankers and cargo ship from Asia move to Europe and cross the Atlantic via the Red Sea, Suez Canal and the Straits of Gibraltar linking the Mediterranean and the Atlantic.

The collapse of the Somali state structures and its location very close to the Red Sea has increased the vulnerability of ships to attacks by pirates. The attack on an American destroyer USS Cole on 12th October 2000 and French oil tanker Limbourg on 6th October 2002 off the Yemeni coast highlights the dangerous coast it has become for shipping. Actually the first attempt to attack an American ship was made on 3 January 2000 on US Sullivan which had moored in Aden port for refuelling. The attack boat which had been laden with bombs sank before it could attack the US ship. One Islamic group said: "The Aden Islamic Army pledges to destroy US possessions and bases that are being equipped in Socotra, Al-Hudayadah and Aden". Also the recent attack by pirates on a luxury cruise liner off Somalia highlights the need for cooperation on maritime security in the Indian Ocean area.

The US intervened in Somalia but due to heavy losses it withdrew by March 1, 1994.This was seen as proof by Osama bin Laden and his Al Qaeda that they can defeat the US. In an interview with Robert Fisk of the Independent, Osama bin

Laden said: "We believe that God used our holy war in Afghanistan to destroy the Russian army and the Soviet Union…and now we ask God to use us one ore time to do the same to America to make it a shadow of itself. We also believe that our battle against America is much simpler than the war against the Soviet Union, because some of our mujahidin who fought here in Afghanistan also participated in operations against the Americans in Somalia, and they were surprised at the collapse of American morale. This convinced us that the Americans are a paper tiger". To the *Al Jazeera* he said: "Based on the reports we received from our brothers, who participated in the Jihad in Somalia, we learned that they saw weakness, frailty and cowardice of US troops. Only eighteen US troops were killed. Nonetheless, they fled in the heart of darkness, frustrated after they had caused great commotion about a New World Order".

Many foreigners have also been taken as hostages in Yemen lately. More daring was the recent abortive attack on US naval ships in the Gulf of Aqaba from Jordan. The recent escape of the prisoners from a high security prison in Yemen high lights the breakdown of some authority in Yemen. This can be linked to US invasion and occupation of Iraq as the suspects belonged to Iraq based in the Hashemite Kingdom. Although both India and Australia have held naval exercises and political relations are gradually maturing but divergences in approaches to maritime security cooperation persist.

Whereas the conservative government of John Howard has strongly supported the US in the war on terrorism and has sent troops to Iraq and Afghanistan as part of the coalition to stabilize both the countries, India, though equally concerned about terrorism and the spread of religious extremism, has refused to send Indian troops to Iraq and Afghanistan. Of course, it has joined the US in promoting democracy elsewhere. Although India is aware of the Islamic groups in Malaysia, Singapore, Philippines, Indonesia and Thailand which are active, organized and some of them armed but it is sceptical whether they have active links with Al Qaeda of Osama bin Laden and promote international terrorism. In most of these states domestic insurgencies are widespread, cross-border terrorism is growing and Islamic groups have become assertive and better organized due to regional economic disparities. India's growing military cooperation with the US including naval exercises and identification with US project to spread democracy is a completely new element in recent Indian foreign policy. Since India pursued non-aligned policy as also due to past policies of the US with a marked tilt towards Pakistan, joint naval exercises were ruled out.

Now Indian Navy regularly conducts naval exercises not only with Australian and US navies but also Chinese, Russian, Israeli, Omani, Iranian and others. But it is interesting to note that exceptions were made during the Janata Party rule in 1977-78 and later in 1989. Given India's proximity to the oil and gas rich Gulf region and the instability and insecurity coupled with rising religious extremism and terrorism there, new prospects are emerging for cooperation between India, European Union, Australia and the US, especially in the sphere of maritime security in the Indian Ocean and especially in the Red Sea and Persian Gulf area. Due to European Union's support to the US war on terror and also close identification with other western policies, both have been victims of terrorist violence.

Both can co-operate to contain maritime insurgency to acts of piracy and armed robbery on ships. The upsurge in naval activities/attacks should propel the governments to be alert to probable low intensity conflicts, mercenary activities, drug and gun running, hijacking and piracy and take step to contain them. In order to enhance maritime security cooperation both can organize more frequent joint naval exercises involving the US or other navies, coordinated patrols of select vulnerable choke points, and both can consider participation in UN peace-keeping operations like near the Somali-Yemeni Coast, joint naval operations like helping Tsunami victims or earth quake or other natural disaster victims, and also identify new areas of cooperation in maritime security which is fast becoming complex and expensive. As the US spreads its presence in the oil rich Gulf area the resistance and attacks on US are bound to increase especially due to open US support to Israeli policies of oppression of the Palestinians. The Iran nuclear crisis has made it clear that even the US needs the help of Russia and China at the UN Security Council thereby indicating that the world is moving towards a multi polar world in which India will also find its due place soon. [21]

Conclusion

US domination in the Gulf region is mounting pressure on the states in the region as also on SAARC especially India. The Gulf rulers have become nervous due to US-Israeli incited developments but despair and discontent among the unemployed youth in the region is also mounting to take one example of Yemen. After September 11 attack, Gulf States were started to look to the East particularly the South Asian states for great many things including investments and food security. As India has come to establish good ties with all Gulf Cooperation Council states especially more recently with Saudi Arabia this would be useful to solve the long festering Kashmir issue and also the issue of terrorism from Pakistan. Many have said that Kashmiri militants derive inspiration from the unresolved Palestine issue as also the Kashmiri militants accuse Indian government of using Israeli tactics and experience in tackling Palestinian violence to suppress them. The Kashmiri protests which erupted in the summer of 2010 and their suppression by Indian security forces by force in which over 100 civilians were killed was compared to Gaza and Palestine.

Referring to the Kashmiri protests the Pakistani foreign minister at the UN General Assembly had called upon India to hold plebiscite to resolve the problem. Referring to foreign minister S M Krishna's UN speech that India is holding plebiscite in Kashmir every five years (i.e. Assembly Elections), the Peoples Democratic Party (PDP) President Mehbooba Mufti said people have lost faith in the Indian state. "You talked about the Assembly in United Nations but as representatives of this House we feel ashamed to visit people as we have nothing to offer them," she said. "As solidarity with those killed in the Kashmir, we have decided to boycott the entire session". The PDP president compared the "siege" in the Valley with the siege of Gaza by Israel. "A boy was beaten to death here by the forces," she said. "A child had a toffee in his mouth when he was beaten to death and some boys were chased by the police and drowned to death".

This was obviously compared to the high handed Israeli military tactics used against Palestinians in Gaza and West Bank. It need not be mentioned here that the Islamic revolution of Iran grew from Palestine Liberation Organisation training camps in Lebanon. The destruction and huge loss of life in Palestine, Iraq, Afghanistan and elsewhere acts as a magnet for militants' world wide. Many see the USA using wealth from Gulf Cooperation Council states to further its foreign policy objectives and hence friends of the USA are also targeted. Saudi Arabia also has a crucial role to play in Afghanistan along with Pakistan. As new threats emerge in the Gulf region which would destabilize the area as also South Asia it is imperative for India to further engage all the states in the region at a much broader and higher level. It would be in the long term interest of India to have a balanced relationship with all the Gulf States including Iran and Turkey.

Any over-identification with one group of states is not in our long term interest. Just as blind support to Israel has de-stabilized West Asia, US support to Pakistan is hindering greater cooperation in South Asia. Pakistan's old and failed attempt to isolate India in West Asia has not worked and is unlikely to work in future. Sadly, Pakistan continues to paint India in dark colours at international forces particularly UN and Organization of the Islamic Conference (OIC) on violation of human rights and killings in Kashmir, treatment of Indian Muslims and of India being hegemonic in South Asian affairs. Most West Asian states have realized the client status relationship of Pakistan with the US. In view of the setback US has suffered in Iraq and Afghanistan, most states in West Asia as also the US look to India for cooperation to maintain security and stability in the Gulf so essential for trade and suppressing the threat of growing violence or terrorism. Of course there are bound to be pulls and pressures between US and Gulf Cooperation Council and Iran on the one hand and India and the broader SAARC. But an independent Indian approach has much greater chance to broaden and deepen relationship between SAARC and the Gulf States. Outside support to religious minorities, ethnic groups and to members of former ruling families is becoming sharper in the Gulf region. Should India be unaware of these momentous developments which have a direct bearing on its future interaction with this vital energy rich-region?

While continuing the fight against terror, and focusing on problems like ending Israeli occupation of Arab lands and US occupation of Iraq and Afghanistan among many other local concerns, India needs to constantly review its policies emerging from a strategic and volatile area and explore new and dynamic ways of overcoming the mounting constraints which need to be addressed with a sense of urgency. Terrorism and violence will continue to thrive in West Asia as long as injustice prevails in Palestine, Iraq and other areas. These injustices should persuade states to address genuine grievances which terrorists exploit by mindless violence. As David Clark, former British Labour government adviser said: "In each case the terrorists failed in their objective and the authorities conceded no more than what was right and those who indulge in condemnation to the exclusion of everything else have failed to produce a single useful policy prescription" that might deal more effectively with terrorist threat.

It needs to be emphasized that India needs to charter its

energy security policies independent of the US and other Asian powers so as not to compromise its long term energy and security interests. Despite the challenges as discussed above like terrorism, religious extremism, maritime piracy, nuclear Iran, US factor, Arab-Israeli conflict, ambitions of Iran, Iran-Pakistan-India (IPI) gas pipeline, gulf security, Iraq invasion, border conflicts, instability due to dependency syndrome, Pakistan's attempt to isolate India in the region, emerging challenge from China among other factors, it is surely possible for India to strive for good ties not only between West Asian states and SAARC but also with the US and Israel (without of course over-identifying with their agenda in West Asia and elsewhere). Indian diplomacy needs to rise to the occasion as it has both challenges and opportunities in South Asia and also in the energy rich but unstable Gulf region which is after all India's extended neighbourhood. [22]

End Notes

1. The CIA, Saudi and British intelligence organized bomb attacks on a Shia leader accused of complicity in terrorism in Beirut on March 8, 1985. The bomb was placed outside a mosque, timed to explode when Muslim worshippers left. Nora Boustany reported that about 250 girls and women in flowing black chadors, pouring out of Friday prayers at the Imam Reda Mosque, took the brunt of the blast: The bomb also burned babies in their beds, killed children as they walked home from the mosque and devastated the main street of the densely populated West Beirut Suburb Nora Boustany, *Washington Post Weekly,* 14 March 1998, Bob Woodward, (1987). *Veil: The Secret Wars of the CIA, 1981-1987,* New York: Simon and Schuster, 396. For Sheikh Fadlallah's views on *Islam, West and Israel* see chapter 7 in Ibrahim M. Abu Rabi, (1996). (eds.) *Intellectual Origins of Islamic Resurgence in the Modern Arab World,* New York: Albany: State University of New York Press: 220-247. The Hezbollah leader Sheikh Fadlallah Lebanese Shia leader was the target as the CIA saw him connected to all three bombings of US facilities in Beirut. See also Muhammad Muslih, (1992). *History of the Israeli-Palestinian Conflict* in

Elizabeth Warnock Fernea and Mary Evelyn Hocking, (eds.) *Israelis and Palestinians: The Struggle for Peace* Austin: University of Texas Press: 62-74.

2. Israeli Prime Minister Shimon Peres sent Israeli force bombers in Sept-Oct. 1985 to attack PLO activist's houses killing 75 people with smart bombs that tore them to streds. Not only the US cooperated with Israel by failing to warn its ally Tunisia that the Israeli bombers were about to attack Tunis but US Secretary of State George Shultz informed Israeli Foreign Minister Yitzhak Shamir that Washington 'had considerable sympathy for the Israeli action', but drew back when the UNS Council unanimously denounced the Israeli bombing as an 'act of armed aggression'. The US abstained in the vote. For details see *New York Times,* 17,18 October1985, Geoffrey Jansen, *Middle East International*, 11 October 1985; Bernard Gwestzman, *New York Times,* 2 October 1985. Cited in chapter 11, Noam Chomsky, (2002). *Who are the Global Terrorists?* in ken Booth and Time Dunne, (eds.), *Worlds in Collision: Terror and the Future of Global Order*, New York: Palgrave Macmillan:128-137. The 'Iron Fist' policy of Shimon Peres in March 1985 reached new depths of 'calculated brutality and arbitrary murder' as IDF shelled Lebanese villages, carted off the male population, killed dozens of villagers in addition to many massacred by paramilitary associates, shelled hospitals and took patients away for 'interrogation', along with numerous other atrocities. The targets were described as 'terrorist villagers'. The operations against them must continue because the IDF must 'maintain order and security' in occupied Lebanon despite' the price the inhabitants will have to pay: Like Israel's invasion of Lebanon in 1982 in which over 20,000 were killed, this invasion was not for self defence as Begin and Sharon claimed but rather purely for political ends. The same is true of Peres invasion of Lebanon in 1996. According to Noam Chomsky all these Israeli military operations relied crucially on US military and diplomatic support. Accordingly, they too do not enter the annals of international terrorism. Ibid: 131. How the Zionist's used terrors a deliberate strategy against the Palestinians, see Rosemary Sayigh, (1979). *Palestinians: From Peasants to Revolution,* London: Zed Books: 68-77.

3. Ibid: 27. For more details on this see Walid Mahmoud Abdel

Nasser, (1994). *The Islamic Movement in Egypt: Perceptions of International Relations 1967-1981,* London: Kegan Paul International.

4. For details see A.K. Pasha, *Arab Response to Peace Process, World Focus–Palestine Israel Conflict,* Vol. 23, No. 3, March 2002:14-19. See also Bernard Reich, (1995). (ed.) *Arab-Israeli Conflict and Conciliation: A Documentary History,* London: Praeger: 229-262; *The Hindu,* December 15, 2005.
5. Ibid: 178-179, see also Laurie Mylroie, (2001). *The War against America: Saddam Hussein and the World Trade Centre Attacks, Washington:* Reagan Books, Harper Collins, see also A.K. Pasha, (2010). *September 11, 2001 Attack on US and West Asia,* in M. Saleem Kidwai (ed.), *US Policy towards the Muslim World: Focus on Post 9/11 Period,* New York: University Press of America: 77-177.
6. See Riyaz Punjabi and A.K. Pasha, (1998). (eds.) *India and the Islamic World* New Delhi: Radiant Publishers, see also Afsir Karim *Pak sponsored Terrorism, AGNI: Studies in International Strategic Israel,* Vol. 1, No. 2, May-August 2002:81-99; See Phyllis Bennis, (1996). *Calling the Shots: How Washington Dominates Today's UN,* New York: Interlink: 211-230; see also Yonah Alexander, (2002). (ed)*Combating Terrorism: Strategies of Ten Countries*, Ann Arbor: University of Michigan Press: 227-259 and 301-336; see also *Frontline,* vol. 20, No.8, 13-26 April 2002 :20, Claire Sterling,(1981). *The Terror Network: The Secret War of International Terrorism,* New York: Holt, Rinehart.
7. According to Avi Shlaim's estimates the US since 1967 has given Israel more than $92 billion in aid to Israel. Ken Booth and Tim Dunne, No. 2: 182; see also *Frontline,* 1 March 2002: 59; A.K. Pasha, (1999). *Aspects of Political Participation in the Gulf States,* New Delhi: Kalinga Publishers, Noam Chomsky, (1999). *World Orders: Old and New,* Cairo: American University. X, Francois Burgat, (2003) *Face to Face with Political Islam*, London: IB Tauris. Johan F. Murphy Jr. (2002) *Sword of Islam: Muslim Extremism from the Arab Conquests to the Attack on America,* New York: Prometheus Books, Glean E. Schweitzer and Carole C. Dorsch, (1988).Super-Terrorism: Assassins, Mobsters and Weapons of Mass Destruction, New York: Plenum.

8. Ibid.: 180;, Dilip Hiro, *War without End, Ziya us Salam In Conversation, Exposing Dichotomies, The Hindu, Literary Review,* 2 February 2003, See also Times of India, 3 November 2004.
9. Ibid.: 32; For details how Israel's Mossad trained and supplied arms to LTTE terrorist groups in Sri Lanka see Claire Hoy and Victor Ostrovsky, (1991). *By Way of Deception: An Insider's Devastating Expose of the Mossad*, London: Arrow Books, : 67-69and 127-131
10. Ibid, see also Prince Turki al Faisal, *Allied against Terrorism, As Sharq al Awsat, Arab News,* (Jeddah), 17 September 2002: A 21. See also Mai Yamani, (2002). *The New Generation in Saudi Arabia: Cultural Change. Political Identity, and Regime Security*, in Lawrence G. Potter and Gary G. Sick, (eds.) *Security in the Persian Gulf: Origins, Obstacles, and the Search for Consensus*, New York: Palgrave: 207-216; see also Milton Viorst, (2002). *In the Shadow of the Prophet: The Struggle for the Soul of Islam*, Boulder, Colorado: Westview Press: 204-236; Dilip Hiro, (1989). *Holy Wars: The Rise of Islamic Fundamentalism,* New York: Routledge, Chapman and Hall, *The Guardian Weekly,* 12-18 August 2005, India's Top Police Officer says "no state has ever eliminated terrorism without winning the hearts and minds of communities from which the terrorists come" and warns that "military action alone will not solve the problem", see Agwani, No. 3 :25.
11. Telha mi, no.3:33-34; see also Shibley Telhami, *The Persian Gulf: Understanding the American Oil Strategy, The Brookings Review,* 20, 2 Spring 2002:32-35. Anwar Ibrahim, the deposed and jailed Deputy Prime Minister of Malaysia observed: "Osama bin Laden and his protégés are children of desperation; they come from countries where political struggle through peaceful means is futile. In many Muslim countries, political dissent is simply illegal". Farish Noor, a Malaysian Scholar of Islam, establisher a direct link between terrorism and authoritarian politics: "It is the absence o democratic culture and practices in the Muslim world in general that leads to the rise of self-proclaimed leaders like the Mullahs of (the) Taliban, Osama bin Laden...And as long as a sense of political awareness and understanding of democracy is not instilled in the hearts and minds of ordinary Muslims the world over...We will remain

hostage to a bunch of bigoted fanatics who claim to speak, act and think on our behalf without us knowing so". Cited in Amitav Acharya, *State-Society Relations: Asian and World Order after September 11*, Chapter 17, Ken Booth and Tim Dunne, No.2: 198-199; According to Fred Halliday, Saudi Arabia finds itself in an uncomfortable situation due to the prize of pro-Qaeda sentiment amongst young people after 9/11 (as also in other GCC states). Moreover, Saudi population has strongly anti-American attitudes. This population is also increasingly critical of the ruling family because of unemployment and the elite's disproportionate take of oil and investment revenues. Ibid.:. 238; see also MJ Akbar, (2002). *The Shade of Swords: Jihad and the Conflict between Islam and Christianity,* New Delhi: Roli Books: 280-288, Jay Robert Nash, (1998). *Terrorism in the 20th Century*, New York: M Evans and Co., James J Zogby, *Present Road Map will only lead to dead end*, *Gulf News,* April 7, 2003; Mustapha Karkouti, *A Road Map without Proper Directions*, *Gulf News,* April 1, 2003; *Do not Trust Israel*, *Gulf News,* April 1, 2003.

12. Vikra m Sura's interview with Yasser Arafat, *Frontline* (Chennai) Vol. 19, No. 19 September 14-27 2002:21-23. Neta Golan an Israeli-Canadian asked the Israeli soldiers at Check point in West Bank. The soldier replied: "They are animals? "(Palestinians). "Really? Is this woman here an animal? "No, no, it's not like that its' just when they're all in a crowd"... because you're not letting them through". "They are terrorists. These people here? This woman here is a terrorist? This child?" Justin Podur, "Occupation and Resistance", *Frontline,* Vol. 19, No. 17, 17-30 August 2002:57-60.
13. U ma Iyenger (2007). (ed.), *The Oxford India Nehru,* New Delhi: Oxford University Press : 471 and 511; A.K. Pasha, *India and Israel: Growing Cooperation, World Focus,* Vol. 14, No. 8, August 1993:19-2; See also A.K. Pasha, *Gulf-Asia Historical Relations: An Overview, World Focus,* Vol. XXX No.5 [353] May 2009:. 183-196; RR Sharma, (2005). (ed.) *India and Emerging Asia*, New Delhi: Sage, Publications:12-79; See also Mahavir Singh, (2005). (ed.) Building a New Asia, New Delhi; Shipra, Hari Sharan Chhabra, (1989). *Nehru and Resurgent Africa,* New Delhi: Africa Publications, A.K. Pasha, *Asian Security: Flash Points in the Gulf Region, World Focus,* Vol. 26,

Nos. 10-12, October-December 2005:25-33; A.K. Pasha, *India and West Asia, World Focus,* Vol. 25, October-December 2004: 41-46, M.S. Agwani, (1976). *India and the Arab World,* in BR Nanda, (ed.), *Indian Foreign Policy : The Nehru Years*, New Delhi : 72-73,A.K. Pasha, *Tipu's Sultan's Diplomacy in the Gulf Region, Gulf Studies Program, Working Paper* No. 10, February 1997, CWAAS, SIS, JNU, New Delhi; A.K. Pasha, (2003).*South India and the Gulf: Trade and Diplomacy during the late 18th Century* in N.N. Vohra (ed.), *History, Culture and Society in India and West Asia,* New Delhi: Shipra, 11C:237-49; A.K. Pasha,(2007). *India's Cultural Diplomacy in West Asia*, in M.H. Ilias and P.J. Vincent (eds.) *India-West Asia Relations: Understanding Cultural Interplay's*, New Delhi: New Century Publications:39-58; A.K. Pasha, *Nehru and the Crises in West Asia, Détente,* New Delhi, Vol. 9, No..1, May-June 1990: 4-9; A.K. Pasha, *Indo-Egyptian Ties: Retrospect and Prospects, Third World Impact*, Vol. 2, No. 20/23, November 1991: 23-27; AK Pasha,(1993). *Tipu and the Ottoman Empire* in B. Sheik Ali, (ed.), *Tipu Sultan: A Great Martyr,* Bangalore University: Prasaranga: 219-32.

14. A .K. Pasha, (2008). *India's Cultural Diplomacy in West Asia and North Africa*, in Anwar Alam (ed.), *India and West Asia in an Era of Globalization,* New Delhi: New Century Publications, During 2007-08 India paid almost $50 billion for oil and products imports; A.K. Pasha, *Rediscovering Old Bond with Egypt, The Pioneer,* December 23, 1991; A.K. Pasha, *A Great Leap Forward Taken by India and Israel*, *India Abroad*, New York, 17 January 1997: 2-3; A.K. Pasha, (2007). *India-Saudi Relations: Past and Emerging Challenges*, in G. Dietl, G. Pant, A.K. Pasha and P.C. Jain (eds.) *Contemporary Saudi Arabia and the Emerging Indo-Saudi Relations,* New Delhi: Manak Publications:143-166; A.K. Pasha, *Safety and Security Aspects of Hajj, The Pioneer,* 24 May 1997; A.K. Pasha, (2007). *India's Cultural Diplomacy in West Asia*, in A.K. Sinha and A.K. Singh (eds.) *New Horizons in History, Classics and Inter-Cultural Studies,* Delhi: Amanika Publications:295-310, External Affairs Minister S.M. Krishna at the Ministerial Meeting of the NAM Committee on Palestine, New York, 25 September 2010 recalled the last meeting of the committee at Sharm el-Sheikh in July 2009, where India renewed its commitment to the just cause of

the Palestinian people and, to seeking progress in the peace process. 2. In line with our support for UN Security Council Resolutions 242 and 338, India renews its support for a negotiated solution resulting in a sovereign, independent, viable and united State of Palestine living within secure and recognized borders, side by side at peace with Israel as endorsed in the Quartet Roadmap and UNSC Resolutions 1397 and 1515. We have also supported the Arab Peace Plan, which calls for withdrawal of Israel to pre-1967 borders, along with recognition of Israel and the establishment of the State of Palestine with East Jerusalem as its capital. 3. We have also called for an end to illegal Israeli settlements in the occupied Palestinian territories and for an early and significant easing of restrictions on the free movement of persons and goods within Palestine. On the events of 31 May 2010, India deplored the tragic loss of life and the reports of killings and injuries to people on the boats carrying supplies for Gaza. There can be no justification for such indiscriminate use of force, which we condemned. We extended our sympathies to the families of the dead and wounded. It is our firm conviction that lasting peace and security in the region can be achieved only through peaceful dialogue and not through use of force. 4. We welcome the 'direct talks' between the Israelis and the Palestinians, which have resumed after a hiatus of almost two years. We are hopeful that the talks and negotiations would continue, leading to a comprehensive peace process for final resolution of the Middle East conflict. 5. India's continued developmental support to Palestine and last year, we enhanced our annual contribution to United Nations Relief and Works Agency for Palestine Refugees in the Near East [UNRWA] to US$ 1 million, besides, making a special contribution of US $ 1 million to UNRWA in response to UNWRA's flash appeal. Last year and this year, India contributed US$ 10 million annually as untied budget support to the Palestinian National Authority. This year's budget support followed from discussions between H E, President Mahmoud Abbas and PM Dr. Manmohan Singh in New Delhi in February 2010. These exemplify India's continuing commitment to Palestine. During the visit of President Mahmoud Abbas of Palestine National Authority on February 11, 2010, Prime Minister had reiterated India's commitment to the Palestinian cause and urged concerted action for achieving a durable, just and comprehensive settlement of the Middle East conflict. During the India-Brazil-South Africa Summit (IBSA) in Brasilia, the Ministers of IBSA issued a joint communiqué on 15 April 2010 on the situation in the Middle East that, inter alia, stated that concerned by the continuing deterioration of the humanitarian situation in Gaza, the Ministers called on Israel to alleviate circulation restrictions on the movement of people and goods, both in Gaza and in the West Bank. It is our firm conviction that lasting peace and security in the region can be achieved only through peaceful dialogue and not through use of force. Source: MEA, New Delhi.

15. Musta fa Alani, Dhafer Al Ani and Mahmood Sariolghalam, *Developments in Iraq and Iran*, in *Gulf Research Centre Year Book 2004,* Dubai: 249-272; A.K. Pasha, *India's West Asia Policy: Continuity and Change*, Strategic Analysis, Vol. XVI, No. 6, September 1992:783-804; A.K. Pasha, (2007). *India and West Asia: Past and Future* in NS Sisodia and Ashok K Behuria, (eds.) *West Asia in Turmoil: Implications for Global Security,* New Delhi: Academic Foundation: 441-470; A.K. Pasha, *Yemen-Saudi Security Relations: Implications for India*, *Third Concept,* Vol. 8, No. 87, May 1994:33-36; Dilip Hiro, (2008). *Blood of the Earth: The Battle for the World's Vanishing Oil Resources,* New Delhi: Penguin Books, A.K. Pasha, *Indo-OIC Relations: Perspective and Trends*, *Journal of Peace Studies,* Vol. 1, No..3-4, March-June 1994: 22-50; A.K. Pasha, *The Recent Gulf Crisis: India's Options*, *Strategic Analysis,* Vol. XVII, No. 10, January 1995:127-86; Mustafa Alani, *The Curse of oil and the disintegration of Iraq*, *Gulf Monitor,* GRC, Vol. No. 4, June 2007:8-9.
16. In Saudi Arabia where pro Al Qaeda, anti-American and anti-ruling family sentiments are growing, the Saudi regime has tried to offset this by reducing cooperation with the US, but in doing so it has deeply antagonized the country the country on which it relies for its ultimate survival. Time has, in a way, overtaken the cautious, and often indecisive, rulers. Washington may belatedly be getting the military facilities and some of the information on terrorist suspects and finances it has asked for from Riyadh, but no US President will find it easy to risk American lives to defend the House of Saud. Strategists in Washington are already thinking the unthinkable: if Saudi Arabia enters a serious crisis,

it may as did two other states form around the same time in the 1920's Yugoslavia and the USSR, break up. The question then become how to preserve the Western, and global economic, interest in the oil and gas regions of the (Gulf without remaining embroiled in the domestic politics. It has not come to this, but it may]. Fred Halliday, *A New Global Configuration*, Chapter 21, in Ken Booth and Tim Dunne, No.2:239; see also Fred Halliday, (2000). *The World at 2000,* Washington: Palgrave; Chapter 6. Key members of Al Qaeda came from wealthy Saudi families, including Osama bin Laden, who came not from the royal family but a very prominent one close to it. Osama was so popular among Saudi youth that the rulers refused to freeze his assets despite US pressure, fearing a rebellion. It is said that he was even financed by some elements of the royal family which feel that unquestioned Saudi loyalty to the US is harmful to their own interests. The international channels of Osama's finances were so deeply connected with those of many a prominent Saudi finances that the US could not isolate his accounts. It was starting to think of freezing a good number of Saudi accounts in US banks, which is said to have precipitated a surge of Saudi withdrawals which in turn is said to have contributed to the recent fall in the value of the dollar. Meanwhile, the ruling family has watched Sharon's policies in Palestine which are creating such distress among Arabs that it cannot forever support all US polices. Experts believe that Saudi Arabia is on the brink of an anti-monarchist revolution. Aijaz Ahmad, *In the Shadow of Permanent War, Frontline,* Vol. 19, No. 20, 28 September -11 October 2002:20. The former CIA Director James Woolsey apparently had prepared a plan to partition Saudi Arabia into three parts as states: Hejaz- which would include Jeddah, Mecca Medina, Islamic holy places; Najd–from where the Saudi-Wahhabi combination originally came to eventually dominate most of the Arabian Peninsula, and Al Hasa–the oil rich Shia dominated eastern part. The US would eventually dominate Al Hasa due to its oil like Kuwait in the event of Saudi Arabia's disintegration. *The Hindu,* February 9, 2003, Jessica Stern, (1999). *The Ultimate Terrorist,* Cambridge: Harvard University Press.

17. US State Department of State, 2000, *Patterns of Global Terrorism Report* released April 2001 by the Secretary of State

and the Coordinator for Counter-terrorism., Ne w Delhi: US Embassy, 2001. See also MS Agwani, *Islamic Fundamentalism in India Chandigarh: 21st Century India Society,* 1986; Khalid Bin Sayeed, (1995). *Western Dominance and Political Islam: Challenge and Response*, Albany: State University of New York Press.

18. See Riyaz Punjabi and AK Pasha, (1998) (eds.) *India and the Islamic World,* New Delhi: Radiant Publishers, see also Afsir Karim *Pak-sponsored Terrorism, AGNI,* Vol. I, No. 2, May-August 2002: 81-99.

19. Accordin g to Avi Shlaim's estimates the US since 1967 has given Israel more than $92 billion in aid to Israel. Ken Booth and Tim Dunne, No. 2:182; see also *Frontline,* March 1, 2002:59.

20. A .K. Pasha, (1999). *Aspects of Political Participation in the Gulf States,* New Delhi Kalinga Publishers, Noam Chomsky, (1994). *World Orders: Old and New,* Cairo: American University, Francois Burgat, (2003). *Face to Face with Political Islam,* London: IB Tauris, Johan F. Murphy Jr. (2002) *Sword of Islam: Muslim Extremism from the Arab Conquests to the Attack on America,* New York: Prometheus Books, Glean E. Schweitzer and Carole C. Dorsch, (1988). *Super-Terrorism: Assassins, Mobsters and Weapons of Mass Destruction* New York: Plenum, *The Guardian Weekly,* July 29-August 4, 2005, *Yahoo News,* October 1, 2010.

21. 21.Laurie Mylroie, (2001). *The War against America: Saddam Hussein and the World Trade Centre Attacks*, Washington: Reagan Books, Harper Collins, See Gilles Kepel, (2002). *Jihad: The Trail of Political Islam,* London: 1B Taurus: 299–322; Yossef Bodansky, (1993). *Target America: Terrorism in the US Today,* New York: SPI Books,; Yossef Bodansky, The High Cost of Peace: How Washington's Middle East Policy left America Vulnerable to Terrorism, New York: Forum, Prima, Random House, see also *Frontline,* Vol. 20, No. 8, 13-26, April 2002:16; see also Graham E. Fuller *As killing Mounts, who'll Blink First*, *Los Angeles Times* 3 April 2002, *Frontline* 1 March 2002:55.

22. For details how Israel's Mossad trained and supplied arms to LTTE terrorist groups in Sri Lanka see Claire Hoy and Victor Ostrovsky, (1991). *By Way of Deception: An Insider's*

Devastating Expose of the Mossad, London: Arrow Books: 67-69: 127-131, It has been known for several years that India has acquired over 4,000 Galil 7.62 mm super sniper rifles, and night vision sights, laser range finders and other targeting equipment. This is not an infantry rifle, but the ammunition is the same as an Indian INSAS and an AK-47, purchased from Rumania. This is also all separate, of course from thermal imaging equipment, satellite transmission of such images and use of Unmanned Aerial Vehicles, better known as drones. All from Israel in the main. In fact India takes up more than 50% of Israel's arms exports. Selective assassination, use of UAVs, missile attacks on selected homes and sniper fire has been a hallmark of the Israeli Mossad and Defence forces, not only in Gaza and the West Bank, but also in different parts of the world including South America, Iran and Europe. For the past several years it is now well-known that India has entered into very close collaboration with the IDF and over 32 non-disclosure arms and security agreements have been signed with them. The Mossad has titillated gun-and ammo freaks and underhanded counter-insurgency nut jobs with their secretive killing techniques. Assassination and murder that goes undocumented, un-prosecuted and never brought to light, when the Mossad is involved. The CIA fumbles, trips and gets blown up. Not the Mossad. That is why India has chosen them to deploy dirty tricks on India's citizens. India for Selective Assassination of its Own Citizens? By Trevor Selvam, 31 January, 2010; Counter currents. Org; See also PRK Swamy, *Relations with Israel: The UPA and the Indian left, MEI, Occasional Paper,* New Delhi: No.16, 30 August, 2010.

References

1. Findlay, Pawl, *Liberating America from Israel, Young Muslim Digest,* November 2002:48-49.
2. Gunaratna, Rohan, *International Terrorism and Al Qaeda: Still Threatening, The World Today*, London, 59(1), January 2003: 19-21.
3. Kepel, Gilles, (2002). *Jihad: The Trail of Political Islam,* London: 1B Taurus: 299-322.
4. Kronenwetter, Michael, (1988). *The War on Terrorism,* New Jersey: Simon and Shuster.

5. Pasha, A.K., (1999). *India and West Asia: Continuity and Change,* Delhi: Gyan Sagar.
6. Pasha, A.K. (2000), (ed.), *India, Iran and the GCC States: Political Strategy and Foreign Policy*, New Delhi: Manas Publications: 263.
7. Pasha, A.K., (1995). *India and OIC: Strategy and Diplomacy,* New Delhi: Centre for Peace Studies.
8. Telhami, Shibley (2002), *The Stakes: America and the Middle East: The Consequences of Power and the Choice for Peace,* Colorado: Westview Press: 18.

14

India's Quest for New Partnership in West Asia: The Case of Israel as a Strategic Ally

K.M. Sajad Ibrahim

India's relation with Israel since 1992 has been viewed as an outcome of the post-Cold War scenario. With the demise of the Soviet Union, India lost its long time military supplier and principal diplomatic crutch. It has also grown increasingly disenchanted with Arab sympathy for Pakistan on the Kashmir issue. As a result of the diplomatic relations, India showed keen interest in developing high level military and commercial links with Israel, especially during the period of BJP led government of 1998-2004. Israel is now the largest supplier of arms to India surpassing Russia recently. It provides India with missile radar, border monitoring equipment and other similar high-tech military hardwires. In addition, several thousand Indian soldiers have been provided with "anti-insurgency training in Israel". The latest in the series was the launching of Israel's spy satellite by India in April 2009 to enhance Israel's intelligence-gathering capability. The geopolitical implications of the collaboration between India and Israel are grave and manifold. India's close collaboration with Israel is fundamentally to woo the United States as well as to build a new strategic relation vis-à-vis Pakistan and China.

India's West Asian Policy Principles

India's relation with the West Asia was formulated by Jawaharlal Nehru in 1930s. Although Nehru took an impartial view regarding the Arab-Israeli differences in the initial period, he later took the stand of supporting the Arabs by taking into account of the denial of justice to the Palestinians. In the 1939 Resolution adopted by the Indian National Congress, it stated that "in Palestine the Jews have relied on British armed forces to advance their special privileges". [1] Even Gandhiji was not ready to recognize the Jewish nationalism, which was artificially created in Palestine at the cost of indigenous Arab population. [2] Nehru indicted Zionism for fostering Jewish settlement in Palestine at the expense of the Arab population. Jai Prakash Narayan stated:

"No doubt the Jews were entitled as a persecuted people to compassion and some compensation for the wrongs heaped upon their innocent heads through the centuries. But it was certainly not the Arabs, least of all the Palestinians, who were the persecutors. If the Christian peoples and powers of the West, some of whom had tried mercilessly to exterminate the Jews, were anxious at least to salve their conscience and do a good turn to their victims, they had no right to do it at the cost of the Arabs". [3]

Nehru in his letters to his daughter, Indira, during his prison days commented the British tactics in Palestine in favour of the Jewish immigrants violating the rights of the Palestine as another face of a colonial power. He saw the English in Palestine pitting "Jewish religious nationalism against Arab nationalism, and (making) it appear that (their) presence is necessary to act as an arbiter and to keep the peace between the two". [4] All these were some of the basic perspectives of Indian leaders regarding the Jewish colonialism in the pre-independence period.

The first task before India in its post independence period was to examine an appropriate solution to the Palestine question by becoming a member in the Special UN Committee. India supported the minority plan which recommended a federation of two Arab and Jewish states by opposing the partition plan of Palestine (During this period the third world countries have not emerged as members of the UN

General Assembly). [5] The decision of India was influenced by the perception of Indian leaders on the Palestine question as well as the partition of India.

When Israel became a reality in 1948, India had several reservations in granting recognition to it. Nehru openly stated the reason as a gesture of supporting the stand of Arab countries. [6] Moreover, India opposed U.N. membership for Israel in 1949. By 1950 a series of efforts had been made to influence the Indian government to recognize the state of Israel by the Jewish lobby as well as its counterpart in India. Finally, India accorded its recognition to the State of Israel in late 1950 without establishing any formal ties until 1992. [7]

India's Support to Palestinian Movements

When Israel invaded Sinai on October 29, 1956 as a reaction to Egypt's decision to nationalize Suez Canal, India condemned it as a re-imposition of European colonialism in the Afro Asian world. India cosponsored resolutions in the General Assembly urging the withdrawal of French, British and Israeli forces from Egypt. In fact, the Suez crisis drew Egypt and India closer together and its relation with Israel to low point and ended all possibility for a bilateral tie. [8]

India's hostility towards Israel increased even more after the death of Nehru in 1964. It was evident from India's refusal to accept Israeli assistance in redeveloping the barren wastes of Rajasthan. Similarly, Israeli offer of famine relief given in response to a plea by the UN Secretary General, U. Thant was declined by India for political reasons. [9] India condemned the Israeli invasion of Arab lands of Palestine in the 1967 Arab-Israeli war. In December 1967, D.P. Dhar, a member of Indian delegation to the UN Special Committee, reiterated Indian position, which recognized the Palestinian as a people and not merely as refugees. It also emphasized the need of for a lasting solutions to ensure the just rights of the Arab people of Palestine on the basis of UN resolution 194 (III). [10]

In the meantime, the Indian political atmosphere was not

fully supporting the views of the government stand. The opposition parties in India, except the Communist parties, demanded a cautious approach in the 1967 War, promoting a neutral stand. The parties like Swathanthra Party and Jan Sangh openly supported Israel. It happened on account of the neutral policy of Egypt during the Sino-Indian War of 1962 and Indo-Pak War of 1965. [11] Similarly, the Indian press also took a negative approach to official Indian position in the 1967 war. The news papers like Times of India, Indian Express, Statesman and The Hindustan Times made critical remarks on Indian policy of supporting the Arabs. [12]

The first setback to India's relation with West Asia came in 1969 when India was denied participation on the Rabat conference of Islamic leaders due to the opposition of Pakistan. The meeting was convened to condemn the burning of Al-Aqsa Mosque in Jerusalem. Moreover, under the initiative of Pakistan the meeting also condemned the communal riots in Ahmedabad. As a reaction to these developments, India recalled its Senior Envoys from Morocco and Jordan. Further, Indian Foreign Affairs Minister, Dinesh Singh held a meeting with his Israeli counterpart, Abba Eban in New York, as a first sign of improving relations with Israel. [13] During the Indo-Pak War in November 1971, countries like Egypt and Syria took a neutral stand while countries like Kuwait, Jordan and Saudi Arabia condemned India. However, Israel took a pro-India stand by criticizing Pakistan actions in East Bengal. [14]

However, India continued pro-Arab stand even in the 1973 Arab-Israeli war. At the same time India gradually moved away from the policy of supporting individual Arab countries by focusing exclusively on Palestine question. [15] Hence, in the post-1973 war period India gave more importance to support the struggles of the Palestine Liberation Organization (PLO) led by Yasser Arafat. In this respect, India played considerable role in the UN to support the PLO's bid for observer status in 1974. India became the first non-Arab government to extend formal diplomatic accreditation to the representatives of the PLO in January 1975. Moreover, India was a cosponsor of General Assembly Resolution 3379, which equated Zionism with racism in November 1975. [16]

When Janata Party came to power in 1977, there were speculations about the shift of India's policy towards Palestine. It was during this period Moshe Dayan, Israeli Foreign Minister made an unofficial visit to India. [17] However, there was no official action in supporting the relationship with Israel. When Camp David Accord was signed in September 1978 between Israel and Egypt, India opposed it along with the Arab world. In 1980, Indira Gandhi returned to power with the continued support of Palestinian struggle. It was during this period India accorded full diplomatic recognition to the Office of PLO in New Delhi. Moreover, Yasser Arafat paid state visits to India in 1980 and 1982. [18] This line of Indian policy continued until early 1990s. The situation in West Asian witnessed a sea change when Iraq invaded Kuwait in August 1990. It was during this period the Soviet Union was disappearing from the world map marking the era of unipolar world. In the meantime, the P.L.O. lost its prestige in West Asia on account of its support to Saddam Hussain. The United States took the initiative of holding international Middle East Peace Conference immediately after expelling Iraq out of Kuwait in 1991. This marked new era in West Asia due to different varieties of diplomatic manoeuvring. As a consequence to these developments, India also made drastic changes in its policy towards West Asia.

Ties with Israel and Shift in India's Foreign Policy

The decision of establishing formal ties with Israel was taken by P.V. Narasimha Rao, the Prime Minister of Congress government in January 1992. The decision was a surprising one, although it looked like a long awaited decision, as remarked by Indian media. In fact, the decision of India to start formal relation with Israel was based on changes in the international scenario. It was the beginning of post-Cold War period with the disintegration of the Soviet Union, India's strong ally for a long period. In the new situation, India desired the support and collaboration with major international powers like the United States, especially in the wake of the political turmoil in Kashmir. In this respect, India had two objectives in promoting its relation with the US. Firstly, to overcome the propaganda unleashed by Pakistan on Kashmir situation. Secondly, India required strategic cooperation with the US due to the demise of the Soviet Union, the leading exporter of arms to India. It was imperative for India to modernise Indian weaponry. At the same time India was fully aware of the complexities in establishing strong ties with the US. In this context India found Israel as a best option of appeasing the US line of policy. It is to be noted that India announced its decision to formally establish relations with Israel on the eve of Prime Minister Narasimha Rao's visit to the US. [19]

Moreover, the P.L.O. had already recognised the state of Israel to join as a party of the peace process in the Middle East. So India found a favourable occasion in justifying its ties with Israel. It was also remarked that India's normal relation with Israel was helpful to get the status of a mediator in the on going peace negotiations. India's relationship with Israel also marked the shift of India's foreign policy from the traditional line of anti-colonial and anti-imperialist to economic and strategic developments. In the decade following this normalisation of ties, successive governments of both the centrist Congress and the rightist BJP, irrespective of party ideology, have rapidly forged extensive military, economic and political relationship. In fact, the shift within the Indian ruling classes from the official position of non-alignment and state-centred economic development towards a pro-United States policy facilitated and encouraged this change attitude towards Israel.

Milestones in the India-Israel Relations

The most important outcome in the Indo-Israel relationship

was that in 2008 Israel surpassed Russia as the main defence supplier to India after breaking the US$ 1 billion mark in new contracts signed annually over the past years. Israel is not, as Minister Antony claims, just one among 45 countries with which India has defence deals. A Jerusalem Post article on February 15, 2009 had a screaming headline: "Israel now India's top defence supplier". [20] Although India's relation with Israel started at a low profile, a sea change took place after the NDA came to power in 1998. India soon became Israel's closest ally in Asia with strategic, defence and intelligence cooperation growing rapidly. India became the biggest market for Israeli arms. Israel supplied not only military hard wares but also several high-techs, critical weaponry such as wide array of surveillance items, electronic warfare systems, a ground based Green Pine ABM radar, and phalcon airborne warning and control systems. These arms sales were part of a declared NDA policy to forge an alliance among India, United States and Israel. [21]

The United States has given clearance to Israel's delivery of phalcon reconnaissance aircraft to India, in marked contrast to Washington's vigorous opposition to supplying them to China in 1998. The US forced Israel to cancel the deal to sell the phalcons to China out of concern altering the balance of power between China and Taiwan. In February 2003, an agreement was made to supply advanced Israeli avionic systems for the Indian Air Force's new MIG-27 combat aircraft. There were reports about the collaboration between India and Israel on a missile defence system based on the Israel Arrow technology. [22]

India-Israeli partnership has intensified since 1998 and later led to the visiting of India's Home Minister, L.K. Advani and India's External Affairs Minister, Jaswant Singh to Israel in quick succession in mid 2000. The delegates of the Indian team with L.K. Advani consisted of Heads of India's intelligence agencies, RAW, IB, and Central Police Organisations fighting terrorism. In addition to this, India's

National Security Advisor, Brijesh Mishra and Services Chiefs have paid their visit to Israel since 1998, underlining the growing strategic cooperation between India and Israel. The top officials of Indian Navy also conducted goodwill visits to Israel. [23]

The Israeli aid during the Kargil War in 1999 was considered by India as a cementing factor in the Indo-Israeli relationship. It was during the visit of Shimon Pares to India in January 2002 India and Israel made major agreements to fight 'terrorism'. Ironically, the word 'terrorism' used by Israel was about the national liberation struggle of the Palestinians, which had been strongly supported by India until late 1980s. An Indian Foreign Ministry Spokesman said during the visit of Pares: "India finds it increasingly beneficial to learn from Israel's experience in dealing with terrorism". [24] This line of Indian policy was in contradiction with the fundamental principle of Indian foreign policy, supporting all national liberation movements.

The most significant event in the Indo-Israeli relationship was the visit of Israeli Prime Minster, Ariel Sharon to India in September 2003. In fact, the visit engineered much controversy in the wake of the assassination of Palestinian leaders by Israeli military forces during the period. There were series of protests in different parts of India against the Israeli Prime Minister. However, the Indian government adopted a cautious step of either displeasing Sharon or giving much honour against the public sentiments. [25] At the same time, there were many agreements during his visit as Sharon was accompanied by a large delegation of about 30 influential businessmen, eager to forge new contracts and open new markets in India. [26]

When the UPA government under the Congress leadership came to power in mid-2004, it decided to follow the same line of the policy adopted by the earlier NDA regime. During the NDA rule the Congress party had criticised some of the close cooperation between India and Israel. But UPA government followed its relations with Israel without changing any policies. India's Navel Chief Admiral Suresh Mehta visited Israel in January 2008 to finalise several key defence projects. It was reported that Mehta had reviewed efforts to enhance the Israeli-origin Barak missiles defence system. [27] On January 21, 2008 an Indian space launch vehicle lifted off from the Sriharikota spaceport on the Indian Ocean to put into space Israel's most sophisticated spy satellite ever launched, the Polaris. The commercial launch of Polaris by the Indian Space Research Organization (ISRO) underscored the growing military and intelligence connections between Israel and India. The United States helped inspire this relationship and has a strong interest in its success. Though unique in the military cooperation realm, this is but one of several evolving relationships between Israel and great or emerging powers that deserves attention. [28]

The launching of an Israeli made satellite on April 20, 2009 came close on the heels of an opaque missile deal of India with an Israeli company under investigation both in India and Israel, raising further questions about India's Israeli ties and its implications. A.K. Antony, India's Defence Minister, found it hard to answer questions related to these deals while campaigning for the Congress party in the Parliament elections in his home State of Kerala. India signed a massive US $ 1.4 billion deal with the Israeli Aerospace Industries (IAI) for the supply and joint development of medium-range surface-to-air missiles (MRSAM). The deal signed on February 27, 2009, just two days prior to the notification of elections to Parliament, was wrapped in secrecy till the Israeli Aerospace Industries officially announced it. The company explained that "early disclosure was liable to cause material difficulties in execution of the contract and even result in its cancellation", according to the Israeli business daily Globes. The company has claimed that the Indian Government wanted the signing of the contract to be kept secret. [29]

Major Implications in the Indo-Israeli Relationship

The most important outcome in the Indo-Israeli relation is the aberration in the fundamental principle of Indian foreign policy. In the first four decades after independence, successive governments sought to project India as country dedicated to decolonisation. This posture offered the basis for the principled foreign policy of Nehruvian state which drew its own legitimacy from the tumultuous anti-colonial struggle that brought about independence for the subcontinent in the late 1940s. But when India decided to establish its ties with Israel, it had far reaching implications including military and intelligence cooperation against Pakistan and Islamic terrorism. In fact, India's relation with Israel was not a normal one as it expanded into different vital fields, even foiled India's traditional relations with Arab countries and Iran. It was viewed as a tactic used by the US to bring India into its strategic orbit. As a result, it lost its independent foreign policy initiatives in the post-Cold War period.

The traders and business lobby in India and Israel played a crucial role in fostering the ties between the two countries for promoting their interests. The Indian business lobby was not interested any matters regarding the case of Palestinians. Since Palestine has little to offer financially or technologically, while Israel can sell to India what the US refuses to India, these pragmatists insisted that New Delhi had no option but to court the more "valuable" Israel. [30] The official Israeli figures show that Israel exports to India valued US$ 1.270 billion in 2006 and imports US$ 1.433 billion to Israel. Agricultural, water and IT technologies in addition to fertilisers and diamonds are major mutual trade concerns. The State Bank of India became the first foreign bank to open a branch in Israel's diamond exchange. [31]

The India-Israeli alliance strengthens the US strategic designs for India and the region. India holds significant place in the September 20, 2002 National Security Strategy of the US, a policy document to support the actions of the current US

President, George Bush. [32] Like Israel in West Asia, the US needed a close ally in South Asia to confront terrorists in Afghanistan and Pakistan as well as to overcome the challenges posed by China. The Indo-US nuclear deal is the most significant outcome of this kind of policy initiatives of the United States.

"Pakistan factor" was another aspect which cemented the relation between India and Israel. For India, the growing nuclear arsenal of Pakistan and its support to terrorism in Kashmir and different parts of India were most important challenges. In the case of Israel, the nuclear capability of Pakistan and its support to Palestinian extremists posed a threat to its security. In this context Pakistan was a common threat to India and Israel and any alliance in this direction was considered as most valuable. There were reports about the Israeli clandestine support to Indian nuclear explosion, Pokhran II in May 1998. [33] Even the Sangh Parivar was demanding for an alliance with Israel way back in 1960s and 1970s to face the "Islamic threat" from Pakistan and Kashmir.

India's relationship with the West Asian countries, most specifically Iran, has been a point of contention in the Indo-Israeli partnership. Israel's relationship with Iran is extremely antagonistic and unstable. Israel viewed Iran as the most important threat to its security in the region due to the kind of support it extended to Hezbollah and Palestinian extremists. In the case of India, Iran is considered as the most important ally in the region. India paid a lot of respect to Iran on account of its support to Kashmir issue against Pakistan. So India treated Iran as an ideal power in the region to counter Pakistan influence in West Asia. But with the inception of Indo-Israeli ties India's traditional relationship with Iran badly damaged. [34] Israel's spy satellite, Tecsar (Polaris), was launched by India in January 2008 to enhance Israel's intelligence gathering capability. In fact, the real objective behind the launching of the satellite was to undermine the Iranian nuclear programme. Moreover, India voted twice on the IAEA governing body against Iran under the compulsion from the United States. All these created rifts between India and Iran. [35]

However, it is not possible to follow a negative policy towards the Arab countries by taking into account of many realities. It is estimated that more than five million Indian expatriate work in the Arab countries. Moreover, nearly US$ 25 billion worth of Indo-Arab trade, including 60 per cent of Indian oil and gas imports worth US$ 20 billion, is the basic support of Indian economy. [36] In this respect, India had to follow a soft policy towards the question of Palestine. In order to overcome this dilemma an attempt had been made by Indian foreign policy makers to separate its Israeli policy from the Arab-Israeli conflict. To realise this objective, India has taken a more tactical neutral position on the Palestine question, publicly stating its continued support for the Palestinian case and making deliberative effort to further strengthen ties with ties Arab neighbours. [37]

India considers Israel as a role model of counter terrorist strategies. However, even after 60 years of military actions against the Palestinians, Israel still lives in an atmosphere of fear. Israel's counterterrorism strategy has been a complete failure which the Israeli government has been trying to hide by brutally using its fire power against innocent Palestinians. Two years ago, Israel marched into Lebanon thinking they would destroy the Hezbollah but ended up retreating in disgrace. It is not in India's interest to emulate Israel counterterrorism strategy as this would pose a serious threat to the stability of the entire South Asian region. Instead of accusing and threatening Pakistan, India should investigate the local support which enabled the attackers to carry out this gruesome act of terrorism. Both India and Pakistan are nuclear states and should understand the repercussions and consequences of war. [38]

Conclusion

As a result of India's new foreign policy decisions, its

traditional line of supporting national liberation movements and anti-colonial and anti-imperial stands has fizzled out. The Palestinians have been waging a struggle for their nationhood for the last six decades against Israeli illegal occupation of lands. India was one of the leading countries which extended all support to the Palestinian cause. India has always opposed the continued illegal occupation of West Bank and Gaza. However, India's changed policy since 1992 is a blatant contradiction to its avowed policy of supporting the Palestinian cause due to the transformation in the international politics resulted in the disintegration of the Soviet Union. Moreover, India had enough justifications in establishing ties with Israel by taking into account of the factors like the recognition of Israel by the P.L.O. and some Arab countries. However, the current phase of India's relation with Israel goes beyond the level of normalcy and reached a stage of much clandestine cooperation for defence and strategic purposes. Ironically, India wants to borrow the ideas of Israeli tactics of eliminating the Palestinian leaders in its efforts to combat terrorism in Jammu and Kashmir. For a long period, India had been condemning these Israeli policies against the Palestinians. Now the cooperation in the same field with Israel is against its foreign policy principle and the support to the Palestinian struggle.

Moreover, India never used its relation with Israel to resolve the issue of Palestinians. At present India is in a commanding position of using its good offices to influence Israel. However, no attempt was made to pressurise Israel to withdraw its forces from the occupied territories. It is very unfortunate that on many occasions since 1992 India was not ready to condemn Israeli atrocities against the Palestinians by sticking to a passive stand of supporting a 'peaceful solution' to the crisis. The new diplomatic initiatives of India target only its vested interest against the traditional principle of solidarity with the third world countries. The current trends indicate India's keen interest to develop close ties with imperialist global powers like the United States for economic and defence benefits undermining its values and principles. In other words, Indian foreign policy lost its direction as it is dictated by the external powers to realise their objectives.

In fact, there were widespread concerns about India's burgeoning support to the war economy of Israel, the chief victims of which are Palestinians. The spy satellite, also made by the controversial Israeli Aerospace Industries fits into this. The defence and intelligence nexus between India and Israel has strategic implications not only for West Asia but also for South Asia especially through their collaboration in the US-led war on terror. While continuing to pay lip service to the Palestinian cause India is subsidizing Israel's war against Palestinians.

End Notes

1. N.V. Raj Kumar (Ed.), (1952). *The Background of India's Foreign Policy,* New Delhi: Indian National Congress: 57.
2. Leonard A. Gordon, (1975). *Indian Nationalist Ideas about Palestine and Israel, Jewish Social Studies,* 37:223.
3. Jai Prakash Narayan, *The Arab-Israeli Question*, *Indian and Foreign Review,* Vol.6, 15 July 1969:1-2.
4. Jawaharlal Nehru, (1962). *Glimpses of World History,* Bombay: Asia Publishing House: 789.
5. For details see United Nations, *Official Records of the General Assembly,* Second Session, Supplement No. 11, Document A/364 (UNSCOP Report)
6. G. Parthasarathi (ed.), (1986). *Jawaharlal Nehru: Letters to Chief Ministers 1947-1964,* Vol. 2, 1950-52, 1 October 195, (Delhi: Oxford University Press for the Jawaharlal Nehru Trust,), p. 217.
7. Subhash Kapila, *India–Israel Relations: The Imperatives For Enhanced Strategic Cooperation,* South Asia Analysis Group : Papers, cited at *http://www.southasiaanalysis.org/papers2/paper131.html retrieved on 12-09-2008.*
8. Sudha Rao, (1972). *The Arab-Israeli Conflict: The Indian View,* Delhi: Orient Longman: 60.
9. Arthur G. Rubinoff, *Normalisation of India-Israel Relations:*

Stillborn for Forty Years, Asian Survey, Vol.35, No.5, May: 1995: 493.
10. Krish n Gopal Swamy, (1981). *West Asia and North Africa,* New Delhi: V.I. Publications: 278-279.
11. Farah Naaz, (2005). *West Asia: Changing Perspectives,* Delhi: Shipra Publications: 95.
12. See *Indian Opinion on the West Asian Crisis,* Bombay: Indo-Israeli Friendship League, 1967.
13. Art hur G. Rubinoff, op. cit: 498.
14. Ibid.
15. K.R. Singh, (1999). *India and West Asia: Retrospect and Prospects*, Nancy Jetly (ed.), *India's Foreign Policy: Challenges and Prospects,* New Delhi: Vikas Publishing House: 227.
16. Raja Swamy, *The Case against Collaboration between Indian and Israel, MR Zine,* 30-08-06 cited in *http://mrzine.monthlyreview.org/swamy300806.html,* retrieved on 11-09-08.
17. Moshe Dayan, (1978). *Breakthrough: A Personal Account of the Egypt-Israeli Peace Negotiations,* New Delhi: Vikas Publishing House: 28.
18. *Hindustan Times,* New Delhi: 27 March 1980.
19. *New York Times,* 30 January 1992.
20. Nina n Koshy, *India-Israel Defence Nexus Deepens, Mainstream,* Vol XLVII, No 20, 2 May 2009.
21. Nina n Koshy, *India and Israel Eye Iran, Foreign Policy in Focus,* 13 February 2008, cited at *http://www.fpif.org/fpiftxt/4959* retrieved on 10-09-2008.
22. Nina n Koshy, *US plays matchmaker to India, Israel, Asia Times on line,* 10 June 2003, cited *http://www.atimes.com/atimes/South_Asia/EF10Df03.html* retrieved on 21-09-2008.
23. Subha sh Kapila, op. cit.
24. Nina n Koshy, *US plays matchmaker to India, Israel,* op. cit.
25. Bansidhar Pradhan, (2008).*Globalisation and the Shift in India's Palestine Policy*, in Anwar Alam (ed.), *India and West Asia in the Era of Globalisation,* New Delhi: New Century Publications: 296-297.
26. Harsh V. Pant, (2004). *India-Israel Partnership: Convergence and Constraints*, *The Middle East Review of International Affairs,* Vol. 8, No. 4, December, cited at

http://meria.idc.ac.il/journal/2004/issue4/jv8no4a6.html.

27. Nina n Koshy, *India and Israel Eye Iran,* op.cit.
28. *Israel and In dia New Allies* see *http://www.brookings.edu/profile/Portfolio/PortfolioHelper.aspx?ProfileItemId=e187dc42-b737-46c3-b21c-3ad0c62dffd0.*
29. Naina n Koshy, *India-Israel Defence Nexus Deepens*, op. cit.
30. Ra mtanu Maitra, (2003). *Palestinians Pay for Indian Ambitions, Asian Times on line,* 10 September 2003, cited at *http://www.atimes.com/atimes/South_Asia/EI10Df03.html,* retrieved on 25-09-2008.
31. Nicola Nasser, *Indian-Israeli Ties Could Neutralize Delhi's Palestinian Policy, Arabic Media Internet Network,* 12 July 2007, cited at *http://www.amin.org/look/amin/en.tpl?idLanguage=I&IdPublication=7&NrArticle=41334&NrIssue=I&NrSection=3* retrieved on 09-09-2008.
32. Nina n Koshy, *US plays matchmaker to India, Israel*, op. cit.
33. S.R. Chaudhari, *Indo-Israeli N-Nexus*, *The Hindu,* 10 February 1999.
34. Ada m C Castillo, *India and Israel: A balancing alliance*, *International Relations and Security Network,* cited at: *http://www.isn.ethz.ch/news/sw/details.cfm?ID=19199* retrieved on 23-09-2008.
35. Nina n Koshy, *India and Israel Eye Iran*, op. cit.
36. Nicola Nasser, op. cit.
37. Frederick Stakelbeck, Jr., *India and Israel Shape a New Strategic Relationship*, *Global Politician,* cited at *http://www.globalpolitician.com/2345-israel.*
38. Mah wish Hafeez, Indo-Israel Relations and the Mumbai Attacks, *Reflections,* No. 1: 2009.

15

India's Look East Policy: The China Factor

B. Venugopal

India's Look East Policy, which is culminated in the FTA with the ASEAN, is the result of India's realization of the international political realities. Since 1962, we were losing opportunities to emerge as an Asian leader, mainly because of our short sighted policies and the inability to cope with the emerging situations. We closed our eyes to the developments in the outer world. And we could not see the economic and political developments in our continent. Now ASEAN+3 constitute the Asian economic might and have emerged as a fast growing and powerful economic alliance. Though we have close cultural and civilizational links with the Southeast Asian countries, we did not give much importance to the economic and political relationship with this region. But China, who once openly opposed the formation of the ASEAN, gave much importance to this region and used every available opportunity and made its presence strong in this part, thereby relegating India into just a South Asian player. Even in South Asia, China could make inroads by making links with all our neighbours, thereby isolating India.

But since the disintegration of the Soviet Union and the end of the Cold War, we can see a sea change in the policy perspectives of India and out look towards the neighbouring countries. It became ready, in spite of the strong opposition from China, to forge alliances with almost all the Southeast Asian states and it became a dialogue partner in the ARF. This is also resulted from its awareness of the consequences of China's growth.

China factor is an important constituent in India's Look East Policy and that is why India, through this policy tries to counter China economically and politically. China does not favour a strong Indian presence and influence in the Southeast Asia. China is aware of the linkages between India and Southeast Asia which could naturally attract the two regions to come closer. China knows that India is the only country that could possibly challenge its hegemony in Asia and therefore tries hard to keep India under pressure. India needs to adopt an aggressive stance economically and politically to compete with China. On the other side, though there is a cordial relation with China, the Southeast Asian states basically dislikes China's undue interventions in the region and wants India, a democracy to come as a balancing force. Thus seen, India's Look East Policy may be conceived as an external security trajectory, whereby India would develop a sophisticated array of security relations in the Southeast and East Asia with an eye to project India's legitimate power and resist the growing Chinese domination of the region.

This paper analyses the China factor involved in India's relation with the Southeast Asian countries. The paper does not go into the economic arrangements between the two, but highlights the factors, mainly China, which induces India to forge a close alliance with the Southeast Asian Countries and vice versa. Also, the paper examines the areas in which India can overcome Chinese obstacles and the conditions favourable to India's intervention in Southeast Asia.

To begin with, "Look east" is a new orientation in India's foreign policy towards the Southeast Asian nations. India's policy of rediscovering the Southeast Asian nations for better economic co-operation, security considerations and for the revival of traditional cultural ties through a comprehensive approach is termed as India's Look East Policy.

The Southeast Asian region comprising of Myanmar, Malaysia, Thailand, Indonesia, Singapore, Brunei, Philippines, Vietnam, Laos and Cambodia is rich in resources, is an emerging economy and is strategically located and also act as a link in Asia-Pacific Region. In spite of different political systems, these states are now united into an Economic Union namely ASEAN which was formed in 1967. Today ASEAN+3 (China, Japan and South Korea) constitute Asia's economic might and have emerged as a fast growing and powerful economic alliance. Unlike the European Union, the Southeast Asian states have formed an economic union without any political unity or military alliance system. ASEAN is already in an advanced stage of economic integration. [1]

India's close civilizational links with the Southeast Asia go back over a millennium. Historically, India and Southeast Asia have been linked by culture and commerce. The cross fertilization of human experiences and the spiritual interaction between India and this region has left an indelible mark on regional art, architecture, language and culture. By the First Century AD, Indian princes, priests, poets and artisans triggered off cultural efflorescence in Southeast Asian countries. AngorWat, Lara Djong Grag and Boro Budur stand testimony to the benign cultural interaction between India and Southeast Asian countries. [2] Later with the growth of maritime trade with Southeast Asia, merchants from Gujarat, Bengal and Tamil Nadu settled down in the port cities of this region. They gradually got assimilated with the local people. The Gujarati Muslim merchants, mainly of the Sufi variant played an important role in the Islamisation of the Malay Peninsula and Indonesian Archipelago. The Malacca Chettis, who are the descendants of the Tamil Chettiars who went to Malay Peninsula during the Malacca Sultanate, still retain elements of Hindu religion and culture.

However, with the coming of the Muslim rulers, there came an end to this cultural transaction as the East was never in the political picture of the Muslim rulers. The interaction between the Southeast Asian countries and India got revived again by the coming of the British and some parts of this region were inseparable parts of the British Empire. Migration to the Southeast started again but unlike to the other parts of the world, most of the migrants to this region composed of the lower class of unskilled labourers. And they could not make any inroads into the political, social or economic set up of the countries to which they migrated.

After Independence, there was a slow down in the relationship between India and the Southeast Asia. Southeast Asia was another world as far as India was concerned. It did not come into the foreign policy frame work of India. Though we spoke of Asian Unity, Asian Resurgence, Asian Civilization etc., India could recognize only two worlds in the cold war era and Nehru was dreaming of a Non-Aligned World. As most of the Southeast were close to USA, they were not in the NAM picture as well. As India was close to USSR, both the parties looked at each other with suspicion. More, Nehru was trying to woo China at any cost and this 'helped' India to divert its eyes from other parts of Asia. And again, Southeast Asia at that time was not an economic power to get recognition from other states of Asia. Thus, in the Cold War era, "India-Southeast Asia relation remained mostly dormant and lacking in substance; in fact, there were very few strategic or economic convergences at that time, which could have brought India and Southeast Asia closer". [3] On both sides, there was apathy, indifference and lack of interest in forging deeper ties, and their relationship lacked any substance.

In fact, India was losing an opportunity to forge ties with the rising economic power of the Southeast Asia during this period. India had ties with the Communist bloc countries of Southeast Asia—Vietnam, Cambodia and Laos, but as these countries were poor and impoverished, this relation brought little benefits to India. In the meantime, other countries of Southeast Asia had gone forward to become rapidly developing countries and eventually became modern, industrialized states with developed and sophisticated economies. India was missing the opportunity to get related with these states during the Cold War era.

When ASEAN was formed in 1967, China strongly opposed and criticized the formation of such an organization as China felt it to be an out and out counter revolutionary alliance rigged up to oppose it. New Delhi did not enthusiastically welcome the idea but at the same time did not get aligned with those countries which openly condemned the formation. India's attitude was rather indistinct. As India was looked upon with suspicion by many of the Southeast Asian nations, the ASEAN was not ready to invite India to the new formation. It was only in 1973 India formally welcomed ASEAN.

New Delhi's lack of depth in political relations and weak economic linkages with AEAN were caused due to their differences in perception and behaviour in security and other related issues of great power activities in the Southeast Asia. India's linkage with Soviet Union and its inclination towards Vietnam and Cambodia irked the Southeast Asian nations. Its recognition of the Samarin Government in Cambodia was a further setback to the ASEAN members. India was not at all ready to surrender its close alliance with the Soviet Union and its allies, which was strategically more important a relation with ASEAN.

Its defeat in the 1962 war made India very inward looking. India's preoccupation with its own security problems kept it away from building up a strong relation with the Southeast. The successful intervention in Bangladesh worsened the matter as the Southeast Asian states had their own reservations about India's role in the East Pakistan. The ASEAN states regarded India's involvement in the Bangladesh war as an uncalled for interference in Pakistan's affairs. They were never free from anxiety about the consequences of a dominant, Soviet backed India.

Another factor which came as a block between India and the ASEAN was the irrelevance of India in economic terms. The inward looking economy of India and the rapidly changing economic strategies of the ASEAN states pushed them away from one another. India's meagre joint venture presence in the region and the near impossibility of augmenting any trade with regional states created further distance. In comparison, countries like Japan, Taiwan and South Korea were regarded as more relevant economies for the region. In any case, most of the regional states' investment and trade ties were with the West and this was something they wanted to preserve and promote more than anything else. India therefore did not loom much in their calculations.

In the economic and social spheres of the Southeast Asian states, India's role or part is quite negligible and these states need not give any importance to India. Most of the Indian diaspora in the Southeast Asia is of the 'Coolie' class and they have no strength to influence the policy makers. While the economic achievements of the Chinese in the region are out of all proportions to their numbers, Indian contributions do not count at all. For example, in Indonesia, the Chinese are less than 4 percent of the population but they have 75 percent of the wealth. In Thailand, the Chinese represent 8 percent of the population but control over 80 percent of the wealth. In Philippines their population is less than 2 percent but the Chinese have control over 70 percent of the wealth. Unfortunately, the contributions of the Indian minority groups to the economic transformation of the Southeast Asian region are negligible. Actually the Indians did not take roots in this region. The Indians today own only 1.5 percent of Malaysia's national wealth. The per capita income of a Singapore citizen of Indian origin is less than the national average. Socially also the Indians are not a factor in ethnic politics.

India's interest in the Southeast Asia began during the pre-emergency Indira regime. The visit of Singapore Prime Minister Lee Kuan Yew to India in 1966 and 1970, visit of Indian Foreign Minister M.C. Chagla to Malaysia and Singapore in 1967, President V.V. Giri's visit to Singapore (1971), Malaysia and Thailand (1972) and Indonesia (1975) can be considered as the beginnings. But it was A.B. Vajpayee as the Foreign Minister in the Janata Government who gave an official green signal to the new Southeast Asia policy. The declaration of the "Genuine Non-Alignment" by the Government was a welcome change to the Southeast Asian States. And the Indian Government convened a conference of the Indian envoys accredited to the East and Southeast Asian States in Delhi to discuss the new policy. But nothing concrete came out of these developments as the Janata Government fell down and with the coming of Mrs. Gandhi back to power, relations between India and Southeast Asia became cold again. [4]

In the early 90's, the global and regional politics underwent qualitative changes. The collapse of the Soviet Union led to the resolution of the Cambodian crisis and the liberalization policy introduced by the Indian Government led to significant alterations in India's foreign relations. Actually economic liberalization policies introduced by the Narasimha Rao Government brought the Indian economy in line with the economies of the Southeast Asian States. The disappointing pace at which the SAARC was developing as a regional organization due to the strained Indo-Pak relations coming in the way of its smooth evolution also propped up the Indian policy makers into expanding the focus of their attention and the aspirations regarding India's future role beyond the narrow confines of South Asia.

By this time, China began to emerge on the International scene as a major player, especially in the Asia-Pacific region. Southeast Asia, now deprived of the western security cover and facing the new challenge from China, was compelled to evolve a new strategic doctrine. India was redefining and rediscovering her foreign policy options in the changing climate. For ASEAN, the potential strategic reassurance provided by a rapidly growing military and economic India was a factor in changing its policies towards India.

Thus, under P.V. Narasimha Rao, the new Look East Policy began to take shape. India started looking at Southeast

Asia with a changed outlook. The domestic economic situation in India also helped to propel the Look East Policy. For India, it was imperative to extend the domestic and regional economic space, and the ASEAN seemed to be the most appropriate arena for this extension. India's liberal approach attracted several Southeast Asian States and they found India a very attractive destination for its export of goods, services, technology and capital. It was precisely this economic relationship which made India becoming a sectoral dialogue partner in 1996 and a full dialogue partner later. This enabled India to be a political ally of ASEAN, enabling India to participate in the Annual Meetings of ASEAN Regional Forum (ARF), a forum to discuss issues relating to peace, stability and security in the region.

The culmination of the Look East Policy was the signing of the FTA on August 13, 2009. This Accord, India's first with a trade bloc, will cover eleven countries with a combined GDP of over two trillion. Under this Agreement, ASEAN members and India will reduce import tariffs to zero for more than 80 percent of their total imported goods between 2013-16, while import tariffs for sensitive goods will be reduced to 5 percent by 2016. India has agreed to special and differential treatment to ASEAN group and aligns its peak tariff levels. India will reduce its tariff for Brunei, Cambodia, Laos, Indo-china, Malaysia, Singapore, Thailand and Vietnam in 2011. It is expected that FTA might well result in a boom in bilateral trade that can easily cross 50 million dollars by 2010. The FTA is bound to open a huge market for our goods. India can benefit from services trade with the ASEAN. The FTA is likely to be our most ambitious trade agreement as it will spur India's drive eastwards.

And it must be remembered that ASEAN has embarked on an ambitious integration process, which will culminate in the creation of an ASEAN Economic Community (AEC) by 2015. This means a single market and production base, a highly competitive economic region, a region of equitable economic development and a region fully integrated into the global economy. As far as India is concerned, this is going to be a great business opportunity.

India's Look East Policy is not a mere political or economic slogan. It was and is not a mere response to the changed global equation and trends of post-Cold War period. It is a search for political and economic convergence with a large dynamic region evolving into a critical mass of global political and economic power. A scrutiny of this policy reveals that it is not simply meant to improve relations with the Southeast Asian nations but there are a number of other dimensions too. It has become a multi faceted policy with a multi-pronged approach to establish strategic links with as many countries as possible. It is an external security trajectory, whereby India would develop a sophisticated array of security relations in the East and Southeast Asia with an eye to project India's legitimate power and resist growing Chinese domination in the region.

China does not favour a strong Indian presence and influence in the Southeast Asia. China is aware of the various cultural and historical ties that India shares with Southeast Asia, which could naturally attract the two regions to come closer. China knows that India is the only country that could possibly challenge its ascendancy and potential hegemony in Asia, and therefore it makes for China to try hard to keep India under pressure. Traditionally, china has been very dismissive of India, which it treats as a mere South Asian player. However, for the last decade or so, the Chinese have been somewhat puzzled and intrigued by the steady rate of India's economic growth and its political stability.

An important factor driving the Look East Policy is the need to counter China economically. The 'open door' policies of China has seen meteoric rise of an economic giant in Asia and is now competes with India in the political, economic and military spheres and has established military links with all the neighbouring countries of India. China is trying hard to extend its influence-economic as well as military-in Southeast Asia and all these facts warrants India to adopt an economically aggressive stance to compete with China to link itself with international market forces at work in the region. It has become necessary for India to look for new markets in order for India to become powerful economically and militarily and thus to counter China's policies and intentions.

It is true that China has much better conditions conducive for economic investments and developments attractive to Southeast Asian investors. This includes a larger, educated workforce in quantitative terms, cheaper material resources in abundance and relatively stable governance free from any significant internal or external security threat. The simple fact of consumer behaviour gravitating towards a better choice in terms of cost and quality ensures that Southeast Asia turns first to China for trade and investment rather than other countries.

However one major weakness exists for China. Its long history of Socialist rule results in a tightly controlled state with little room for political manoeuvring or reform. This meant China is a state that plays by its own rules and is not answerable to non-state actors like foreign investors. Foreign investors must adapt to local conditions instead of expecting adherence to international law and trade conduct.

India in contrast, having less to offer in tangible terms like man power costs and resource abundance, however enjoys the reputation of being a democracy which respects consumer rights and international law governing trade and foreign investments. Also, India's long standing recognition of English as the official language breaks down language and cultural barriers in trade communications, and in theory accelerates business procedures. This is an advantage over China and should be exploited to the full to gain an edge.

China has, in truth, a less than savoury reputation in its foreign relations with its neighbours with regard in pursuing its own economic interests. It deals from a position of strength with regional partners, and usually ends with the latter having to compromise with a lesser share of the cake. Two clear examples were its past records of the Suzhon Project in Singapore and the occupation of the Spartly Islands. India, however, starts with a clean slate in terms of economic co-operation with regional partners, putting it in a favourable position to win and maintain trust with its partners.

For ASEAN, India is relevant and significant. India is seen as a counterweight to other partners, especially China and Japan. India's technological co operation with southeast Asian states in the military and civilian sectors serve as an alternative as well as additional source of purchases of sophisticated military technology and equipment. Again, India's strategic positioning as well as development of naval facilities in the Andamans are clearly designed to protect and promote the commercial, maritime and security interests of India and are an added attraction to Southeast Asian states. [5]

ASEAN has strong apprehensions over China's emergence as a regional military power and this has been endorsed by the US military presence inn the Asia-Pacific. China's future role, interest, capabilities and influence are a major concern to ASEAN as they are to India. India sees itself as co-equal with China as a nuclear power. The modernization of China's military especially the Navy has enabled Beijing to adopt a more assertive posture in South China Sea. China has got 888 ships (in 2005) that can easily be brought anywhere in the pacific region. The People's Liberation Navy also occupies and has naval facilities in several convenient and strategic island bases in Southeast Asia waters which may act as spring boards to easily dominate and control sea lanes from Southeast Asia to the coasts of China. These are growing concern for ASEAN states, especially Malaysia, Vietnam, Brunei, and Philippines. China's assertiveness in foreign policy led to a sense of insecurity and vulnerability among the other regional states. Even USA had to intervene in a number of times to deter Chinese military moves. [6]

How China handles its behaviour and growing military

power in the region would likely to influence the strategic responses not only of the regional claimants but also of the other Asian powers. Chinese moves are linked to the balance of power considerations in the Southeast Asian regional security. It is here India's role and participation in Southeast Asian regional politics becomes relevant. Most of the Southeast Asian states would be ready to welcome India to balance Chinese interference.

It is firmly believed that economic co-operation and integration between India and the ASEAN will enhance the security and peace in the Region. India's democratic system is viewed with a feeling of security by the Southeast Asian societies. No doubt, India's economic co-operation will act as a "building block of security" and Indian democracy as a system can serve as a confidence building mechanism in India's interactions with the ASEAN states. Though China liberalized its economy, its politics remain under iron curtain and democracy is alien to China. China's economic power without a liberal political order threatens ASEAN members. This gives India an edge over China and all the ASEAN states look upon India with great expectations. [7]

Conclusion

Domestic and external developments dictate pragmatism in getting India to play a game of international trade and economics with free market rules. Unlike China, which enjoys a number of economic and military advantages over India in tangible and qualitative terms, India cannot rely on FDIs as a springboard toward achieving a well developed economy thriving on service sector and tertiary industries. As such, it is necessary it looks to other tangible factors to form a niche for itself to off set the regional competition. Its main advantage over China lies in the official recognition and use of English, the language of international trade and technology and it's relatively clean slate of records in economic co-operation with Southeast Asia is an added advantage.

Currently, Southeast Asia's attention remains focused on China for potential economic development. Relatively free trade and large scale investments are still currently taking place, bringing mutual benefits for both the investors and China itself. Historical experience, however, has shown that China will eventually wish to take its historical place of dominance in Asia and also the full control of its economic destiny in the manner of a huge empire-like state. Simultaneously, China will wish to restore bilateral relations with other Asian states in mutually beneficial but unequal trade and economic status just like the tributary states in pre-modern times.

Already, China's open intentions of preventing Taiwan from declaring independence were obviously backed by threats of use of force if necessary. More recently, China has publicly protested against the US move to sell arms to Taiwan. Frequent military and naval manoeuvres against Taiwan are putting unnecessary strains on the Region's interstate trade dynamics and causing fluctuations in the regional stock markets.

India's advantage over China lies in the fact of its abstinence from ambitions towards a regional hegemony, making it less threatening to states in the Southeast Asian Region. Should other nations in the region discover that, in a future scenario, options of trade and investments with china become unfeasible, countries in the Southeast Asia naturally will then turn towards the next obvious and available option-India. Thus, India should get prepared itself to meet such a potential development in future.

End Notes

1. Syamala. K. and K. Jayaprasad, *Look East: Re discovering India's Policy Towards the Southeast Asian Nations, Review of Social Sciences,* January-June 2006.
2. Surya Narayan.V, (2005). *Neglected Dimensions of India's Look East Policy*, K. Raja Reddy (ed.), *India and ASEAN-Foreign Policy Dimensions for the 21st Century,* New Century

Publications.

3. Ram A.N., (2005). *India's Look East Policy* in K. Raja Reddy (ed.) op.cit.
4. Khanna V.N, (2007). *Foreign Policy of India,* New Delhi: Vikas Publications.
5. Prakash Nanda, (2003). *Rediscovering Asia,* New Delhi: Lancer Publishers and Distributors.
6. Gopinath, Aruna, (2005). *Strategic Relations in Indo- ASEAN in the 21st Century: An Asian Perspective* in K. Raja Reddy (ed.) op.cit.
7. Samala. R. and K. Jayaprasad op. cit.

Index

Index

A
A.K. Antony, 263
Abba Eban, 258
Administrative Reforms Commission, 50
Akali Dal, 140
Al Qaeda, 237
Al-Aqsa Mosque, 258
Anna Hazare, 129
Anwar Sadat, 193
Ariel Sharon, 198
Armed Forces Special Powers Act of 1958, 53
Asian Development Bank, 102
Association of South East Asian Nations, 25
Atal Bihari Vajpayee, 150

B
B.C. Roy, 45
B.R. Ambedkar, 32
Bahujan Samaj party, 96
Bay of Bengal, 47
Biju Janata Dal, 97
BIMARU states (Bihar, Madhya Pradesh, Rajasthan and Uttar Pradesh), 79
Biodiversity Convention, 165
British Common Law, 121
British North America Act, 16

C
C Rajagopalachari, 39, 42
C.S. Jha, 39
Camp David Accord, 259
Cauvery Dispute, 124
Central Bureau of Investigation, 165
Central Police Organisations, 262
Ceylon Citizenship Act of 1948, 38
Ceylon Workers Congress, 41
Cold War politics, 171
Cold war, 271
Communist Party of India, 42
Comprehensive Test Ban Treaty, 181
Conference of Cantonal Governments, 6
Congress Party, 97
Constitution (Amendment) Bill, 1993, 28
Constitution for Australia, 17
Council of the States, 138

D
D.P. Dhar, 257

Democratic Republic of Congo, 178
Disturbed Areas Act in North-East, 53
Doha Development Agenda (DDA), 165
Dominion Parliament, 17
Dravida Munnetra Kazhagam, 42
Dudley Senanayake, 38

E
European Union Directives, 129
European Union, 8, 80, 102

F
Federal Assembly, 7
Federal Council, 2
Financial Action Task Force, 164
First World War, 35
Foreign Relations Committees, 2
Francis Fukyama, 80

G
Gamal Abdel Nassar, 171
Gazetteer of Ramnathapuram, 44
Geneva Conference on Disarmament, 181
George Fernandes, 28
George Soros, 86
George W. Bush, 197, 182
Gujarat High Court, 21
Gulf Cooperation Council, 230, 232
Gulf of Mannar, 47

H
Helsinki Rules, 119
Human Development Index, 86

I
India-China Agreement of 1954, 149
India-EU Security Dialogue, 163
Indian Council for Cultural Relations, 219
Indian Council of World Affairs, 210
Indian National Congress, 256
Indian Renaissance, 171
Indian Space Research Organization, 263
Indian Tamils, 36
India-Sri Lanka Maritime Agreement of 1976, 47
Indira Gandhi, 45, 148, 259
Indo-American Civilian Nuclear Agreement, 152
Indo-ASEAN Free Trade Agreement, 147
Indo-Bangladesh Treaty of 1972, 149

Indo-Nepalese Treaty of 1951, 149
Indo-Sikkimese Treaty of 1950, 149
Indo-Soviet of Treaty of 1971, 149
Indo-Soviet Trade Agreement of 1971, 149
Indo-US Nuclear Deal, 135
Insurance Regulatory Authority, 98
Intellectual Property Rights, 19
International Atomic Energy Agency, 182
International Monetary Fund, 81, 176
International Water Laws, 118
Inter-state Water Disputes Act (1956), 122
Islamic Jihad, 192

J
J.N. Dixit, 149
Jackson Report, 37
Jai Prakash Narayan, 256
Janata Dal-Secular, 97
Janata Party, 259
Jaswant Singh, 150
Jawaharlal Nehru, 37, 171, 173, 255
John Kotelawala, 39
Joseph E. Stiglitz, 176
Joseph Frankle, 143
Josip Broz Tito, 171

K
K.R. Narayanan, 186
Kamaraj Nadar, 39, 40
Kargil War in 1999, 262
Kewal Singh, 44
King Abdullah of Jordan, 193
King Feisal of Saudi Arabia, 193
Krishna Iyer, 29

L
L. K. Advani, 182
Lal Bahadur Shastri, 39, 40
Larry Diamond, 85
Lee Kuan Yew, 276
Liberation Tigers of Tamil Eelam, 192
Lok Sabha, 46, 173
Look East Policy, 271

M
M. Hidayatullah, 21
M.C. Chagla, 148
M.G. Ramachandran, 45
Madhu Limaye, 44
Madras Prcsidency, 42
Malacca Sultanate, 273
Manmohan Singh, 101, 145
Mastrich Treaty, 80
Mayawati, 96
M.C. Setalvad, 45
Middle East Peace

Conference, 259
Montek Singh Ahluwalia, 86
Moshe Dayan, 259
Mulayam Singh, 96

N

Narasimha Rao, 170
National Democratic Alliance, 170
National Liberation Front, 192
Nationalist Congress Party, 98
Nehru-Liaquat Agreement of 1950, 149
Nehru-Noon Agreement of 1958, 149
New Global Order, 170
Non-agricultural Market Access, 165
Non-aligned Movement, 179
Non-alignment policy, 82
Non-navigational Uses of International Watercourses, 120
Non-resident Indians, 101

O

Occupied Arab Territories, 197
Organization of Arab Petroleum Exporting Countries, 221
Osama bin Laden, 205, 237
Oslo Accords, 195

P

P. Ramaswamy, 40
P.V. Narasimha Rao, 182
Palestine Liberation Organization, 192, 216
Palk Bay region, 42
People's Liberation Navy, 281
Persian Gulf, 239
Persons of Indian Origin, (PIO), 94
Pieter Kuneman, 38
Pokhran nuclear test, 150
Politics of Immigrant Labour, 37
Popular Front for the Liberation of Palestine, 199
Post-Cold War International Environment, 170
Praja Socialist Party, 172
Provisional Irish Republican, 192

Q

Quebec Province, 89

R

Raja of Ramnad, 42
Rajiv Gandhi, 150, 181
Rajya Sabha, 138
Rashtriya Janata Dal

(Bihar), 97
Red Sea, 239
River Boards Act (1956), 122, 123
Roman legal system, 119

S
Samajwadi Party, 96, 97
Sarkaria Commission, 28
Sarpanch Popat Pawar, 129
Satyaprakash Malviya, 28
Schengen Treaty, 10
Second World War, 171
Sharm El Sheik, 171
Sheikh Hasina, 24
Simla Agreement of 1972, 149
Sirimavo Bandaranaike, 46
Sirimavo-Shatri Pact, 36, 41, 48
Som Nath Chatterjee, 153
Soulbury Report, 1947, 37
S.P. Jagota, 44
Special Economic Zone, 106
Strait of Hormouz, 230
Suez Canal, 257
Supreme Court, 21
Swaran Singh, 39
Swiss Cantons, 32
Switzerland Constitution, 4

T
Tashkent Agreement of 1965, 149
Thakachi Madam, 43
Third World, 85
Thomas Fleiner, 108
Tony Blair, 207
Trade-related Intellectual Property Rights (TRIPs), 165

U
U Thant, 257
U.S. House of Representatives, 8
UN General Assembly, 181
UN Security Council Resolutions, 164
United National Party, 38
United Progressive Alliance, 170
Uruguay Round of GATT, 22

V
Vertical Federalism, 13
V.K. Krishna Menon, 42

W
World Bank, 94, 102, 176
World Economic Forum, 86
World Trade Centre, 208
World Trade Organization, 165, 176

Y
Y2K issue, 83
Yasser Arafat, 192, 197

Y.B. Chavan, 47
Yitzhak Rabin, 193